MY YEAR 2000:
LEAVING SOMETHING BEHIND

T0017529

SELECTED BOOKS BY THE AUTHOR

My Year 2000:

Leaving Something Behind

READINGS

EVENTS

MEMORIES

by
Douglas Messerli

GREEN INTEGER
KØBENHAVN & LOS ANGELES
2018

GREEN INTEGER
Edited by Per Bregne
København / Los Angeles
(323) 937-3783 / www.greeninteger.com

Distributed in the United States by
Consortium Book Sales & Distribution / Ingram Books
(800) 283-3572 / www.cbsd.com

LIBRARY OF CONGRESS CATALOGING-IN-PUBLICATION DATA
Douglas Messerli [1947]
My Year 2000: Leaving Something Behind
ISBN: 978-1-55713-443-1
p. cm – Green Integer 255
I. Title II. Series

Green Integer books are published for Douglas Messerli
Printed in Canada

Table of Contents

Looking Backward in Order to Safely Go Forward: An Introduction

THIS VOLUME OF *My Year*, representing the shift into the new millennium, will be the last episode in the back and forth rock of what I have been describing as "out of the cradle." Henceforth, I will only swing forward—and we all know the inevitable result of that! At some point I will surely simply fly into space and these cultural memoirs will come to a close.

Like the volumes from 2001 and 2002, the 2000 volume was composed somewhat "after the fact," and, accordingly represents essays written over a fairly broad period of time which, put together, seemed to represent my slightly nostalgic subtitle, "Leaving Something Behind." I am, after all, a product of the 20th century, despite the fact that I hope to continue fairly far into the 21st. Many of the pieces in this cultural memoir thus represent events of the past century: readings, films, travels (to both Brazil and the Soviet Union), and theoretical works and interviews which I wrote as a younger man. A long piece selects great moments of dance in 20th-century American film musicals. Essays on the films of Renoir, Tarkovsky, and Bresson, as well as on American westerns and the works of Samuel Beckett, all look backward to the century through which we had just passed.

In a strange way, however, many of the pieces—despite the fact that when I wrote them I had not conceived of an annual series of cultural memoirs—were created contemporaneously. During the year, I had planned a volume covering the year's works of fiction, to be called *Fiction 2000*, which I had hoped to continue as an annual series—in some respects an ur-form of my 2003-conceived *My Year* volumes. For that never-realized publication, I read numerous volumes of fiction published during the year, including works by John Updike, Franz Hellens, Jane Unrue, Eliseo Alberto, Antonio José Ponte, Peter Handke, Daniela Fischerová, Fran Ross, and J. Rodolfo Wilcock. So, in some respects—at least with regard to fiction—a significant number of the pieces were written during the year about works also published at the turn of the century.

Particularly within these works there was a strong sense of the century just finished, despite the recognition of its horrific wars and terrifying ideologies. Indeed, I would argue, my own after-the-fact discussion of films, theater performances, and other fictions such as the brilliant *The Melancholy of Resistance* by László Krasznahorkai (the translation published in 2000, but Messerli read and wrote about it the following year) strongly revealed the sense of the ambiguous transition into the millennium. If this 2000 volume is, thus, not precisely a "natural" product of experiences and cultural events of the year, it clearly embraces many works I read and saw during the Millennium. While I would still characterize it, as I did in the 2001 and 2002 volumes, as a fictional representation of the year—although using only truthful reactions and perceptions—it is also, to my way of thinking, a fairly accurate one.

As late as 2014, viewing Agnés Vardas' wonderful documentary/memoir of the same year, *The Gleaners and I*, I perceived the perfect match to my pre-determined title of this year's volume. Seeing Raúl Ruiz's vision of Proust's *Remembrance of Things Past* during that same year, I felt the issues of the past and change in his *Time Regained*, a film that appeared in the US in 2000, should also be included. The death of director and acquaintance Paul Bartel led me to look again at his *Eating Raoul*, which, in turn, helped me to recognize how much of a salute it was to a past period which, while he clearly satirized, he also loved.

Perhaps I should characterize the major activity

of 2000 as being not only one of transitioning into the new century, but of trying to recall and piece together the world out of which we had just come. Knowing one cannot return to the past, and would not even want to, it is important—so it seems to me—nonetheless, to remember it. Unlike the volume of the following year, where it became necessary, in order to go forward, to keep history a secret, in 2000 it seemed important—as we stepped into new territory—to look backward in order to safely go forward. If, hereafter, I am only moving forward, I can still recognize what I expressed in my review of Ponte's 2000 collection of stories, *In the Cold of the Malecón*: "Death becomes the only relief, something from which the survivors have no choice but to walk away in a kind of silent envy and respect, leaving the door open."

There is, finally, a sense of possibility along with a sense of sadness in the works of *My Year 2000*. All possibility lay before us, but we could never be certain that we wanted to go there. In fact, looking back now on what I have written about the first 16 years of the new century, many of the qualms I felt were highly justified. As awful as it was, the previous century, at least, was something that we knew and comprehended. And there were, we all must admit, wonderfully exciting moments!

From the very beginning, I now realize, I had marvelous friends and supporters who helped me to create this volume, even if they did not know they were contributing to a series that has now spanned nearly two decades. Among them are Erland Anderson, David and Eleanor Antin, Nelson Ascher, Don Askarian, Tom Beckett, Charles Bernstein, Régis Bonvicino, Haraldo de Campos, Clark and Susan Coolidge, Gene Corman, Lígia Cortez, Horácio Costa, Arkadii and Zina Dragomoshchenko, Ostap Dragomoshchenko, Nicholas Frangakis, Cola Franzen, Rebecca Goodman, Lyn Hejinian, Fanny Howe, Mary Klaus, Abram Lerner, Joe Martin, Deborah Meadows, Lorna Messerli, Harryette Mullen, Cristina Mutarelli, Martin Nakell, Larry Ochs and the ROVA Saxophone Quartet, Michael Palmer, Marjorie Perloff, Joe Ross, Rod Smith, Pat Thieben, Carolyn L. Tipton, Peter Vilms, Frederick Wasser, Don Wellman, Mac Wellman, Mary Woronov, and my companion Howard Fox, who read several of these pieces, particularly the long series on dance, and commented extensively. Once more, this volume could not have been possible without the careful proofreading and brilliant typography of Pablo Capra, who now probably knows my life better than even I do.

LOS ANGELES, JULY 5, 2013, JANUARY 4, 2016

Before the Curtain Rises

JOHN UPDIKE **GERTRUDE AND CLAUDIUS** (NEW YORK: ALFRED A. KNOPF, 2000)

WHY AMERICAN CRITICS and prize-givers have been so enthusiastic about John Updike's work (he has won the Pulitzer Prize, the National Book Award, the American Book Award, the National Book Critics Circle Award, and the Howells Medal) and readers so faithful (this is his 18th novel) have always been a mystery to me. I have my theories, but they shall have to wait for another occasion. Regarding his most recent novel *Gertrude and Claudius,* however, I can only assert—in contrast to the several appreciative reviews that have proceeded this one—that it is little more than a work of restrained mediocrity.

The problems are many, not the least of which is the fact that Updike has chosen to write in the shadow of a great work of art that we all know and love, only to leave off at precisely the moment the other begins.

That is, he has chosen to narrate the events of Shakespeare's play up until the very moment Hamlet gets underway. Certainly, the story of Gerutha (later Geruthe and finally Gertrude) and Feng's (later Fegon and ultimately Claudius) adulterous relationship fits nicely into an *oeuvre* obsessed with adultery. And in the hands of a greater artist—Tom Stoppard has shown us in *Rosencrantz and Guildenstern Are Dead* what can be done with Shakespeare and his sources—this might have been an entertaining fiction. But in Updike's hands there is no sustaining story. Gerutha is forced by her father Rorik to marry Horwendil (King Hamlet); she finds him unsubtle and lacking in the finer sensibilities of bedroom behavior, and from childhood has been attracted to his brother, Feng. When Feng returns from his multifarious travels (undertaken primarily to remain away from his brother and Gerutha, to whom he too has been highly attracted), they develop a relationship that quickly shifts from a play of wits to a drama of secretive and romantic love. When the King discovers their treachery, Feng (with the help of the Lord Chamberlin, Corambus [spelled throughout the novel also as Corambis, later Polonius]) poisons the King and takes over the throne, marrying his lover. Enter Hamlet.

Of course, great works of art have been written with much less of a story to go on. But Updike's work—at least in this novel—is highly dependent upon plot, and with so little to work with he fills the book with what I am sure he believes are deep insights into his characters: Gertrude is an independent woman who has no other choice in her society but to be pliant and supple; King Hamlet is a man of good deeds, a good King, a good Husband, but has no sensitivity whatsoever, and hence, is referred to by Gertrude and Claudius as "The Hammer"; Claudius is a true romantic and is capable of great subtlety in love, but also is deceitful and capable of murder. In repeating these qualities again and again throughout this short work, however, Updike becomes less than subtle himself and hammers his characters' qualities into the poor reader's perceivèd thick head. Gertrude is described over and over as "surrendering" (even as late as page 200 in the 210-page work); King Hamlet is The Hammer throughout, Claudius a clever but too subtle man. One might overlook some of these simplistic characterizations had Updike filled his yarn with some true adventure, but it is almost as if the author could not decide what to fill it *with*. Time and again in the book, he devotes paragraphs and entire passages to various arcane subjects: a short treatise on falconry, a description of the various toiletries available to a Scandinavian queen of the day, a list of the foods they eat, a short historical compendium of the Byzantine empire, a brief explanation of the Nordic *råd* and *thing*. Many readers enjoy historical fictions precisely because of what they can glean from such information. In the hands of a Lagerlöf, of an Undset, or a Yourcenar these kinds of facts are thoroughly embedded in the stories themselves; here Updike features it as if proving to the reader that he has done his research or used his imagination; or perhaps again he feels that few readers could possibly have knowledge of such things. One can almost see the scraps of loose jottings spread across his writing desk as he determined what to include and what not.

That said, there are a few delightful moments in the plot, as when Gertrude (having obtained from Polonius the use of his castle for her rendezvous) requires the middle-aged Claudius to climb through the tower window, which she must help to pull him through. The couple later have a hot groping session—with their heavy clothes on. Yet Updike, doubting, so it appears, that the reader may not recall the event, repeats it later, as Claudius—fresh from emptying his vial of poison into the ear of the King—climbs for his escape through a window (reminding him of the earlier one) into the castle latrine. Get it?

The paucity of plot might be less of an issue if Up-dike's style—for which his work is most often touted—were not so embarrassing. He begins the novel in a kind of fake Shakespearean language "bespoken" with "bewitchments, be-botherments, and bewildernesses" and some inverted syntax that, fortunately, he quickly drops. But what replaces it is, at times, even more embarrassing. After a discussion between Gertrude and Polonius, the author waxes poetic:

> O the days, the days in their all but unnoticed beauty and variety—days of hurtling sun and shade like the dapples of an exhilarated beast, days of steady strong cold and a blood-red dusk, tawny autumn days smelling of of hay and grapes, spring days tasting of salty wave-froth and of hearth-smoke blown down from the chimney pots, misty days...days of luxurious tall clouds...days when the shoreline of Skåne lay vivid as a purple hem upon the Sund's rippling breadth...[this continues for another page]

One can almost see, as in a grade B film of the 1940s, a montage of calendar pages being ripped away one by one. How one longs for a simple, elegant, "Time passes."

Indeed, there is a kind of hack cinematic quality in

many of Updike's images and words. Each character is described at some point as if the camera were embracing their faces in a closeup, perspiration forming on their upper lips ("A ridge of dew appeared on Geruthe's upper lip, which bore transparent down he had never noticed before"). But the language of much of Updike's work is that of the soft porno novel. Penises are referred to as "horns," "members," or—when the action gets truly racy—"spouting cocks" ("I should beat you. I should pound the pale slime of that spouting cock from your gut."). Just before this ridiculous statement Updike devotes a whole page, again emphasizing Gertrude's oft-cited submission to men, to a description that summarizes the quality of much of the book:

> Whereas Fengon was content to loiter in a twinned concupiscence, telling Geruthe over and over, with his tongue and eyes and rethickened horn, all the truth about herself that she could hold. He uncovered in her not just the warrior but the slave. Had he bid her lie down in pigshit she would have squeezed her buttocks together in the clench and rejoiced to be thus befouled. At night, reliving the afternoon's embraces, she would lick her pillow in hunger to be with her lover again—her redeemer from lawful life's deadening emptiness, her own self turned inside out and given a man's bearish, boyish form. Her father's court held no more eager slut

than she.

Had Hamlet read this version of his mother's secret life, he might have stayed in Germany.

LOS ANGELES, 2000
Reprinted from *Green Integer Blog* (January 2009).

The Moment to Say No

TOM STOPPARD **ROSENCRANTZ AND GUILDEN-STERN ARE DEAD** (NEW YORK: SAMUEL FRENCH, 1967)
TOM STOPPARD (WRITER AND DIRECTOR) **ROSEN-CRANTZ AND GUILDENSTERN ARE DEAD** / 1990

STOPPARD'S BRILLIANT 1967 play takes the two minor characters of *Hamlet* through an existentialist journey made up of language, a world in which these two anti-heroes, inexplicably called into being by a court messenger, can participate only through linguistic games as they try to explain their existence and purpose. The marvel of this play was its youthful wit as the two original actors, Brian Murray and John Wood, attempted to best each other with rapid-fire language games:

> ROS: We were sent for.
> GUIL: Yes.
> ROS: That's why we're here [*he looks round, seems doubtful, then the explanation*]. Travelling
> GUIL: Yes.

ROS: [*dramatically*] It was urgent—a matter of extreme urgency, a royal summons, his very words: official business and no questions asked—lights in the stable-yard, saddle up and off headlong and hotfoot across the land, our guides outstripped us in breakneck pursuit of our duty! Fearful lest we come too late!

[*small pause*]

GUIL: Too late for what?

ROS: How do I know? We haven't got there yet.

GUIL: Then what are we doing here, I ask myself.

ROS: You might well ask.

GUIL: We better get on.

Their "getting on," however, is harder than one might expect as they encounter a group of actors performing a play very similar to the play they are living within. Once they do reach Elsinore, moreover, Hamlet himself is playing with "words, words, words," as large groups of people come and go, vaguely ordering the pair to note Hamlet's behavior and comments. Yet, since these minor figures have few encounters with the Danish Prince: most of what they observe is "offstage," through the cracks of walls, leaving them more confused than ever.

One of the great delights of Stoppard's play is this couple's inability to know even which of them is Rosencrantz and Guildenstern, what their relationship is

 to each other (they are simply a "couple," although the playwright in determining that suggests perhaps something more than a deep friendship), or what their true relationship is to Hamlet. They are simply told they are old school friends.

The irony, of course, is that the audience already knows their fate—the fate of nearly everyone within the play—which the playwright (just in case someone might have never read *Hamlet*) announces in the title itself. Consequently the substance of the play depends upon their *not-knowing*, despite their intense cleverness, revealed, particularly, in their philosophical and scientific thinking. The great pleasure of *Rosencrantz and Guildenstern Are Dead*, in short, is its Beckett-like representation of two clueless everymen who trip through the language like clowns in their attempts to comprehend their imposed reality.

It may be a basic trope—played out in numerous characters from Bouvard and Pécuchet, Vladimir and Estragon, and even Abbott and Costello—but it works, on stage and page, because of its basic dialogical rhythms, which are at the heart of theater.

At the heart of film, however, is the image, and

transforming a work of "words, words, words," despite the fact that the playwright remained in complete control of this film, is most difficult. While the play begins immediately with the toss of a coin (reinstating the themes of game and chance), Stoppard's movie version begins with a long ride through time and space, with an even longer vertical dip by Guildenstern to reach down for a coin he has spotted upon the ground. In these visual maneuvers, everything changes, and what once was clever and witty—what once was based on "timing"—is slowed down in narrative pace. By the time Rosencrantz and Guildenstern get into their dialogue, the audience has lost attention, and the characters seem leaden.

I never saw the original production (my companion, Howard, did see it, however, at the Alvin Theater

 in New York), but I am certain that behind the verbal gymnastics of the original actors was a great deal of joy; in the film, although Gary Oldman (as Rosencrantz) and Tim Roth (as Guildenstern) are fine actors, they seem to approach their verbal roles so diffidently that they appear more as dolts rather than swordsmen of language.

The busy costumes and sets of the players, moreover, distract us from any comments with which the two may joust. The abused child-actor Alfred is converted into a knowledgeable drag-queen, removing some of the naughty sting of the original. And by the time the couple reaches Elsinore, with its cavernous spaces, almost any linguistic arousal has been dampened.

Strangely, Stoppard encourages this even further by having the seemingly less intelligent Guildenstern express his intelligence in a series of visual puns surrounding various physical principles such as Newton's cradle, Newton's law of universal gravitation, the Greek principle of steam power, and the creation of a bi-wing plane. At moments, these actions seem entertaining, but once more they slow down the language which is the essential engine of Stoppard's play.

Several critics have argued that the film failed because of its attempt to bring such a high level of language to the screen. But I would argue just the opposite; it is almost as if the playwright, determining to make the work a visual manifestation of his story, pulled the plug on the very source of its energy.

In fact, what Stoppard does is to turn the play *Rosencrantz and Guildenstern Are Dead* inside out. Instead of allowing the obscure figures to become the focus of the play, his cinematic intrusions of time and space refocus our attentions onto *Hamlet*. Richard Dreyfuss as the Lead Player, Iain Glen as Prince Hamlet, Ian Richards as Polonius, and Joanna Miles as Gertrude are such fine actors that, speaking Shakespeare's lines, they dominate the play; and like this Rosencrantz and Guildenstern, we are more attracted to the action going on "onstage" (which might have been described as "offstage" in the original) than we are to the shenanigans of the sparring couple. In short, the movie entirely loses the focus of the original play, ending up within the dead center of what was once a vortex, where, as Wyndham Lewis described it, art becomes abstract.

Accordingly, I believe the language-bound original was less abstract than Stoppard's visualization of his work, which is far more representational than the very human rendering of complex ideas of the original.

By comparison with the "still-lives" portrayed by

Rosencrantz and Guildenstern, the lightness of Iain Glen's acting seems anything but morose. Even Polonius seems more light on his feet than the two actors at the center of this filmed version.

Perhaps a "staged" film might have generated more excitement than this camera-busy "representation" of what once was a verbal delight. The death of Rosencrantz and Guildenstern, unfortunately, does not occur at the end of Stoppard's film, but in its very earliest scenes, and we can only wonder, as does the comic couple, whether there was a time at the beginning when they might have said "no" to their excruciating voyage.

LOS ANGELES, JULY 4, 2013
Reprinted from *World Cinema Review* (July 2013).

Leaving Elsinore

FRANZ HELLENS **MEMOIRS FROM ELSINORE,**
TRANSLATED FROM THE FRENCH BY HOWARD CURTIS
(NEW YORK: PETER LANG, 2000)

ALTHOUGH HE IS little known today—even in his native Belgium—Franz Hellens was a recognized novelist of the 1920s through the '50s in his homeland; without Hellens' existence, fellow Belgian Henri Michaux said that he would never have written his own first book. Author of over 100 books of fiction, poetry, essays, plays, art criticism, and other genres, Hellens' most noted works are the surrealist-fantasy *Mélusine* of 1921, *Le Naïf* (with an introduction in the Italian edition by Giuseppe Ungaretti), and *Moreldieu* of 1946.

Memoirs from Elsinore (1954) is the kind of novel where you know the narrator is not only unreliable but is going to precipitate a great many disasters, and, accordingly, an uneasy feeling settles over this book from its first pages. The young Hamlet of this novel,

Théophile, is a chubby and extremely healthy terror, whom his parents immediately dub as "the monster." His relationship with his mother is nearly incestuous; but it is his shock at seeing his work-horse of a father unexpectedly cry in his presence that haunts him throughout the early part of his life. The father soon dies and the uncle quickly enters the scene to marry the widow. Not unlike Hamlet, young Théo is as suddenly sent off to a Jesuit boarding school in Antwerp. Fortunately (or unfortunately for the other figures of the book) Théo is allowed visits with his mother's cousin, Jean, a local canon, but also a free-thinking alcoholic with a live-in maid-mistress, the bosomy Toinette. Expectedly, Théo makes trouble at the school, forcing a young schoolmate to steal for him a poisonous snake he has seen at the zoo, and, with money from the Canon, he is off on a truly monstrous career. He returns home (snake in hand) only to have his arm blown away by an old grenade in the attic. His revenge on his step-father is now determined, and, having put the snake in the protection of his beloved Séraphine—the gardener's daughter—he plots patricide. But before it can be completed, his Ophelia dies by the sting of the viper. Now in revenge for his own father's cuckolding, his mother's honor, and his young beloved's death, he plants the snake in his uncle's bed and the inevitable occurs.

Ousted from Eden, Hellens' young Hamlet begins his voyage through life. Théo escapes to sea, where he is entrusted by the Captain of the *Slonsk* to keep a diary-log of the ship's many voyages. On their very first voyage, Théo murders a woman aboard who toys with his and others' affections, and begins a long life aboard the ship lived mainly in fevers and forgetfulness. He awakens just long enough for the mad captain to tell him of the existence of his goddess-like daughter, Upanisha, of whom he catches a glimpse in his feverish sleep. Hellens seems almost unable to sustain or, perhaps, explain the surreal circumstances of Théo's love-hate relationship with Upanisha; but suffice it to say that this strange portion of the novel ends in his destroying the woman and the boat. He is saved; how we are never told.

Returning home to his mother, he is suddenly forced to face a new rival in the previously unreported step-brother Victor, who is attempting to sell the lovely house and grounds in order to create a factory that will make him his fortune. The brothers, innately hating one another, are further embittered as Victor's intended bride, the mayor's daughter Amanda, increasingly falls in love with and outwardly flirts with the older

Théo. But when the mother dies, in part because of an argument with Victor, Théo simply packs his bag and leaves. Just as he mystified Upanisha's murder and the destruction of the boat at sea, so Hellens turns to fable at novel's end, as Théo trudges off into the snow, never to be seen again.

It is difficult to know what to make of a novel in which the major events of the book are clouded over, and other actions are presented "off-stage" or in brief glimpses. Yet the psychological portrait Hellens paints of his anti-hero is a strong one, at times extremely moving and touching and at other times enormously frightening and unsettling. And that alone makes it worth reading this most unusual work.

LOS ANGELES, 2000
Reprinted from *Green Integer Blog* (March 2008).

Despite my companion Howard Fox's attempts back in 1998 to entice me to the theater to view Shakespeare in Love, *I remained unconvinced. I was assured that it was a lovely fiction, but I was so tired of* Masterpiece Theatre *classic revivals of Elizabethan dramas and their numerous Shakespearian references that I just couldn't be tempted. One should recall that the Sekhar Kapur-directed* Elizabeth *appeared in the same year; I am equally certain of its merits, but perhaps I was just exhausted by those well-performed costume dramas. I faced Cate Blanchett as Elizabeth on the cover, every day, of my* Time Out Film Guide*! I have to admit it slightly intimidated me; I probably wouldn't have done well in her no-nonsense, slightly male-repugnant reign, despite my admiration for her long-before-feminism admonitions. I've never been a courtier.*

It wasn't until 2014 that I broke down and bought Howard a DVD version of the film for his birthday in October or, if my memory's mistaken, for a Christmas gift (along with numerous other DVDs). And it wasn't until the following June, in 2015, that I finally spent a joyous morning watching it.

From the moment it began I realized that this film, from the now "other side" of the century, belonged among the early essays I had written for My Year 2000, *along with Updike's fictional version of* Hamlet, *the Belgium writer Franz Hellens' fiction* Memories from Elsinore, *and Tom Stoppard's earlier manic Shakespearian send-*

up, Rosencrantz and Guildenstern Are Dead.

And yes, as Howard had long ago predicted, I did very much enjoy this film by the director John Madden; but I also realized I'd needed the experiences of older age to allow me entry into this loving, and also slightly sentimentalized viewpoint on the significance of Shakespeare to the issue of true love—particularly since it had little to do with the life of the actual playwright, for whom I'm still waiting for a gay or, at least, bisexually-conceived reconstruction.

Meanwhile, given Marc Norman's and Tom Stoppard's lovely mash-up of fact and fictional machinations, I'll accept the slightly Moonstruck-like similarities between the love of Gwyneth Paltrow (a far prettier if less convincing Cher) and Joseph Fiennes (a more innocent and less savage Nicolas Cage). As I suggest below, Shakespeare is simply a name in this genre-defying piece, so it hardly matters whether or not he is at all similar to the few bits of knowledge we might have gathered about the great author's reality through the centuries. In the end, it's a blissful blarney piece about the great bard of Avon that doesn't need or pretend to need any collaboration with historical reality. Besides, we hardly have a historical reality to refer to, do we? As this film seems to insist, not unlike Mike Leigh's topsy-turvy send-up of Gilbert and Sullivan of the same period, it's all in the work.

LOS ANGELES, JUNE 11, 2015

A Historical-Romantic, Tragi-Comical, Post-Modern, Sentimental Mystery

MARC NORMAN AND TOM STOPPARD (WRITERS, BASED ON A SCRIPT BY MARC NORMAN), JOHN MADDEN (DIRECTOR) **SHAKESPEARE IN LOVE** / 1998

IF POLONIUS WERE alive today—and he is by many other names—he might well describe Marc Norman's and Tom Stoppard's script in the manner with which I've titled this piece, for director John Madden seems, in his very busy narrative, to have wanted to include everything one could in one work about the young Will Shakespeare and his times.

Unable to write and, apparently, sexually unfulfilled, the young, lonely Will (Joseph Fiennes) in London is having a difficult time of it, shifting between acting and writing, while having to appease the theater owners' commitments and the actors' vanity—particu-

larly in the instance of Richard Burbage (Martin Clunes). Promises are made and broken, producers are tortured for non-payment, and behind-the-curtain deals are made, while the government, in the form of The Master of the Revels, Edward Tilney (Simon Callow), threatens to close down all theaters.

Although he has a vague idea for a comedy, *Romeo and Ethel, the Pirate's Daughter*, Shakespeare can find no words to express it. Fortunately, his friendly rival, Christopher "Kit" Marlowe (Rupert Everett), suggests that he make it an Italian story, with a love interest of a young girl from a warring family with a brother named Mercutio. His pirate story, in short, has begun to shape up into what we now know as *Romeo and Juliet*—if only he had a young Romeo or Juliet to inspire him to write.

Shakespeare finds both in the daughter of a wealthy businessman, Viola de Lesseps (Gwenyth Paltrow), who comes to him dressed as a male, Thomas Kent, hoping to play the lead. Smitten with theater and with Shakespeare's writing, Viola cannot appear onstage as a woman, so must win over the playwright as a man, which she immediately does with her convincing acting. Yet at the very moment of charming him, after he demands that she remove her hat that hides her golden curls, she rushes off, with the charmed Shakespeare on the chase.

Their run leads to the home of Lord and Lady de Lesseps, who are about to marry off their daughter to the crude and money-hungry, yet royally-connected Lord Wessex (Colin Firth). In search of the young actor Kent, Shakespeare interlopes upon the party, coming face to face with the beautiful Viola in a dance, and thunderously falls in love. Threatened by the jealous Wessex, the playwright gives his name as Kit Marlowe, thus unintentionally threatening the other's life, which later becomes a major element of the plot when Marlowe is killed in a bar, with the young Will believing he was the cause.

Indeed by the time the story has gone this far, there are so many avenues down which the authors' take the plot that it's hard to know how to untie their knotted entwinements. It hardly matters that at moments their story is filled with the same sophomoric humor that one might encounter in *Airplane!* or any number of

bad-boy bromances (at one moment, for example, Shakespeare is seen drinking from a cup inscribed with the words "Souvenir of Stratford-upon-Avon"), while at other moments the film presents itself as a witty commentary on Shakespeare's time; the central story follows much of the plot of *Romeo and Juliet* without the Capulets (although there are plenty of sword fights), interweaving the fictional affair offstage of Will and Viola with the onstage tragic love tale of Shakespeare's lovers. The next generation's popular playwright, John Webster, makes a cameo as a nasty boy actor (Joe Roberts), while the highly esteemed actor Burbage finally comes round to help out Shakespeare by allowing him to use his theater.

Married off to Wessex, Viola nonetheless escapes to watch the play, in which, when news spreads that the male-Juliet is ill, she suddenly discovers herself again acting, this time playing out onstage what the couple has been exploring in the wings. Even Queen Elizabeth (in the form of the magisterial acting of Judi Dench) enters the scene to save the day and award Shakespeare the money from an earlier wager that theater can some-

how be true to life.

If the film seems to be a grand pastiche, it would appear that the authors have gotten their point across. For the charm of this work is that, despite its declarations for realist theater, it is a post-modern mish-mash that works against most realist conventions, tossing numerous anachronisms, illogical plot developments, snippets of lines from other Shakespeare and Elizabethan dramas, ridiculous skits with dogs, and the shit and slops of the London streets all into the same pot. That it all somehow works, coming together to provide its audience with a truly wry lark, as theater producer Philip Henslowe (Geoffrey Rush) keeps insisting, is a mystery.

LOS ANGELES, JUNE 13, 2015
Reprinted from *World Cinema Review* (June 2015).

A New Way of Seeing

JANE UNRUE **THE HOUSE** (PROVIDENCE, RHODE
ISLAND: BURNING DECK, 2000)

THE NARRATOR OF this beautiful poetic text describes,
in its various aspects and relationships with its inhabit-
ant, a modernistic house, a house of great architectural
style "built on narrow supporting columns arranged
on a geometric grid...pierced around by windows."
But while the house is almost wondrous in its ability
to reflect illuminated light and receive sunlight, there
is something almost sinister and dark about the constructed box.

At several points, the narrator—in her detailed descriptions of moving up and down its staircases and in
and out of its rooms—lashes out in desperation, seeking
"a new house" or a complete immersion in the nearby
lake. Indeed, at one point in her frustration, she seeks
a new vantage-place by entering the matching house attached and looking out from its windows just as she has

done from her own.

Much of her movement throughout this geometric grid is, perhaps, an attempt on the part of the narrator to find a new perspective. And, as her masturbatory fantasies increase along with brief memories of sharing the house with another, the reader begins to perceive the very sterility of this glass container in which the narrator is entrapped.

There are no narrative punches or even near-explanations in this work, but the beauty of the language and the emotional effect the author achieves through it should delight anyone for whom plot is not the major device of fiction.

LOS ANGELES, 2000

Leaving the Door Open

ANTONIO JOSÉ PONTE **IN THE COLD OF THE MALECÓN AND OTHER STORIES,** TRANSLATED FROM THE SPANISH BY COLA FRANZEN AND DICK CLUSTER (SAN FRANCISCO: CITY LIGHTS, 2000)

THE TITLE STORY of the volume of stories *In the Cold of the Malecón* by Cuban Antonio José Ponte is indicative, perhaps, of the subtlety and themes of these short tales as a whole. In a fashion that might remind one of a short dialogue by Beckett or even Ionesco, a wife queries her husband concerning his visit to their son—not only about the look of his apartment and the food they ate, but how it was cooked, and, most particularly, about their activities after dinner. It is apparent from the start of this dialogue, however, that the wife has already heard it many a time, and when, at the tale's end, she asks her husband to repeat a section, we know it is a never-ending ritual, that the recounting is something they repeat over and over to wile away their

own empty lives, their own loneliness. But for the reader, the details of the visit reveal, on the surface, very little. The son lives in so small of an apartment, his father claims it could almost fit into one of their rooms. There is no evidence of any other person in their son's life. The son chopped the meat they had brought him into small pieces and had eaten it rare, not wanting "to lose the blood in cooking." After dinner, the father—in what appears as an absurd request—asks to see the "whores again." He is told that it is a bad night for walking along the Malecón, the sea, with the surf so high; they may not see any. Yet the two do go out and spot a few prostitutes along the sidewalk. One of them looks at the son, for just a moment, the father explains, "Like when you mistake someone in the street and realize the mistake immediately." The two then return home for a welcome cup of coffee.

It is the very "strangeness" of this seemingly meaningless tale, retold over and over by the couple, that forces the reader—at least this reader—to reread the tale in search of greater significance. Obviously, since

the father has brought the meat which the son so carefully cooks, it is something precious; as we discover
throughout these tales, nutritious food, as well as space,
is a rare commodity in contemporary Cuba. But why
the fascination with whores? The woman realizes her
mistake in even looking at the son: is he that disinter-
ested in appearance? Is he gay? And why has the father
insisted upon seeing them? Quite obviously they represent something outside normality, something unusual
in the parents' experience, something, perhaps, not
only sexual and immoral, but—in their illegal activity—more open and free? Ponte provides the reader no
explanations. The parents' conversation is, *in fact*, absurd; but then, as the author makes quite apparent, so
too is contemporary Cuban society.

In another story located by the beach, two brothers, awaiting the return of their father (the parents have
evidently gone off to care for a sick relative or friend),
rearrange the furniture each night, forcing them to
return each evening into a totally dark room through
which they must pass without bumping into the rear-
ranged furniture to reach the light. Ponte pushes this
slight tale into nearly metaphysical dimensions, as the
reshiftings of the room come to represent a break in the
relationships of objects, of past to present, of action to
life, as at story's end the older of the two boys discovers in the dark a door "that's never been there before,"

which he opens and "advances among the souls."

In "Station H," an old man arrives by train at a desolate station to play a game of chess with an unknown opponent, who turns out to be a young boy. But the old man never meets him, the game is never played. The old man disappears and the young boy makes away with the chess set the old man left. "This Life" is about individuals who ride the trains, almost like hobos of the American 1920s and 1930s, with no fixed destination and no apparent reason save poverty and utter boredom. The best story in this collection, "Heart of Skitalietz," goes even further in its absurdity than the others, as a despairing employee of an "institute" misses days of work only to discover, upon his return, that his office has been moved, most employees let go, and his own job terminated. Like the "disinherited wanderers of Russia," the Skitalietz, he begins to wander the streets of Havana, encountering a dying woman—an ex-astrologer who he first met via a crossed telephone connection—with whom he develops a strange relationship. But as their wanderings through often blacked-out sections of the city verge more and more on anarchic behavior, they are arrested and taken away to clinics where they might be resocialized. Released, the hero is called to take away his friend, now near death. They return to her apartment, stripped of all objects in their absence, where he places her against the wall and rushes out to buy a bed.

By the time he has returned, she is dead.

Ponte's tales in this volume are not just about purposelessness, about individuals fed-up with their lives seeking pleasure and freedom; in the world this author conjures up everything has been shifted about so completely, so many times, there is no definition even of what enjoyment and freedom might look like. What is change in a society that, while incessantly shifting, never changes? What is freedom in a world in which the individual is left only sexuality as an independent political act? In a world in which great actions have led to nothing, little acts mean everything—while resulting equally in nothing at all. Death becomes the only relief, something from which the survivors have no choice but to walk away in a kind of silent envy and respect, leaving the door open.

SAN FRANCISCO, 2000
Reprinted from *Green Integer Blog* (April 2008).

Ricochet

MICHAEL HANEKE (WRITER AND DIRECTOR) CODE INCONNU: RÉCIT INCOMPLETE DE DIVERS VOYAGES (CODE UNKNOWN: INCOMPLETE TALES OF SEVERAL JOURNEYS) / 2000

CODE UNKNOWN BEGINS with a sense of urgency and trauma which grows and grows throughout the film until the final scene, resulting in a disconnect with almost all the film's figures.

As she leaves a building, Anne Laurent (Juliette Binoche) is hailed by her boyfriend's young brother, Jean (Alexandre Hamidi), a disaffected boy who announces that he has just left his home on the farm. He's come to Paris, evidently, to speak with his brother, Georges, hoping for help in his escape from his hard and uneventful life.

Georges (Thierry Neuvic), Anne reports, is in Kosovo where he has been sent to photograph the war. She, an actress, has an appointment; she has no

choice but to share her building code with him so that Jean has someplace to stay the night. She quickly stops into a small store to buy a couple of pastries, knowing that the boy must be hungry, before they part.

No sooner than she is out of sight, Jean, having finished his sweet, rolls up the wrapper and tosses it into the lap of an older woman begging on the street. The rude behavior is witnessed by a young teacher from Mali, Amadou (Ona Lu Yenke), who grabs the youth and demands he apologize to the beggar, a Romanian woman encamped in front of a posh store. A street scuffle ensues and a small crowd gathers around them, as Jean attempts to escape. Some have seen his actions, but when Amadou and others try to explain the situation to the arriving police, they release Jean and arrest both Amadou and the Romanian woman.

Amadou's arrest horrifies his parents, an over-worked taxi driving father, and a caring mother who we witness telling her tale of woe, along with a torrent of tears, to a Malian aminate. This is, evidently, not the first time he has gotten into trouble. Maria, the Romanian woman is escorted to a plane and forced, as an illegal immigrant, to leave the country.

In short, through a simple ball of paper tossed away in anger, an entire series of unfortunate events ricochets, affecting all those around them,  setting the tone to a film in which each of the figures grows increasingly more isolated.

Similarly, the director isolates these events through his presentation of the film's scenes, as if he has dropped in to each household for a few minutes, scanning the figures briefly before moving on to others, signified with a black-out. Through this process, Haneke forces us to connect these dissociated fragments in order to evaluate his shadowy characters and to comprehend their problems in the context of the larger difficulties facing the society as a whole.

Some, like Jean's farmer father, to whom Jean temporarily returns, seem to have been already isolated before this primary event. With his wife dead, he sits basically in a brooding silence. Although it is clear that he loves his son, at one point bringing him home a motorcycle as a gift, with the heavy chores, early hours, and other taxing conditions of his life, he has no way to help his son adjust. By film's end, Jean has left the farm again, none of his family knowing where he has gone.

Similarly, when Georges returns from his photo-graphic assignment where he has clearly witnessed the terrors of the horrifying Balkan struggles, he seems relatively unaffected and is criticized both by another friend and Anne of lacking empathy and feeling for his fellow beings.

Others such as Anne, Amadou, and Maria seem to have too much feeling, involving themselves in situa-tions in which they are unable to significantly help, opening them to abuse. Anne plays just such a figure in the film on which she is currently at work, a thriller in which she portrays a woman touring an apartment where she is suddenly lured into a "music room" and threatened with her life. This terrible scene—in which the would-be murderer reports that he wants to watch her die—since we do not yet know that she is an actress, appears at first as if it might be a "real" event. The threat that gas will soon be filling the room, moreover, echoes with the deaths of millions of such women in the Nazi concentration camps.

Amadou, who desperately wants to be become as-similated into French culture, feels racially slighted and abused at nearly every turn. He works with deaf chil-dren, who have clearly their own problems with their own sense of being cut off from the world.

Maria, who was almost catatonic in Paris, comes alive as a grandmother and neighbor back in her native

Romanian city. Yet the poverty and drabness of her life there clearly makes one comprehend why she may wish to escape her country again.

The breaking point for Anne comes when she is accosted by a young Algerian boy on the subway, as he sexually toys with her, venting his own sense of anger and dissociation from the dominant and, in his mind, wealthy society in which he exists. The most frightening aspect of this assault is that the other riders look away, pretending as if the event were not occurring. Only one rider attempts to help.

Accompanied in the soundtrack by the heavy drumming of a performance of Amadou's deaf children, Anne returns home after her ordeal. Soon after, Georges is about to join her, but finds the code to her apartment no longer works. A telephone call from across the street results in no answer. Anne, too, has apparently recognized the failure of their relationship and their lack of true kinship. But in refusing him, she also has removed herself from the active loving and caring she, along with Amadou and Maria, have formerly committed to. We cannot but be fearful that if things do not change—if the codes of society are not resolved—the young Malian teacher and the older Romanian woman may ultimately close themselves off from others as well.

LOS ANGELES, FEBRUARY 3, 2011
Reprinted from *World Cinema Review* (February 2011).

Responsible Parties

ELISEO ALBERTO **CARACOL BEACH**, TRANSLATED FROM THE SPANISH BY EDITH GROSSMAN (NEW YORK: KNOPF, 2000)

AT THE HEART of Eliseo Alberto's terrifying and mesmerizing novel, *Caracol Beach*, first published in English in 2000, is a mad ex-soldier, Alberto Beto Milanés, a man of Cuban descent who fought in Ibondá de Akú, Angola in a Cuban detachment, of which he was the only survivor. Plagued by horrifying memories of his fellow soldiers and a seemingly real, if invisible, Bengal tiger, Beto Milanés, who has tried and failed at suicide, is determined to find others to help him die.

By coincidence a group of students just graduated from the nearby Emerson Institute, have traveled to the wealthy spit of land named Caracol Beach in Florida to celebrate at the home of their fellow classmate, Martin Lowell, who has invited his friends to the house without his parents' knowledge. Martin, the best student at the Institute, has just discovered his love for a young girl, Laura Fontanet, of Cuban heritage. She is also the girlfriend of the school athlete, Tom Chávez, and a rivalry

between the two boys lies at the heart of their concerted effort to save her life when she is later threatened by the ex-soldier.

In short, the series of events which ends so sadly with the deaths of both boys (deaths foretold and reported throughout even the earliest chapters of this fiction) seems terribly random. Had they only not run out of beer and wine, had they only not happened to visit the liquor store at the same moment that Beto Milanés was prowling the neighborhood, had they simply refused to go along with the mad man's horrible demands, had the local Sheriff, Sam Ramos, been in his office instead of a new deputy, Wellington Perales, when the calls concerning the boys' activities first came through...if only.... At first this tale seems so utterly meaningless, a series of random encounters which ends in a tragedy and painful memories that later lead others to self-destruction as well. But it is at precisely this point that novelist Alberto, the son of the great Cuban poet Diego Alberto, makes it clear that his fiction is not a thinly-veiled retelling of real events, that it is not even a truly realist fiction.

Caracol Beach, in fact, had its roots in Gabriel García Marquez's script-writing course at the International School of Film and Television in San Antonio de los Baños, Cuba in 1989. As the assistant for that course, Alberto shared stories with the students, one of which, a tale in which young Puerto Ricans were pursued for an entire night by an unknown assailant, clearly became the embryonic center of this novel. In the class, various students suggested wild alternatives for the attending plot, including suggestions for the inclusion of an Armenian, a drug addict, a Bengal tiger, and other elements, many of which found their way into Alberto's work of 1998.

And parallel to its development, one might argue, *Caracol Beach* is not at all a story of *random* acts, but like the collaborative process which helped bring it to life, is ultimately a story of tightly interlinked events, of human actions and failures that are so interwoven that, at the close of this story, one sees the young boys' deaths as strangely fated.

The mad ex-soldier, first of all, is not just a misfit who has found his way to the Beach salvage yard where he lives. Ramos, a former soldier himself, was the man who watched over the recovery of Beto Milanés, and developed such a close relationship with the unfortunate young man that, when it came time to part ways, the survivor felt betrayed. It is not entirely accidental, accordingly, that when Ramos retires from the army and comes to work at the Caracol Beach Police Department, the young soldier has moved nearby. Perhaps if Ramos, instead of ignoring the suicidal soldier, had befriended him again, Beto Milanés' killing might have been prevented.

But Ramos, himself, has problems. The night of these events he is not only busy training a clearly inept new deputy, the son of another army buddy, but is plagued by the behavior of his own son, Nelson (who uses the name Mandy), a transvestite whom he has not seen for weeks, and who, as a judo and black-belt expert, has not only just beaten his own lover, Tigran Androsian, but attacked a man who attempts to make advances toward him at the local bowling alley and bar. It is this series of events, along with the nuisance call by the town busybody, Mrs. Dickinson, that takes Ramos away from his desk during the crucial hours during which the young boys are forced by the soldier to destroy an automobile, kill a dog, and attack a prostitute, Gigi Col, a friend of Mandy and Tigran's (it is notable that the mad soldier's son was also a prostitute). And it is Ramos' decision to visit his estranged son that puts the young deputy in charge during the attack upon the two boys who enter the junkyard to save their beloved Laura.

Laura, who is at the center of the boys' world at the moment of these events, is, herself, a kind of lost soul, having witnessed as a child the wasting away of her Cuban-born mother, a woman she imagined watching over her when she was young, and who, herself, loved to visit Caracol Beach. As she enters the area to attend the party, she conjures up her mother, who pounds at the car window to tell her not to go to the Martin home.

The wealth of Martin's parents, moreover, draws these young people to his home, and the parents' evident permissiveness, expressed in a telephone conversation never received by Martin, suggests that, despite Martin's own previous sense of responsibility, they might have attended more to his whereabouts that night.

The school gym teacher, Agnes MacLarty, invited to the party at Caracol Beach, and who had had a sexual relationship with her student Tom, might have been able to protect her charges from their destinies; but that night she had a date with a charming poet and scholar (he has written a thesis on the Cuban writer Reinaldo Arenas), Theo Uzcanga, whom she later marries.

In short, as the lover of astronomy, Alberto Beto Milanés, might have said, the events of that night of June 20, 1994, were "in the stars."

As the author himself makes clear, particularly in the passage where Martin and Tom enter the junkyard, fighting each other for a few moments in a combat that encompasses their desires to save Laura, to retreat, and to turn to one another in love:

> When Martin turned and began his retreat, Tom suddenly tackled him and they both rolled down the slope of wrecked metal in the auto salvage yard. They fought hard and senselessly and with love. How can that terrible moment be described if neither of them lived to tell about it?

With that remarkable questioning of his own narrative techniques, Alberto retreats from his seemingly objective narration (something he does numerous times throughout the book) to question not only *his* authorial motives, but the meaning of it all.

> Would it be better to use this page to reflect on the indecency of wars, which do not end when the politicians sign their peace treaties but live on in the survivors, the victims of an arduous campaign that still goes on inside each one of them, between their guts and their hearts?
>
> ...But does that make sense? What good would it do? Tom and Martin won't read this book: if the document exists, this fiction about facts, it is be-

cause they could not rely on the shield of letters, sentences, paragraphs, parapets of words. The only way to change destiny would be to lie, and not even a lie would save men: death, too, is a tyrant.

Alberto here defends fiction as an act of imagination rather than a telling of historical or political truth, which he recognizes would have to be a kind of lie. Life does not represent, after all, an orderly pattern of experience, but is a "totality of coincidences. And accidents" that includes everyone. It is only through the imagination, through a recreation of reality, that forgiveness and redemption can be found.

And this is, at last, a novel of just such redemption. Mandy and her lover return to their relationship, with Ramos' blessing. Agnes MacLarty, at book's end, is pregnant with her second child. Laura, after a period of psychological recovery, is studying psychology at the University of California at Los Angeles. When one of Tom and Martin's young friends is caught up in depression and joins a religious sect, the Children of Heaven, which brings him to the edge of suicide, Ramos, Uzcanga, officer Wellington Perales, Laura's father, and the headmaster of the Emerson Institute secretly travel to Utah, attacking the "monastery" and rescuing the boy.

Out of these seemingly meaningless deaths grows

the awareness within the community of Caracol Beach that everyone is in some way responsible and that they need to admit their failures, forgiving one another and themselves. Perhaps more than any novel since Heimito von Doderer's *Everyman a Murderer*, Alberto's *Caracol Beach* recognizes that we are all, in a small way, "responsible parties." By novel's end, fortunately, "clemency" is finally realized—if only as a crossword puzzle word—and mercy is awarded for those who have survived.

LOS ANGELES, AUGUST 2, 2000
Reprinted from *EXPLORINGfictions* (August 2010).

The Miracle of Our Empty Hands

ROBERT BRESSON (WRITER AND DIRECTOR, BASED ON A NOVEL BY GEORGES BERNANOS) **LE JOURNAL D'UN CURÉ DE CHAMPAGNE** / 1951, USA 1954

ROBERT BRESSON (WRITER AND DIRECTOR) **PICK-POCKET** / 1959, USA 1963

ROBERT BRESSON (WRITER AND DIRECTOR) **AU HASARD BALTHAZAR** / 1966, USA 1970

ROBERT BRESSON (WRITER AND DIRECTOR, BASED ON A NOVEL BY GEORGES BERNANOS) **MOUCHETTE** / 1967, USA 1970

ROBERT BRESSON's third film, *Le Journal d'un curé de champagne*, brought him international attention and awards, including the 1951 Grand Prize at the Venice Film Festival. Like his later film, *Mouchette*, *Diary of a Country Priest* was based on a novel by the noted French Catholic writer Georges Bernanos, and like that later film, this work is a bleak portrait of French provin-

cial life.

A young priest (Claude Laydu), fresh out of seminary, is assigned to the village of Ambricourt in northern France. Innocent and highly idealistic, the priest feels dissociated from and uncomfortable with his often cynical and crude parishioners. These people, according to the seasoned priest of nearby Torcy, are a vengeful and mean folk, going so far—as a local schoolgirl, Séraphita, tells him—to lace wine with drugs upon the priest's visit, just to observe him fall into a stupor upon his return home, which, in their gossip, they can portray as drunkenness. The priest, however, has big changes in mind for his community, which, despite the warnings of the Torcy priest and the local count, he attempts to enact, meeting with resistance and ridicule from nearly all. Even his catechism students involve him in their schoolgirl jokes.

His one regular churchgoing worshipper, Miss Louise, a nanny at the chateau, unintentionally involves him with the family at the chateau. While the husband eventually dismisses the aspirations of the priest, the young daughter of the house further draws him into the life of her family by reporting that her father and her nanny are having an affair. When the priest finally determines to approach the girl's mother, he discovers a woman who, long aware of her husband's infidelities, has determined to forgive them at the expense of her own salvation and happiness.

In a long and fascinating discussion about human will in relation to God's grace, the priest attempts to reconcile the woman to her savior.

> COUNTESS: Love is stronger than death. Your scriptures say so.
> CURÉ D'AMBRICOURT: We did not invent love. It has its order, its law.
> COUNTESS: God is its master.
> CURÉ D'AMBRICOURT: He is not the master of love. He is love itself. If you would love, don't place yourself beyond love's reach.

Miraculously, he succeeds in her returning to her faith, but when she dies that same evening her family and the entire community is even more outraged by his intrusion into this woman's and others' lives.

Meanwhile, the priest himself is suffering not only from severe doubts about the power of his faith and his ability to lead this village, but is unable to eat most foods, surviving primarily on bread crusts and the wine into which he has dipped them; in short, he eats only the elements of the sacrament, bread and wine. A trip to a doctor in a neighboring town reveals that he is terminally ill with cancer, and, upon visiting a seminary  friend living in that town—a man who, having failed to finish his education, leads a desultory and poverty-stricken life as a writer—the young priest dies after apparently coming to terms with his own failures and recognizing that "All is grace," that God himself is grace.

Such a plot summary, however, can give one no idea of the power of Bresson's film, which in scene after scene pits the beautiful, finely-boned, almost monk-like priest (Laydu, a nonprofessional actor, apparently studied the mannerisms of priests and fasted to achieve the wan, fragile look of the priest) against the everyday commonness and earthiness of these village folk. The film begins with an image of a young couple in the midst of a lusty kiss, breaking away from each other as the priest enters their terrain. The nearby priest, a hard-headed pragmatist, has few delusions about the people, and it is clear that he has survived only because he has demanded petty obedience to the church's laws as opposed to sweeping change. The local doctor, Delbende—one of the few men of intelligence of the community—has apparently never heard of Semmelweis and antiseptic techniques. He literally looks and smells of the earth, and returns to the earth by killing himself.

The priest is clearly an aesthete, a man not of action but of symbolic acts and a spiritual language that in contrast to the community he is attempting to serve often appears to come out of nowhere, as if he were speaking in tongues. If nothing else, his highly pitched intensity, revealed in long narrational passages as he is seen writing in his diary, seems utterly at odds with the everyday events and behavior of his surroundings.

As in many later films, Bresson focuses on bodily parts, particularly the hands, to help engage the reader in the priest's sense of displacement. Throughout the film, the priest's hands seem almost to flutter into motion (with many of the sexual connotations that word suggests) while those around him stand stolidly or stomp into space.

The priest, on the other hand, represented significantly by pen in hand, repeats the words of his journal as if they were a sacred text. Repeatedly he signs the blessing. When the countess throws her locket containing the picture of her dead son into the fire, the young priest quickly reaches into the flames to retrieve it.

Moreover, he speaks of the role hands have in his beliefs, recalling the hands of "the virgin rocking the world's cradle," and, as he lifts the countess' veil as she lies upon her deathbed, rhapsodizing: "Oh, the miracle of our empty hands!" in his apparent startlement at discovering the effect—having blessed the countess at the end of their conversation—one can achieve, despite his feelings of inadequacy, with a simple touch.

Part of the dilemma of this man's life is that no one dares to show him love or even encourage his acts. Only once or twice is he blessed by the touch of others' hands, the most important of these moments being when Séraphita discovers him face down in the mud, and he awakens to the touch of her washing away the blood and mud from his face before pulling him into the safety of a temporary hiding place where we can comfortably sleep off the drug-laced wine he has drunk.

The second such event is when a relative of the count invites him to ride on the back of his motorbike, and with hands intently placed upon the handle bars, takes this man of god on a wild ride, so delighting the priest that we suddenly recall he is after all a young boy who might, had he chosen another path, be thrilled by life.

In the isolated village of Ambricourt there is no one to embrace—not only sexually, of course, since he has taken the vow of chastity—but symbolically or spiritually, the only methods left to him. The emptiness with which he is faced is indeed the disease which kills him, a cancer which leaves him equally with an empty stomach. Despite his own dying perception, we can only ponder why he was offered so little earthly grace.

LOS ANGELES, MARCH 19, 2000

PICKPOCKET is one of Bresson's greatest films, although US viewers have often described it as being stiffly-acted with scenes that appear to be "phony." In his introduction to the Criterion release of the film, scriptwriter Paul Schrader explains, in part, why this film was so meaningful to him by discussing how Bresson worked against the genre of the crime story, and, in fact, pushed against traditional narrative techniques.

Through his use of "non-actors"—individuals who have never before appeared in films, who speak lines not as portrayals of "reality" but somewhat flatly and uninflected—through his repetition of the action—often reporting what is about to happen and then showing it again—and through his odd employment of music—stealing it from emotional scenes and bringing it in at seemingly inopportune moments—Bresson works against both narrative and genre; "This is not like a crime movie," Schrader summarizes. The slow movement of the actors, Bresson's "single" or even full-length shots, and the deprivation of emotional expression on the actors' often blank faces, moreover, all work together to create in the viewers a sense of unease that builds up to the final moments when the failure of his life is re-vealed to the "hero," Michel (Martin LaSalle). In short, if to some viewers the film seems stiff and artificial, it is purposely and effectively so.

What Schrader does not describe however, is the even more disquieting relationship this film has with parts of the body, particularly the hands, which lends to the work an uneasy sensation of voyeurism. Indeed, I will go so far as to describe this film as a series of mimed sex acts, most of them homoerotic.

Obviously, we see only fragments of body parts, and the scenes are always played out with clothed actors. We understand, moreover, the "real" action to be a portrayal of robbery.

The situation is simple. A friend of Michel's, Jacques (Pierre Leymarie), tries to help the out-of-work man find a job. "You're good with your hands," he tells Michel. But Michel demures, preferring, so it seems, the emptiness of his shiftless life. We later discover that he has gone as far as to steal money from his own mother.

One day, after witnessing a pick-pocket at work on a train, Michel cannot resist attempting a similar act. When he accomplishes it—out of pure luck, he con-fesses—he feels as if "I was walking on air." Soon after, he is arrested, freed only because the police do not have enough evidence. Like an addict, however, he returns to carry out several other such robberies, that is until he meets up with another man who appears to be follow-ing him, and who quickly becomes an accomplice, soon bringing in a third party as well.

It is at that moment, as the accomplice follows him, and Michel turns back to challenge the stranger, that we begin to perceive in Bresson's work that any plot is basically laid to rest, as the director shifts instead to al-most abstract patterns that are similar to sexual "cruis-ing." Bresson begins, in long repetitive montages, to show us how to steal a billfold, a watch, a purse. In most cases the pickpocket must face the person (most often a male) directly head on, moving as closely to him as possible. The slip of the hand into the pocket (in Bres-son's telling, it is usually the upper breast pocket or the front coat pocket, seldom the back) must be supple and quick, almost as if one were stealthily stroking the individual without him knowing it.

Michel's long, thin fingers sensually dart into pockets again and again, or those same fingers gently curl around the wrist as they remove a victim's watch. The passing of these trophies on to the others is as sudden and lascivious, as if they were sharing some sexual charge carried along with the objects they've stripped from the victims.

Indeed, it is the addiction to these encounters, the fixation on the placement of hands upon the bodies of others that makes this the perfect metaphor for the sexual act, and helps to keep the audience queasily attentive. Without quite knowing it, we feel that we are sharing something that should remain private.

In his public life, on the other hand, in his encounters with the detective, with Jacques, and the woman, Jeanne (Marika Green), who cares for his mother, Michel is a cold fish, arguing vaguely for a kind of anarchy in which "supermen" are permitted to behave as they like. Although it's clear he is attracted to Jeanne, he seems uncaring for her destitute situation and nonplussed by Jacques' growing love of her. Michel gains little, moreover, from his thievery. He readily gives up most of the money to his mother, and would support Jeanne if he could, while living in a hovel, a room that has no reason to exist except for providing him a place to sleep—sometimes for long periods when he becomes exhausted from his acts, just as one might from sex.

On the contrary, in public—at the races, on trains and subways, and in the lobbies of banks where he selects his "clients"—Michel comes alive in his search for something to put into his hands. Unlike the country priest in Bresson's earlier movie, whose hands remain empty in his attempts to express the miracle of life, Michel is seen desperately trying to fill up his hands, reaching out again and again for bodies that he dare not touch, only to discover fists full of watches, billfolds, and an occasional purse. As Jeanne correctly tells him, "You're not in the real world."

After leaving Paris for a time, practicing his thievery elsewhere, Michel returns to find Jeanne alone with a child. For the first time, Michel begins to see her frailty and beauty, and determines to become honest. Jeanne, always the realist, however, knows the truth: "You have to leave me and never come back," she proclaims.

This time his addiction leads him back to Longchamps, the race track where he was first arrested. As he attempts to steal a bundle of money from a man who works with the police, we see a different encirclement of the wrist, a handcuff placed upon it. In prison—a place where, in fact, Michel has metaphorically been all along—he finally comes to see the emptiness of the things he has taken in favor of true physical contact.

Jeanne appears at his cell, and the film ends with her kissing his hands through the prison bars, representing his possible redemption through love.

PERHAPS MY FAVORITE of Bresson's excellent films is *Au Hasard Balthazar* of 1966, maybe because it is one of his richest and yet most forgiving of films. For the characters of *Balthazar*, each suffering or causing others to suffer, are also likeable human beings for whom the filmgoer feels, despite their failures.

At the center of this parable-like tale is the donkey Balthazar, given upon birth to a young girl, Marie (the beautiful Anne Wiazemsky), who lives with her schoolteacher father (Philippe Asselin) and mother (Nathalie Joyaut) on a farm whose owner also has a son her age, Jacques (Walter Green), and a sickly daughter. The three children, particularly the closely knit Jacques and Marie, lovingly care for and pet the animal, even performing over him a kind of baptism, which hints at the specialness of this beast.

When the siblings' mother dies, the father with his son and daughter moves away, leaving the farm to the schoolteacher, who has always wanted to try his hand at farming with modern methods. But as a busy farmer with a now pubescent daughter less attentive to Balthazar, he determines the animal is no longer worth keeping, and sells him to the local baker.

Meanwhile, a small-town thug, Gérard (François Lafarge), and his gang have been sneaking into the farm, torturing the donkey while attempting to attract the attention of Marie. By coincidence, the baker hires Gérard to deliver his bread to outlying regions, using Balthazar as the beast of burden.

One day, while out driving, Marie observes the boy and her former donkey, and stops to pet the animal. Gérard enters her car and refuses to leave, followed by a series of pushes and pulls between the two that ends, predictably, with sex. That incident begins a long and abusive relationship that scandalizes her family and enrages the small town.

Marie's father, meanwhile, has been a topic of gossip for the townspeople, mostly out of envy for his success, and when the gossip reaches the ears of the former owner, he demands a reckoning of accounts. Guiltless, Marie's father refuses to produce them, and the farm is taken from him. Jacques returns to try to reconcile the situation, but Marie's father refuses to speak with him.

Because of Gérard's continual abuse of the donkey, the animal ultimately refuses to move, as the boy ties a newspaper around his tail and sets it on fire. The animal runs off in terror, and when Gérard finds him, he unwillingly moves on. By the next day, however, Balthazar refuses to even rise, as the baker prepares to euthanatize him. A local drunk takes him on, using him and another donkey to bear the burden of his menial tasks. The drunk alternates with love and brutality as well, and, at one point, in the middle of a city street, the animal escapes his tormentor.

The next adventure for the poor donkey is at a circus, where he is introduced to the other animals. Bresson beautifully presents the animals' eye-to-eye contact, the doleful donkey meeting first a lion, then a polar bear, a monkey, and an elephant. A circus trainer perceives the donkey's intelligence and trains him to become a kind of Clever Hans who counts out major multiplications and divisions of numbers with his hoof. The animal is brilliant until he sees the drunk in the crowd and, fearing him, breaks into a braying that ruins the act. Returned to the drunk, the donkey escapes once more, finding his way back to Marie and the farm.

By this time, however, Marie has become so involved with Gérard and his friends, whom Bresson portrays almost as a French equivalent of a gang of hoodlums, that she rarely returns home, and her parents are caught up in their grieving for her and their idyllic past.

The donkey is sent off to a local recluse, who uses the poor animal to grind wheat, beating the beast whenever it pauses in its endless circle of pain.

Miraculously the town drunk receives an inheritance, and celebrates with the young hoodlums and others at a local bar. Gérard, now drunk and almost in a rage, destroys most of the bar, dancing with another girl and refusing to even touch Marie. Marie, finally determined to escape her friends, shows up at the farm of the recluse, begging to stay in the barn for the night. He refuses, bringing her within the house, where she feeds herself—against his will—while discussing his greed. The evening ends with her offering him sex in return for a bed.

Ultimately, Marie returns home, and her mother insists that Balthazar be brought back to console her in

her sorrow. Jacques revisits the family, offering to marry Marie, promising to never remind her of her past. But almost the moment he turns away to confer with her father, Gérard and his gang carry her off, raping her and leaving her naked in a nearby granary. Marie leaves forever, the father left to suffer and, after a brief visit from the priest, to die.

Marie's mother, completely desolate, is visited by Gérard and his friends. They want to borrow the donkey for the night, but she refuses. He is all she has, she insists, and "Besides, he's a saint." Later they steal the animal, using it to traffic goods—chocolates, hosiery, liquor, etc.—across the Swiss border. Authorities cry out, "Customs! Halt!" and begin shooting, the boys running off. The donkey stands alone against the land-scape as the camera moves in to reveal that Balthazar is bleeding.

By the morning the animal is on his knees as a herd of sheep surrounds him. By the time the herd has moved on, we see Balthazar lying upon his side, dead.

For all the tears these last scenes bring to our eyes, however, Bresson's tale, we realize, is not as bleak as it sounds. In part, we readily recognize that all of the individuals of the film, cruel or loving, are humans very much like us. At times each of them is beautiful. Even the wrathful Gérard sings out in a lovely voice in the church and is a stunningly sexual youth. As some critics have pointed out, each of the film's characters, while revealing themselves as potentially caring individuals, seems also to be afflicted by one of the seven deadly sins, a flaw which removes him or her from grace.

The director reveals the complexity of their desires and behavior through images of their legs, eyes, and, once again, most potently, through their hands. From the first images of the children's hands petting Balthazar's body, hands reached out with sugar to feed him, and hands pouring water upon the beast's head, we recognize that it is the empty hand, the open giving hand that signifies love and salvation. But here we simultaneously witness filled hands: hands holding sticks, whips, chairs, and guns, flattened hands that slap, clenched

fists that pummel and beat. In one scene we witness Marie upon a bench, with Gérard crouching behind her, offering his hand in love, which she refuses. While a few images later, we see him and his gang hurling their fists against the donkey's hide. It is precisely this duality of experience, the simultaneous existence of long hands laid to rest, against clenched and closed hands of punishment, hurt, and hate, that is Bresson's central image. Almost every figure of the film has within them the potential to either greedily grab at life or openly accept experience, and it is their alternate decisions of which position to take that result in love or sorrow.

LOS ANGELES, JUNE 4, 2011

ROBERT BRESSON'S 1967 film *Mouchette* (released in the US in March 1970) is one of the most despairing of his oeuvre, yet one of the most celebratory of life. Based, like his *Diary of a Country Priest*, on a novel by Georges Bernanos, *Mouchette,* almost without plot, is the story of a 14-year-old schoolgirl (Nadine Nortier) who lives in a dilapidated farm house with her dying mother, her alcoholic father and brother, and a new-born baby brother, for whose care she is responsible. Unhappy at  home, mocked by her schoolgirl peers, and unable to participate (both financially and spiritually) in any of the limited joys available to her, Mouchette, as Bresson himself described her, is "evidence of misery and cruelty. She is found everywhere: wars, concentration camps, tortures, assassinations."

Like most of Bresson's suffering figures, she nonetheless is more than resilient, ignoring and battling her schoolgirl companions and the neighborhood boys in their taunts. In a stunning scene at a weekend carnival, Bresson reveals the possibilities of her life through the movement of Dodg'em cars: at first her car is simply hit by others again and again, but gradually, as she spots and starts to flirt with a handsome boy in another "auto," she manipulates her car into position to successfully crash into his and others' cars. Later, as she begins to trail after the young man, she is quickly pulled aside by her ever-watchful father and struck in the face.

Bresson films this young woman's abuse with an

almost abstract, "flat," directorial eye, allowing his non-actors (he chose evidently an entirely amateur cast) to reveal their own stories in action, since they are quite clearly a people of few words. Yet the actions in which they engage are anything but uneventful. Luisa, the local bartender, is courted by the gamekeeper Mathieu, but is obviously more attracted to the small-time poacher Arsène. Like Mouchette, who occasionally helps out in the bar to earn her family a few more coins, Luisa's life is one of repetition and boredom, but in her role as the dispenser of what all the men seek—wine and liquor—she is a woman of power, while Mouchette has so little choice over her life that she hardly casts a shadow.

As in his other films, Bresson employs the images of hands in this work—the camera follows Luisa's hands over and over as she pours out the drinks, lingers over Mouchette's attempts to soothe and heal her mother and to hold and change the diaper of her baby brother, and mocks her father's bedtime antics of driving a car—but it is the legs and feet of his characters that dominate: the embarrassing slap of Mouchette's clogs against the earth as she arrives late to school and the later loss of one of those shoes in a storm; the angry crush of dirt into the carpet of an old woman, who, late in the film, demands Mouchette ponder her own death.

What also gives this film such power is the oddity

of its few events, particularly the scene beginning with her journey home from school through the woods. In these woods we have already observed a battle—similar to that of Renoir's *Le Règle de jeu*—between gamekeeper and poacher, between the pheasants and rabbits inhabiting the place and those who would take their lives. Caught up in this struggle, Mouchette is forced to take cover under a tree during a rainstorm. Meanwhile, Mathieu and Arsène encounter one another, a fight-in-the-brewing for some time. At first Arsène seems conciliatory, willing to give up his trap. But when it is refused, he pushes the other into a stream where they briefly fight. Yet it is a ludicrous battle, they perceive, and it ends with them laughing at each other as they share the wine in Arsène's cask.

By the time Arsène comes across Mouchette, however, he is so drunk that he believes he has killed Mathieu. At first he appears solicitous of the young girl, determined to help her find her missing clog, and to have her help him with an alibi. They briefly take cover in a small hut, but after hearing two rifle shots—shots clearly coming from Mathieu's gun—Arsène insists that they wipe away all evidence of being there and takes her to his own house.

Again he seems caring of her situation; but suddenly, in one of the strangest of cinematic events, he undergoes an epileptic fit. As she has previously nursed her mother, Mouchette holds his head, wiping away the blood and spittle that issues from the poacher's mouth. It is as if she can find no other role in her life but that of caregiver; little is ever offered in return. And with Arsène's revival comes the inevitable. She now fears for her own safety and, somewhat lamely perhaps—given both her need for love and her expectations of the abuse—attempts to fend him off before finally, as he begins the rape, accepting him in an embracing hug. In short, it is the very "strangeness" of these scenes that makes them appear to be so inevitable, as if these events were too odd to be anything but the "truth."

When Mouchette finally returns home, the baby is bawling, her mother near death. She cannot even find a match in the house to warm the milk. In the night la mère dies.

The next morning she is determined to go for the baby's milk. But this time she encounters, briefly, people who seem willing to help. A grocer offers her coffee and a croissant, but as she attempts to place another croissant into the girl's pocket, Mouchette backs away—now terrified, evidently, of even human touch. A customer accusingly stares at her as the camera makes apparent what the women observe: the top button of her dress is missing. "Slut," one of the women hisses.

Checking up on Mathieu, Mouchette is surprised to see him still living; seeing her there he insists she

 come into his house to reveal what has occurred during the night. As the game-keeper and his wife begin to interrogate her, she resists, but ends up by declaring Arsène is now her lover.

An old friend of the family invites her in to present her with a shroud for her mother and some dresses for the girl herself. But Mouchette is indignant. What can those things mean to her now? Why didn't the woman help out during her mother's life? The "friend" is, quite obviously, inured to the dead ("I am a friend of the dead") rather than to those who are alive.

In a world such as Mouchette's, love and life are squandered, creating a vacuum that offers only a mean death. As she once again crosses the woods on her way home, Mouchette pauses, checking out one of the new dresses of the "gift"; like all of her other clothes, it too is quickly torn in the brambles. Wrapping herself in it, Mouchette rolls down the hill toward the stream, but her body comes to a standstill as it reaches the bushes at water's edge. With new determination, with a will that represents her attempt to take back her own life, Mouchette repeats the act, rolling in her new "shroud" down the hill once more, this time hitting the mark, her body falling like a stone into the water from where it will never rise.

Has the renowned Roman Catholic director now advocated suicide? some viewers asked upon the film's release. I cannot speak for Bresson. But in such an immoral world, perhaps even self-murder can be seen as a spiritual act.

LOS ANGLES, FEBRUARY 28, 2000
Reprinted from *World Cinema Review* (June 2011).

The People are a Fantasy

JEAN-LOUIS MILESI AND ROBERT GUÉDIGUIAN (SCE-
NARIO AND DIALOGUE), ROBERT GUÉDIGUIAN (DIREC-
TOR) LA VILLE EST TRANQUILLE (THE TOWN IS QUIET)
/ 2000

THE MARSEILLE DIRECTOR Robert Guédiguian presents, in a 360° pan at the beginning of this film, a city
awash in a golden splendor of light, that does indeed
appear to be quiet and calm. The music we hear, De-
bussy, Bach, and works by other composers, is being
played, we soon discover, by a young Georgian boy on
an electric keyboard set up in a park; a sign asks listen-
ers to contribute to his purchase of a real piano.

Union organizers are attempting to stand firm
against dockyard closures and a payout agreement with
the company, but the men shouting out their determination seem tired and look uncertain about their
demands. One, a character we will later follow, Paul
(Jean-Pierre Darroussin), cannot even bring himself to

join in their chants.

On a clear night, a group of city elites celebrates on a rooftop terrace, the host (perhaps a politician) going about his guests to briefly speak with each. One of the most stunning women in the group is Viviane Froment (Christine Brücher), who we later discover is a music teacher currently working with mentally disabled children. Her husband, Yves (Jacques Pieiller), an architect, spends his time chatting and flirting with beautiful women.

So far we see nothing in Marseille that we might not encounter in any large city: Los Angeles, New York, London, Paris. The city is tranquil, or, as an African character later puts it, "The world looks happy from up here."

The irony of Guédiguian's title, accordingly, becomes evident when he takes us down into the streets to follow other denizens of Marseilles' l'Estaque district, the most notable of whom is Michèle (Ariane Ascaride), a woman whose daughter is a drug addict and has a baby born out of wedlock. Her husband is, as the movie puts it, on the "dole," a drunk who sits about all day complaining about his daughter's painful whimpers of withdrawal. To survive, Michèle works as a fishmonger all night, returning in the mornings to feed and care for her baby granddaughter and daughter. When the daughter, Fiona, is not suffering she is out whor-

 ing for money to buy drugs. As Michèle screams out to her daughter, "The drugs you bought last night surely cost more that I can make in a month!" When her husband threatens her, she retorts, "Death would be nice."

For all that, Michèle is filled with determination and the will to survive, and she is the most loving and forgiving character of the film, so desperate to help her daughter, for example, that, after Fiona has used the doctor-prescribed antidote to get high, the mother contacts an old friend, a bartender, Gérard to help her obtain real drugs. When her savings runs out, she is determined even to pimp herself in order to cover the cost.

Into this world comes Paul, who has used his redundancy money to get a loan to purchase a new car and a cab license. Paul, the son of a former partisan father and loving mother, also does not live such a tranquil life. A failure in everything, he represents the millions of individuals who work hard, but seem never to get ahead, cannot maintain relationships, and fall time and again throughout their lives. Claude, the man from whom he has borrowed money, puts it bluntly: (in my summary, imprecise quote) "You will never pay me back and I will

have to do something terrible to you. But I won't be able to because of my respect for your father." A man who seeks love from prostitutes, Paul observes Michèle's dismal failure to find clients, and takes her home without demanding sex. When soon after he loses his cab license for violation of taxi regulations, he returns to Michèle, this time paying her for sex. It is clear that he would like their relationship to go further, but she is too preoccupied to notice his obsequiousness.

Meanwhile, across town a young African, Abderramane (Alexandre Ogou), recently released from jail, observes Viviane teaching her students in an auditorium. He has sought her out because of the memorable experiences he had as a member of a choir she taught in prison, and he is determined to do something better with his life. Like Michèle, Viviane is fed up with her husband, and finds a gracefulness in Abderramane's flattery. Before long, he is helping her students to dance, and the two briefly come together for one night of love. Soon after Abderramane is shot by fascists, who include Michèle's husband, for attempting to swim in the nearby ocean.

Michèle's life continues to spin downward, as her daughter needs higher and higher doses of crack cocaine. She is so exhausted that she misses her workshift for the first time. Fiona continues to cry out in pain.

Gérard, we discover, along with Paul, who mysteriously follows him, is an assassin, whom we watch kill a city notable celebrating on a rooftop party just as we have witnessed early on.

Michèle fires up another dose of drugs for her daughter, this time adding a second packet and yet a third. Smiling in the bliss of relief, Fiona awaits the needle which will result in her death.

Gérard arrives, responding to Michèle's news a few minutes before Paul arrives for another sexual encounter. Despite the fact that he knows he is intruding on some dreadful happening, this time he insists he will not go. What happens, we are never told. But it is clear that they can no longer help one another, that they are both doomed to face the circumstances of their acts.

We witness one such encounter with truth. Gérard, angry with some pedestrians who react to his near-refusal to stop his car to let them pass, picks up a gun as if he intends to shoot them. As he exits the car, however, he turns the gun instead into  his own mouth before releasing the trigger.

In a small street of the immigrant ghetto, a piano is being delivered. Left for a few seconds in the middle of the street, the young Georgian boy, with whom the film began, sits down to play.

Guédiguian's harrowing film is often described as a painfully realist presentation of Marseille, but in its intricacies of plot and its density of coincidence, it is, to my way of thinking, more like a kind of fantasy. Even the most well-rounded character in the work, Michèle, is almost too selfless to be believed; the others are all rather vague, their actions often muddled.

Yet for all that, the film works as a piece of art, for we realize that any attempt to describe the motivations and behavior of real people is a kind of fantasy. Just as Viviane, earlier in the film, suggests her husband's self-proclaimed love of the people belies his complete ignorance of them—"For you the people are a fantasy"—we all can only imagine what is inside each other. The impetus of Guédiguian's film is not realist characterization but a political statement, a presentation, of sorts, of the various social and political positions one might take within any large community. Far from being quiet, life in a city is always noisy, a mess of various voices and demands, which is also why city life is so terrifyingly exciting, creating a place where one never knows what to expect. The town is quiet only when one refuses to listen to its people calling out.

LOS ANGELES, MARCH 16, 2011
Reprinted from *World Cinema Review* (March 2011).

The Frightened Rabbit Flattens Against the Grass

LÁSZLÓ KRASZNAHORKAI **THE MELANCHOLY OF RESISTANCE**, TRANSLATED FROM THE HUNGARIAN BY GEORGE SZIRTES (NEW YORK: NEW DIRECTIONS, 2000)

ONE OF THE major publishing events of 2000 for the US and Canadian audience was the publication of László Krasznahorkai's *The Melancholy of Resistance*. This spellbinding, phantasmagoric fiction is so powerful that even now, weeks after reading it, I feel its effects.

The story is somewhat complex, but not as crucial as it may seem, the characters, the scene, and Krasznahorkai's tumbling sentences mattering far more than plot. Indeed, throughout it is the language that seems to be the subject of this book, the black ink broodingly charging across the page like an army (Krasznahorkai resists periods almost as he might the plague), as opposed to the slightly stumbling amble of its love-

able hero Valuska, who makes his way through the town, head-down, dreaming of the planets and stars.

Valuska Plauf, to most of the townspeople and even to his mother, is an idiot. But observing him in his first scene—as he ducks into a local pub to perform, using the drunks around as actors in a rudimentary theatrical representation of an eclipse—we quickly grow to love this oaf nearly as much as his employer-mentor, the town's composer-genius, György Eszter.

> "We are standing in this...resplendence. Then, suddenly, we see only that the round disc of the Moon..." here he grabbed Sergei and propelled him from his orbit round the house-painter to an intermediary position between the Sun and the Earth, "that the round disc of the Moon...creates an indentation...a dark indentation on the flaming body of the Sun...and this indentation keeps growing...You see?...You see...and soon enough, as the Moon's cover extends...we see nothing but this brilliant sickle of sunlight in the sky. And the next moment," whispered Valuska in a voice chok-

ing with excitement, running his eyes to and fro in a straight line between driver, warehouseman and house painter, "let us say it's one p.m...we shall unexpectedly...with a few minutes...the air about us cools.... Can you feel it?...The sky darkens...and then...grows perfectly black? Guard dogs howl! The frightened rabbit flattens itself against the grass! Herds of deer are startled into a mad stampede! And in this terrible twilight...even the birds ('The birds!' cried Valuska, in rapture, throwing his arms up to the sky, his ample postman's cloak flapping open like a bat's wings)....the very birds are confused and settle in their nests."

Delivering clothes and food for Eszter, who has long before moved out of his dreadful wife's house, Valuska is the caring and loving being whom the great hermit holds near, the one being who represents to him the possibility of salvation for mankind. Valuska's portrayal of a horrifying eclipse, in some senses, is a kind divination of the forces at work around him.

Indeed from the very beginning of this fiction, Krasznahorkai presents a rabble that puts fear into any God-fearing being, particularly threatening Valuska's mother, the orderly Mrs. Plauf, forced to take a train ride, and terrified of the experience. She returns to the comfort of her over-decorated and clearly quite kitschy home to break out the preserves she has long-before

bottled, afraid that her son, whom she has disowned, may attempt to return.

Valuska, too sweet and innocent to see the evil brewing in the world around him, cannot even comprehend the chilling changes that seem to be occurring throughout the town. A great tree has fallen, filth has piled up throughout the streets, and, on the day of this fiction's events, a circus has settled into the main town square, attracting a huge contingent of outsiders, who sit in the dark quietly staring as they wait to see the circus' major attraction: a gigantic stuffed whale!

Eszter's wife, meanwhile, is making plans of her own to take over the town and become a political force. Her plots include Mrs. Plauf, primarily because she wishes to reach her estranged husband through

Valuska; the Chief of Police, with whom she is having an affair; and her husband, who she believes will fortify her position among the city leaders. It is she who has invited the circus to town.

Valuska is awed and slightly terrified by his viewing of the whale, running back to Eszter to tell him what he has seen, only to be interrupted in his voyage home by Mrs. Eszter and her fascistic plans. When Eszter perceives what her intentions are, that she intends to move back into his house and claim her position as his wife, he has no choice—and just like Valuska, finds it difficult to resist the strong forces of evil around him—but, with the boy in tow, to leave his house temporarily for the first time in years! What he sees horrifies him and, ultimately, the reader, as we suddenly are forced to see that the world outside his book-lined, music-loving house has fallen into ugly disrepair. Eszter can hardly bear the appearance of things, and quickly retreats to the house, struggling to erect a barricade of boards from within to protect him from what he has just witnessed.

Valuska returns to the circus, hoping to catch a glimpse again of the whale, but what he sees in the faces of the waiting campers, come to town to see the show, frightens him. Summoned by Mrs. Eszter to her barren apartment, he discovers the Police Chief in a drunken stupor upon the bed, while Mrs. Eszter and other town leaders confer about what they now see as a dangerous situation abrew. Commanded to visit the Police Chief's children and put them to bed, then to return to the square and apprise them of the situation, Valuska is torn between warning his dear friend, György, or carrying out his new "duties."

He chooses the latter, becoming witness to the violence and menacing behavior of the children and overhearing a conversation between the circus manager and a strange unseen figure, The Prince, who speaks in an unknown language, and who apparently is about to use the mob for his purposes of creating chaos.

Transformed by his experiences, similar to Mr. Eszter's shift in focus, Valuska runs off to tell Mrs. Eszter and others of the possible "revolution," only to be grabbed up by one of the leaders of the already destructive mob that has begun the night of terror. By the time the planets have shifted into the following morning, the mob has destroyed much of the town and killed several individuals, including Valuska's mother, who has taken to the streets to find her son.

Although the rabble has worn itself out, the army is called in to aid in the town's protection. Valuska awakens to comprehend that he has played a role in this terrible mayhem, necessitating the realization that the gloriously ordered world of the heavens is all a myth, that there is no natural goodness or objective faith to be found, not even within himself.

Mrs. Eszter quickly takes charge, falling in love with the commanding officer who has temporarily taken over the city and who convenes a criminal court. Valuska has been told to scurry away, and follows the train tracks, but he is caught and, through Mrs. Eszter's decree, incarcerated in the mental hospital.

Eszter retreats to the room where Valuska slept, while his wife takes over the house to begin her not-so-subtle dictatorship. The book ends with her speech over the grave of Mrs. Plauf, the woman she detested, but who now, in her political doublespeak, she describes as the town hero.

In short, evil has won out over those who dream and wonder about the harmonies of the universe. In Krasznahorkai's bleak tale, the world can possibly be cleaned up on the outside, but remains rotten within. Yet we do not fall into despair over his fable, for we have seen something that the others cannot, that the true heroes of this world are the weak, the beings who cannot resist these dark forces, but at least have attempted to reach for the skies. As the title suggests, the resistance of such evil is nearly always a melancholic action, for it "passes," "but it does not pass away." It survives, strangely enough, in those least likely to survive.

LOS ANGELES, JANUARY 23, 2001
Reprinted from *EXPLORINGfictions* (January 2011).

Normalizing Violence

LÁSZLÓ KRASZNAHORKAI AND BÉLA TARR (SCREEN-
PLAY, BASED ON KRASZNAHORKAI'S FICTION *THE MEL-
ANCHOLY OF RESISTANCE*), PÉTER DOBAI, GYURI DÓSA
KISS, AND GYÖRGY FEHÉR (ADDITIONAL DIALOGUE),
BÉLA TARR (DIRECTOR) **WERCKMEISTER HARMONIES**
/ 2001

RELEASED IN 2000 for the Toronto and Chicago International Film Festivals, Béla Tarr's masterful *Werckmeister Harmonies* appeared (at least on US soil) the
same year as the English-language translation of Krasznahorkai's book upon which it was based, *The Melancholy of Resistance* (which I review above).

Although the author was very much involved with
the film version, serving as the co-writer of the screenplay, Tarr has made, at least to my imagination, a very
different work from the dark, broodingly metaphysical
fiction. The film begins with one of the best scenes of
all of literature, the appearance of János Valuska, who

proceeds to take the drunken patrons of the soon-to-be-closed bar through the galactic patterns of a solar eclipse. Valuska,  who plods about the small Hungarian town with a newspaper bag on his shoulder, face to the ground, is fascinated by the heavens, and explains the planetary motions every chance he gets. Like a mad dance choreographer, Valuska positions the men as planets, Sun, Earth, Moon, spinning them around each other with the patience of a theater director attempting to prompt children into synchronized movement.

You are the sun. The sun doesn't move, this is what it does. You are the Earth. The Earth is here for a start, and then the Earth moves around the sun. And now, we'll have an explanation that simple folks like us can also understand, about immortality. All I ask is that you step with me into the boundlessness, where constancy, quietude and peace, infinite emptiness reign. And just imagine, in this infinite sonorous silence, everywhere is an impenetrable darkness. Here, we only experience general motion, and at first, we don't notice the events that we are witnessing. The brilliant light of the sun always sheds its heat and light on that side of the Earth which is just then turned towards it. And we stand here in its brilliance. This is the moon. The moon revolves around the Earth. What is happening? We suddenly see that the disc of the moon, the disc of the moon, on the Sun's flaming sphere, makes an indentation, and this indentation, the dark shadow, grows bigger...and bigger. And as it covers more and more, slowly only a narrow crescent of the sun remains, a dazzling crescent. And at the next moment, the next moment—say that it's around one in the afternoon—a most dramatic turn of event occurs. At that moment the air suddenly turns cold. Can you feel it? The sky darkens, then goes all dark. The dogs howl, rabbits hunch down, the deer run in panic, run, stampede in fright. And in this awful, incomprehensible dusk, even the birds...the birds too are confused and go to roost. And then...Complete Silence.

This scene, the first of 39 slowly paced shots, is totally magic, particularly in Lars Rudolph's boyishly sweet rendition of Valuska's actions. But while in the original novel I imagined the scene to be in a dark, fire-lit bar crowded with revelers, Tarr presents us with just a few late drinkers within a rather clean room, awaiting Valuska's arrival. In the fiction Valuska is equally awaited, but is also taunted by some who see him, as do most the townspeople, as a fool, a mentally-disabled being whose dreams of the heavens only confirms his idiocy.

Throughout the film, Tarr—despite his grim black-and-white palette—opens

up and reorders the landscape of this small town, which, in turn, normalizes it. The gigantic square, with only small groups of men huddled about it, seems far less foreboding than does Krasznahorkai's literary village.

The relationship between Valuska and the noted musical theorist György Eszter (Peter Fitz) is much vaguer here, and the love Eszter feels for the boy remains unspoken in the film until the very end, which invests their friendship with a feeling more of master and servant, rather than mentor and loyal friend. When Eszter is forced to leave the house in order to campaign for his detestable wife, Tünde (here played by Hanna Schygulla), he is not in the least shocked by the filth and debris he suddenly observes; indeed Tarr makes the place look almost respectable, a town that, in summer instead of the middle of cold winter, might possibly be a tourist destination.

Even the truck made of corrugated metal that carries the carcass of a whale into the square seems less menacing than mysterious. Because of the sparseness of the script, in fact, much of the menace and general grubbiness of this world is replaced by a sense of incomprehensibility. In Karasnahorkai's fiction the hidden figure of the Prince, who seems to be at the center of the violence soon to take place, speaks in a high-twittering-voiced, unknown language, but in Tarr's work he speaks, quite normally, in another language. In short the continued normalization of the original often lends the film an even stranger quality. Why is everybody doing what they are doing? To what purpose? To what end?

This is particularly true of the horrific would-be dictator of the town, Tünde Eszter, who in Tarr's hands seems almost, at first, like a slightly interfering auntie instead of the monster that she is. Her relationship with the Chief of Police is presented less as a disgusting coupling of drunkenness and sex than as a kind of quixotic romance. So vaguely is Mrs. Eszter realized in the film that we cannot comprehend what she has in mind by demanding that her husband campaign for her causes; certainly we have no way of knowing that it is she who has brought the terrifying circus act to town.

What Tarr *does* brilliantly convey is the sort of plodding inevitability of the violent riot that takes place. Although the heavy-booted Valuska greets everyone cheerfully as he moves through the city, as if all but the strangers in the square were one large family, he stumblingly marches through his days, just as did the drunken oafs in the bar, symbolizing  the prosaic pace and beat of life in this place.

When the riot does begin, Tarr portrays it almost as a Brecht-Weill opera, with the hostile crowds marching meaninglessly through the streets en masse. Whereas in the author's fiction Valuska himself is caught up in their horrifying actions and himself commits violent crimes, here Valuska simply disappears until after the brutal attack on the hospital and its patients—quite brilliantly depicted in Tarr's work—which literally wears out the assailants.

Just as in the book, Valuska winds up in an insane asylum, but, whereas in the original he seemed to be forever locked away out of Mrs. Eszter's desire, here the poor boy seems truly to have lost his mind in the violence and its aftermath. Mr. Eszter's visit to him presents him and the viewer with a new possibility of redemption that did not exist in Krasznahorkai's fable.

In making these comparisons, I am not necessarily criticizing the film. It is its own work, in which the characters and their actions may be far closer to ev-

eryday life, and, ac-
cordingly, even more
horrifying than the
grotesques of the fic-
tion. Whereas An-
dreas Werckmeister's
harmonic principles
were insistently declared to be wrong in the Kraszna-
horkai work, in Tarr's hands the harmonies might even
be restored with the survival of the beautiful innocence
of the town's sacred fool, Valuska, particularly if Eszter,
as he promises, will again take him in.

LOS ANGELES, NOVEMBER 23, 2001
Reprinted from *World Cinema Review* (May 2011).

A Long Sleep

SUSO CECCHI D'AMICO, PASQUALE FESTA CAMPA-
NILE, ENRICO MEDIOLI, MASSIMO FRANCIOSA, AND
LUCHINO VISCONTI (SCREENPLAY AND ADAPTATION,
BASED ON THE NOVEL BY GIUSEPPE TOMASI DI LAMPE-
DUSA), LUCHINO VISCONTI (DIRECTOR) **IL GATTOPAR-
DO** (THE LEOPARD) / 1963

WINNER OF THE 1963 Palme d'Or at the Cannes Film
Festival, *The Leopard* is certainly one of the most visually beautiful films ever produced. Visconti's Technicolor
evocation of Risorgimento Sicily is perhaps the most
cohesive and convincing aspect of this almost languid
epic, a vision that easily attracts one to the film again
and again. The very beauty with which the director
evokes the falling nobility of this lost world is, in part,
the subject of the book and film narrative, revealing
what is being lost far better than the Prince at the center of this work, Don Fabrizio Salina (Burt Lancaster),
could ever express it.

Don Fabrizio is a sensualist, a lover of the world

he inhabits while simultaneously perceiving—perhaps even reveling in—its faults. His discussion about his wife with the local priest, Father Pinone (comically realized by Romolo Valli), is a sad commentary on domestic life; although he has had seven children with Maria Stella Salina (Rina Morelli), he proclaims he has never seen her navel! Of the Sicilian people themselves, the Prince is only too aware of what he calls their "desire for death":

> Sleep, my dear Chavelley, eternal sleep, that is what Sicilians want. And they will always resent anyone who tries to awaken them, even to bring them the most wonderful of gifts. And, between ourselves, I doubt very strongly whether this new Kingdom has very many gifts for us in its luggage. All Sicilian expression, even the most violent, is really a wish for death. Our sensuality, a wish for oblivion. Our

knifings and shootings, a hankering after extinction. Our laziness, our spiced and drugged sherbets, a desire for voluptuous immobility, that is.... for death again.

Visconti's film begins with a living room mass in Fabrizio's villa, interrupted by the voices of servants who have just discovered the body of a soldier on the estate. Momentarily, news arrives in the form of a letter and newspaper account of an attack on Messina and Palermo by Garibaldi and his "redshirts." The news of the attack terrifies Fabrizio's family, particularly in its suggestion that they shall have to abandon their palace, perhaps even escape Sicily or face exile. Fabrizio, however, greets the news with an amazing placidness, calming his family, and arranging his own travel the next day. His ideas about the "revolution" are summarized in his statement:

> You know what is happening in our country? Nothing...simply an imperceptible replacement of one class for another. The middle class doesn't want to destroy us. It simply wants to take our place... and very gently.

Or as he puts it at another time:

Things will have to change in order that they remain the same.

Indeed it is Fabrizio's sense of inevitability tied up with
his *noblesse oblige* that both protects his family and
dooms it to destruction.

Although the Prince accepts the growing tide—he
has little choice but to do so—his views are nonetheless radically different from his young nephew Tancredi
Falconeri (the dashingly beautiful Alain Delon) who
stops by the palace on his way to join Garibaldi's forces,
determining to help create a new Italian nation that
will mean the nobility's (and, incidentally, his own)
downfall. His rash decisions and immature energy are
both charming and frightful, setting afire the heart of a
lady in waiting, Concetta.

In the end, however, Falconeri is a kind of comic
hero, as he and his friends arrive at the end of a brutal
battle against the soldiers protecting Palermo. For such
a lushly filmed work it is almost shocking to see war
so close up, as the rag-tag squadrons of redshirts rush
forward with hardly any leadership to shoot and kill
the local forces at random. Most of the citizens support
the Garibaldi forces, at one point chasing and running
down a local who is said to have been a police informer.
Despite his attempts to outrun the crowd, we soon see
his body hanging from a nearby post. By the time of Fal-

coneri's arrival there are only a few loyalists remaining, one of whom—almost by accident—shoots the young volunteer near his eye, transforming him suddenly into a hero. We perceive that Falconeri, in all his beauty and bluster, is a man who will take advantage of any situation throughout his life, when, a few scenes later, he shows up in a splendiferous soldier's costume, having abandoned Garibaldi's men for representing the King of Italy's forces.

Fabrizio and his family, meanwhile, refuse to abandon their annual summer pilgrimage to the small town of Donnafugata, a voyage temporarily interrupted by Garibaldi forces, but which is allowed to continue through Falconeri's commands.

Indeed the nephew joins them in their summer retreat, much to the delight of Concetta. Always a realist, however, Fabrizio insists that Concetta will not be suitable as a spouse for his nephew, a man who, he proclaims, will be a world leader visiting other countries. Such a man needs a brilliant and beautiful woman—most importantly, a woman who comes from a wealthy family, particularly since Falconeri and his mother, despite their roles as nobles, are penniless.

Donnafugata offers up just such a woman in the guise of a local wealthy politician's daughter, Angelica Sedara (Claudia Cardinale). Unlike the pious and disapproving Concetta, Angelica is a lusty and open girl, who shocks everyone at the first dinner party with her absolutely joyous laughter at a story told by Falconeri.

The last fourth of the film is devoted to the couple's romance as they chase about the Fabrizio palace in Donnafugata and attend a grand dinner and dance at the home of local nobility. In this scene, Visconti might be said to have staged the final grand gasp of the Sicilian nobility, with all its beauty and grandeur as well as its silliness and stupidity. At one moment, men and woman brilliantly and elegantly perform the local dances, while at the next we observe a gaggle of young women and girls bouncing and consorting about on beds. Malicious gossip is interchanged with witty conversations, grand dishes served up to sometimes unnoticing guests.

In the novel, the later part of the work is devoted to the death of Fabrizio. In the film, the Prince does not die, but simply grows short of breath and feels ill at the grand event, refusing to eat and leaving the party to walk home alone. In the stunning series of events at this ball, the director reveals all to us: it is the beginning of everything new and the end of all the old.

LOS ANGELES, SEPTEMBER 30, 2011
Reprinted from *World Cinema Review* (September 2011).

A Sleepwalker on a Roof

JACQUES PRÉVERT (SCREENWRITER), MARCEL
CARNÉ (DIRECTOR) **LES ENFANTS DU PARADIS** (**CHIL-
DREN OF PARADISE**) / 1945

> "I would give up all my films to have directed *Chil-
> dren of Paradise*."
>
> —François Truffaut

I LOVE MOVIES so much that I don't like picking out my
favorites—there are so many!—but if I were required
to select my very favorite film, I might be tempted to
name *Les Enfants du Paradis*, which I watched with absolute delight once more the other day. Certainly it is
a "stagy" film, a film in a grand theatrical manner, with
dramatically-acted performances that might be said to
represent the very last great example of its own genre.
Later films of the *novelle vague* would be far more
spontaneous, clever, and more deeply involve their
audiences, but none has the luster and polish—like a

perfect pearl—of Pré-
vert's and Carné's tale
of the Paris theater
scene of the early 19th
century. And there
are very few films
made that can match
its sophistication, and

no film that I know has its narrative depth, even though
the storyline is quite simple. *Gone with the Wind*, the
American film to which the French one has been lik-
ened, is a tinny music box by comparison, while *Children of Paradise* sings out like an organ accompanied by
an entire orchestra.

Much has been written about the miracle of the
making of this film during the Vichy rule of France,
when the director and cast feared not only censorship
but Gestapo arrest: one of the leaders of the Resistance
was arrested as an extra on the set, and the film's set designer, Alexandre Trauner, and one of the composers,
Joseph Kosma, had to remain in hiding because they
were Jewish. Starving extras, so Carné revealed in an
interview, made off with food to be filmed on the ban-
quet table, even going so far as to hollow out the bread
from beneath the crust of a baguette.

Yet Carné insists that it was a work largely free
from internal tension, which can only be attributed to

 the high level of professionalism among the entire cast, at the center of which stand the beautiful and calm Arletty, playing Garance Reine, a woman loved by three very different men each in their own manner, a shy romanticist who acts as a pantomime (Baptiste, played by the unforgettable Jean-Louis Barrault), a loquacious and self-assured actor (Frédérick Lemaître, acted by Pierre Brasseu), and a wealthy and snobbish Count (Comte Édouard de Montray, performed by Louis Salou). A fourth man, the true villain of the piece, Lacenaire (Marcel Herrand) might also love Garance if he had a heart, but he is so selfish, so locked within himself that, when he finally acts out his jealousy by killing the Count, it represents more of a meaningless murder than an act of honor.

Surrounding these central characters are numerous other actors, including the gentle Nathalie (María Casares) who deeply loves Baptiste, various street figures—in particular the ragman Jérico (Pierre Renoir) and a blind man who turns out to have perfect sight—a cast of thousands who throng the Boulevard du Crime, and the audiences, particularly those "gods" hovering at the top of the grand Funambules theater. These "gods,"

the poor who shout, clap, boo, and openly evaluate the performances below, are the "children of paradise" who make or break the actors' careers, and ultimately, through the course of this more than three-hour epic, bring both Frédérick and Baptiste to fame.

No one in this Breughel-like world is entirely appealing. Although Garance may be beautiful and desirous to all, she, from the first scene, is presented as a narcissist as she gazes at herself in a tub of water, while men pay to ogle her. She is also witness not only to Lacenaire's robberies, but is told by him of his murderous deeds without her even blinking an eye. The only statement of morality she utters, when Lacenaire declares, "I'd spill torrents of blood to give you rivers of diamonds," is the muted, "I'd settle for less."

Frédérick may be suave and handsome, but he is also a rake, willing even to bed his landlady, Mme. Hermine, in order to keep his room and double bed. The actor is also quite self-centered.

The Count, with whom Garance ultimately and unhappily settles into a relationship, is dismissive of almost the entire world of the everyday people who make up this movie, and is willing to duel with almost anyone at whom Garance smiles. Even the self-centered and truly despicable Lacenaire is more honest than the self-deluded Count.

Although Nathalie may appear innocent in her

true love of Baptiste, she is selfish enough to try to prevent Garance from even seeing him.

It is Baptiste, finally, who we realize is the true "hero" of the piece. He is the only one who, when he speaks of love, truly means it, even though he has never comprehended love's simplicity, only its difficulties, which he plays out time and again in the great pantomimes he performs before us. Like his character, Baptiste is a willing lover, but has no ability to effectively express himself; he is mute, able to express his seriousness only through comic gestures and the pained expressions of his beautifully gaunt face. Yet, it is only he who wins the love of the two central women of the work, Garance and Nathalie.

But even the likeable Baptiste is dishonest, if not with his wife, at least with himself. He is a dreamer always, a man of the moon. As Nathalie aptly describes him when he finally does attempt to consummate his love with Garance: "He is a sleepwalker on a roof," a man who if he is not carefully left to awaken himself may fall to his death.

Several critics and directors, over time, have com-

plained that the film, despite its length, seems attenu-
ated, cut away from a series of deeper stories we still desire even after the rich narratives the film has offered. In
part this is simply because the film, like a Balzac novel
or great Victor Hugo epic, is a fiction that has given us
such a rich palette, we feel slightly betrayed that it must
come to an end. At the same time that I viewed this
movie, I was reading Proust, and the similarities of the
texture between the two are notable.

But also, I think we feel the work is slightly trun-
cated not only because of its narrative density, which
seemingly demands, in turn, more and more stories,
but because we never do observe Baptiste's awakening.
At work's end, the lovestruck "clown" goes rushing after Garance's carriage as she, a seasoned cynic when it
comes to love, determines to awaken him by rushing

back to her wealthy Count (without knowing he has been murdered). The great film ends only with Baptiste's pleading gestures, the welling tears in his eyes (as well as in the audiences' eyes surely); he remains a sleepwalker, a dreamer rather than a skin-and-bones character who might come to terms with the love of his wife and son. The theater of Carné's world, in short, comes to a close with the curtain's fall, and certainly everyone in those 1945 showings must have realized that the world it was depicting, the allegorical presentation of a golden pre-War France, had in fact died. If love was still possible, it was only through the cold vision of more open eyes.

Just as Proust's vision, Carné's was a remembrance of things of the past, allowing little in the way of direction for what lay ahead.

LOS ANGELES, JUNE 18, 2013
Reprinted from *World Cinema Review* (June 2013).

Inside the Wound

ABRAM LERNER **GREGORY GILLESPIE** (WASHINGTON, D.C.: SMITHSONIAN INSTITUTION PRESS, 1977)

THE OTHER DAY, Howard and I read that the artist Gregory Gillespie had died on April 26 of this year, a victim of suicide by hanging. He was found by his wife, Peggy, in his Belchertown, Massachusetts studio.

Howard and I had gotten to know Gregory quite well back in 1977, when Howard worked as an assistant to Hirshhorn Museum and Sculpture Garden director Abram Lerner during their preparation for a retrospective of Gillespie's work that year at the museum. With Lerner, Howard interviewed Gregory during two sessions on March 24th of that year.

Gillespie was born in Roselle Park, New Jersey in 1936, the son of a couple who devoutly practiced Roman Catholicism, to which the artist later reacted in his many transgressive paintings. After high school, Gillespie studied at Cooper Union in New York before

moving with his first wife, Frances Cohen, to San Francisco, where he continued art studies at the San Francisco Art Institute.

In 1962 he received a Fulbright-Hays grant to study the work of the Italian artist Masaccio. Living in Florence for two years and in Rome for six years, Gillespie grew increasingly interested in the works of Renaissance masters such as Carpaccio, Mantegna, and Carlo Crivelli, the last a particular favorite.

With great realist craftsmanship, Gillespie created Roman landscapes that were also filled with surrealist-like images, perverse sexual activity, and adult-children relationships that were difficult to comprehend. Although his painting seemed highly realistic, the heavy impastoing of his surfaces, along with the inclusion of photomontage, collage, and materials such as newspapers and photocopied materials, made his works highly original, and in retrospect fairly postmodern.

As Gillespie recalls his own art-school training, he suggests that he was not truly influenced by any of his teachers: "I was painting tight, and they all believed in spontaneity, openness, and surprise—coming out of my big brush."

Even after the very successful Hirshhorn Museum show, and several shows at the Forum Gallery and in Whitney Biennials, the artist seemed situated somehow outside the US art world. Even his still lifes somehow seemed to be pointing to a strange, outlandish world, a world lying outside of more relatable spaces. Gillespie described his work as coming from the inside of a wound, "and if I'm painting the inside of a wound it feels different than if I were painting on the surface of some other thing. It's a very intuitive, emotional process." Lerner responded:

> It must be exhausting…. When I first looked at your paintings I was struck by their ferocity. They seemed to me to be full of brutality and aggressiveness. And yet, as I became more absorbed in them, I sensed more and more sadness and hurt…suffering, a quiet and chronic suffering in the paintings.....

Gillespie answered: "I think that's true. The feeling of being trapped. My background was Catholic and I

grew up in a very restricted and repressed environment in New Jersey. And there's a lot of anguish and pain in that. Like a delicate organism being born into the world and the kind of *violence* that's done to us as a matter of course." On April 26, apparently, that violence overwhelmed the man.

LOS ANGELES, APRIL 28, 2000
Reprinted from *Green Integer Blog* (July 2013).

In 1980 I was asked by Tom Beckett to make a statement about my poetic writing. It seems amazing to me now that I was so readily willing to do so—but this is often the case with the fearless young, and given my long-time interest in manifestoes, I quickly took on the task. The central sentence of this brief piece—which later was reprinted in a slightly different form as a more assertive epigraph to my poetic manifesto River to Rivet *("I am more interested in the relationship of river to rivet than I am in the relationship of river to bridge.")—became a kind a rallying cry for some friends interested in my early writing. I have slightly adjusted the piece below to reflect works that actually existed as opposed to the mention, for example, of a work-in-progress—*The Red Poems*—which was abandoned almost before it was begun.*

Statement

MY POETRY IS very much located in a "language environment." That's an easy claim to make, for, obviously, *all* poetry is (or at least should be) centered around language. Like several of my contemporaries, however—writers such as Clark Coolidge, Charles Bernstein, Bruce Andrews, Ray DiPalma, Ron Silliman, Bob Perleman, Barrett Watten and others—I am interested in words less as symbols of a preexistent reality, than as signifiers or signs of a whole new reality, a reality which the words (even the syllables and the letters themselves) create. In other words, in my poetry I attempt to *make* (to let the words make) a reality rather than to *reflect* one. In my work (and, it seems to me, in the work of several of the "language" poets), words *spoken to paper* create their own context, their own reference which may or may not have much contiguity with one's everyday experience in the world. The poem is organized by its own semiotic or linguistic logic, the way river is related to rivet more than to barge.

In the past, my own poetry has been more contiguous to experienced reality than are some of these poets' works. And, in that sense, my work has seemed to be more referential. I say "seemed" because, although there is some purposeful reference in my poems (language can never be completely non-referential; and to try to make it so seems to delimit the possibilities of poetry), my work is generally not organized around associations, but around the ear. It's rhythm and sound that dominate. The experience that the poem creates for me often has little to do with the meaning of the words, but rather with what they *sound* like they mean in relation to each other, and how they flow together in a rhythm or pattern of breath. I have moved increasingly away from image and narrative oriented work to a poetry that, without completely abandoning the visual, is grounded in an oral impulse. Even my diagrammatic poems, which appear to rely almost completely on their placement on the page, are organized according to sound, to the sounds of many simultaneously speaking voices. Were I not interested in an audience, I would perhaps move into transrational poetry.

I'm now experimenting with tape-recorded performances with other voices reading along with my own, the way Hannah Weiner has performed her *Clairvoyant Journal*. And in the writing process I've been increasingly resisting the temptation to fall back on what is already known, letting the words take me into their own context. Although I often work by deleting or by pulling language *out* of its ordinary context, the whole process stands against a minimalist sensibility in that the new contexts, the new worlds which this noncontextual language *creates*, appear to be limitless, as if one were standing at the edge of some vast expanse in which anything and everything can/must happen. In such an environment language suddenly reveals itself as something of boundless potentiality, a potentiality in which *it* expresses *us* rather than *us* expressing *it*.

COLLEGE PARK, MARYLAND, 1980
Reprinted from *The Difficulties*, I, no. 1 (1980).

Ah youth! I am touched now by the sense of the limitless potential I then perceived. The "diagrammatic poems" I refer to appeared only in the first edition, primarily destroyed, of Dinner on the Lawn. *Obviously, it was a direction I did not take. I can't actually recall taping any of my poetry—but after seeing Hannah's performance in Washington, D.C., I saw its potentialities. Certainly, I have allowed more performance into my work over the years, at one point performing a play, "Past Present Future Tense," with Fiona Templeton at the famed poetry venue The Ear Inn in New York.*

LOS ANGELES, JULY 9, 2005

Don Wellman's magazine O.ARS/ Toward a New Poetics, *published in Cambridge, Massachusetts, was centered
on poetics in general and, often, on particular poetic topics, and for that reason was perceived by most of us as an
important publication of the time. In 1982 Don asked me
to comment on the subject of Perception and, in particular, the issue of "Mind/World." My response was published
in the second volume of* O.ARS, *along with statements by
Ron Silliman, Craig Watson, and Charles Bernstein.*

Poetry and Perception

IT IS IMPOSSIBLE for me to separate perception from
the speaking/writing act. Certainly one sees things in
the world; there is a visual reality. But that reality has
no meaning and cannot be experienced unless brought
into language/thought. One may see a tree, but that
means little until he experiences it as something being
seen; and in taking this step he has already transformed
the tree from *its* reality into *his*, from a sensation into
a *something* which his society arbitrarily has agreed to
call a "tree." The perception, accordingly, is linked in-
extricably with the thinking/language-making faculty,
is a linguistic property, in fact. The idea that a writer

should or even *could* "reflect" the world around him is a tautology. In the very process of its being perceived, the thing perceived has already been subsumed into the individual mind with all of its public and private codes, signs, associations, and genetic idiosyncrasies.

But what a liberation it is for the poet who comprehends that fact. Suddenly the poet is no longer "put upon" by the world, is no longer made to be passive, but is the creator of a world, is an active participant in the making of *the* world. Speaking/writing/listening/reading take on a new significance as both author and beholder are called upon to bring a reality into perception, a reality of words which—just as that agreed-upon tree—is reality itself. And, in that sense, perception is an artifact.

In saying this, I am not doubting, as did Bishop Berkeley, the tree itself; my claim is only that the agreed-upon tree can be perceived only through the language of thought. Accordingly, if that language is cliché-ridden, too symbolic, or abstract so will be the reality. If our society has forgotten how to speak and write creatively, all of our perceptions will suffer.

On the other hand, if poetry engages this linguistic process, if the poet employs the poem as a ground to unfold the thinking/language process, the poem can be as powerful a force as it was for the ancients, who understood that language did not merely affect the world, but *made* it; who saw poetry as a genesis of experience rather than a reflection.

Perception requires process. If one is to see, if, as in *eidos*, one is to develop a cultural body of knowledge from which to interpret experience, he must permit the mind to unfold itself, to "play" with itself. The "serious poet" (Pound's epithet) is one who permits the language of poetry to generate such knowledge, is one who opens the way for voice and word to determine the poem's succeeding sounds and phrases. For such a process can produce not only a beautiful surface—the "memorable" outline of reality that too many readers have come to define as poetry—but can build a wor(l)dscape which weaves sensations, images, structures, and meanings into an object which loses its objecthood to experience itself.

COLLEGE PARK, MARYLAND, 1982
Reprinted from *O.Ars*, II (1982), special issue titled *Per/ception*.

In 1988, poet and publisher Rod Smith devoted an entire issue of his magazine Aerial, published in Washington, D.C., to my poetry, titling it, "Douglas Messerli Issue." The issue contained essays, poems, and pieces dedicated to me by figures such as Tina Darragh, Tom Beckett, Charles Bernstein, A. L. Nielsen, Gill Ott, Joe Ross, Phyllis Rosenzweig, Joan Retallack, Bruce Andrews, Pater Ganick, Keith Waldrop, Bill Mohr, and others, as well as a selection of my poems and a section of my then-forthcoming fiction, Letters from Hanusse. Marjorie Perloff took time out from her busy schedule to interview me for that issue.

Reading that intereview today, I am startled by how much my publishing has shifted from American literature to the international sector, and that I now devote most of my own energies to non-fiction, having, I guess, found the way to a critical writing that, as I had sought, had "concerns close to me." It is also fascinating to recognize that today I probably write as much drama as I do poetry. Finally, I most certainly would not focus, as Marjorie encouraged, so intensely on "Language" poetry, but would speak of a much broader range of poetic forms—although my relationships with figures such as Charles Bernstein and Bruce Andrews have remained.

LOS ANGELES, JUNE 1, 2011

Majorie Perloff: Interview with Douglas Messerli

(This interview was conducted on November 29, 1986 over lunch at Le Grange restaurant in Westwood, Los Angeles. Despite the clanging of plates and cutlery, the restaurant provided a nice, quiet atmosphere; it was between 2 and 3 p.m. and we had it almost to ourselves.)

MP: Suppose we start with an account of how you came to be a writer and what the first things were that you wrote. Fiction, poetry, or what?

DM: I began writing poetry when I was a teenager and enjoyed writing it a lot—until I showed it to an English teacher who told me, "This isn't poetry." At that point I sort of abandoned it.

MP: Who were your favorite poets at that point?

DM: I didn't really know poetry very well as a teenager. I read poets like Robert Frost, and read lots of prose and fiction writers like Kierkegaard and Marianne

Hauser, who I'm now publishing, and books like *War and Peace*. And I knew theater intently. But I didn't know poetry at all. I didn't quite understand it. And my poetry was of the "teenage mode," one might say. So I began to write fiction, and I wrote fiction quite seriously for many years. I felt that gap that often happens, I think, with people who don't understand or don't want to understand both modes—the sort of thing that results in an interest in only one genre. It wasn't, in fact, until Marjorie Perloff's course [laughter] many years later in graduate school that I really discovered contemporary poetry, and that liberated me immediately and I realized what I'd been missing. Ironically I felt this release with poets with whom I don't have a lot of kinship poetically, people like Frank O'Hara and John Wieners. But in the same course I read extensively Pound's poetics and a lot of other theory, and began to get a good strong basis for my own poetics and my own interest in poetry. I began writing poetry very soon thereafter.

MP: How did you first meet some of the so-called "language poets" you've since published, like Charles Bernstein? Was that while you were in graduate school?

DM: It was while I was in graduate school, but I can't remember the exact incidents or circumstances.

I began a journal, more or less out of the blue. Throughout the early '70s, Howard Fox and I had been discussing the possibility of beginning a journal. *Sun & Moon* was our first enterprise. I hadn't the vaguest notion of what I really wanted to do. I'd read a lot and been teaching courses in graduate school, and taught experimental writing. So I certainly had a knowledge of the kind of poetics that I would eventually come to—in a general way. But I began the journal by corresponding, and the first issue had Gilbert Sorrentino in it.

MP: How did you happen to write to Gilbert Sorrentino? Out of the blue? Did you know him?

DM: I knew his fiction, but I didn't know him. I wrote a lot of people. I wrote Marge Piercy, who is about as far from my aesthetic as one can imagine. But I wrote a lot of people who I thought were writing interesting work, mostly in fiction but some poets also. I got a wide range of manuscripts back immediately. This also made me change our conception of the magazine, which was going to be a mimeographed magazine, to a glossy publication.

MP: How do you explain that established writers like Gilbert Sorrentino would send work to a total stranger who says he's going to start a new magazine? Do you feel there was no outlet for experimental writing?

DM: There had been an outlet, but I think there are always fewer new journals appropriate to one's work than there are works one wants to share with others. I hope that our cover letter also helped encourage contributions because I think it intelligently described what we planned to do—and I think that that helped people feel that this might be the kind of journal that would be something interesting. I had had correspondence with Gilbert Sorrentino. I sent him my essay on John Wieners, to which he responded. So there was that possible connection—he knew that I had some shared interests. But other people—a lot of interesting writers—did send work to me for that first issue sort of out of the blue. We published Leonard Michaels, who, as someone who had published with Farrar, Straus and Giroux at that time, was a very surprising first-issue choice. Journals were, I think, a hot item at that point, in 1976. From the late 1960s on there'd been a real rise in journals. It was one of the healthiest periods for small presses. Everything from mimeographed magazines to more glossy magazines, which we chose to be. But I also think that, often, established poets are interested in helping younger journals get going—and are helpful. And they really will send work. I think that also might have been a motive.

MP: Is it through the journal, then, that you met young fiction writers and poets?

DM: Yes, fairly soon after that I began corresponding with them. I think Bruce Andrews first began to write me. He'd read the journal, and was at that time doing a special issue of Washington, D.C. poetry for *Roof* magazine, to which I had sent some poems. I met Bruce first when he visited me at the University of Maryland, and we had a wonderful chat. I really enjoyed him a lot, and we felt a rapport almost immediately. I met Charles [Bernstein] soon thereafter. We hit it off almost instantaneously, and corresponded for a long period after.

MP: When you say that you began by being interested in poets like Robert Frost and then you got interested in these very different poets, what at that time was your concept of what a poem should be?

DM: I don't think I did have a concept of what a poem was. I wasn't interested in Robert Frost; it's simply that Robert Frost was who was taught. I thought him to be a nice old man, but the poetry didn't relate to me very much. I didn't feel very close to him. I thought his poetry had nice sentiments. I was always sort of against poetry—or writing of any kind—that somehow had "nice sentiments." I was much more interested in philosophy from the start. Charles and I once discussed that both of us had a really strong interest in Kierkegaard, and in philosophy in general. In fact, when I began at the university, my goal was to become a theologian, and to major in philosophy. Not a theologian because of any religious perspective but because I wanted to study religions in general. So I really began as a philosopher, and from there moved into literature. I loved literature and liked reading, and I wanted to write even though I was only writing fiction and didn't quite know where to go. When I say I didn't understand poetry it's because my limitations gave me a notion of what a poem was that had nothing to do with what I was interested in. So what I knew was Robert Frost...

MP: Do you want to say something about what your concept of a poem is now (since you are the publisher of what many people consider "far-out" poets and you seem to understand their work)? What makes something a good poem?

DM: I have no one concept of a poem. I think the primary force behind poetry, the way I am most interested in it, is as a process of mind, of thinking, that gets expressed with an attention to language that we don't find in any other art form. Certainly you can sometimes find as much attention in fiction, when it turns into a *poetic* fiction.

MP: Don't all poets pay attention to language?

DM: Unfortunately not. Certainly not today. But it seems to me that all "great" poets throughout history (and that depends on what one means by great) *did* pay attention to language in a very detailed way. I think most people respect poetry, when they talk about poetry in the broader sense of the word. They are talking about somebody like Shakespeare or Donne or Emily Dickinson, all of whom paid significant attention to language. But I think when it comes down to our own times, a great many of the poets who are most praised or adulated by the general public don't have much interest in language: they're more interested in story or sentiment or self-expression. Often they may also be talented enough to use a clever turn of phrase or linguistic expression. That shows not attention, but awareness of the language. Some don't seem to have any ear at all, or any notion of what language is. But I think anyone who's even willing to write poetry has some special notion of language.

MP: Let's take Derek Walcott, who just received, at the time of this interview, the *Los Angeles Times* Book Award and is a poet widely praised by leading critics. Do you want to comment on what you think of Derek Walcott as a poet?

DM: I don't know Derek Walcott's poetry very well, but the poems I've read are basically stories that have some attention to language but not in a very deep way. What most disturbs me about people like Derek Walcott and Joyce Carol Oates relates to things both have said recently that really irritated me and that express an opposite notion from mine. Joyce Carol Oates recently said that she writes poetry when she feels a great emotional need, as when she feels very depressed. It posits the whole emphasis of the poem as a kind of emotional expression, a primal therapy or something. Derek Walcott, in accepting the *L.A. Times* Book Award, presented another view that I think is just as dismal, and it is very closely related. He got up after several prose writers had given their short speeches (including Maynard Mack [the biographer of Pope], who was very delightful). He said, "The advantage the rest of you have over me is that you write in prose," and therefore he had nothing to say. It's as if somehow poets don't think, poets don't have ideas, poets have nothing to express. I find this sort of sentiment, or Oates' notion of poetry as being primarily a vehicle for the expression of forceful emotion, antithetical to what I believe in.

MP: You say in your manifesto book *River to Rivet*, "I am more interested in the relationship of river to rivet than I am in the relationship of river to bridge." Do you want to comment a little bit on what that means?

DM: For me that's a very particular statement related to a very particular time in my writing. But it also has wider suggestions. I was particularly talking about the relationship of language that a good poet is aware of every second he or she is writing. That is, I'm more interested in the play of the word "river," which with one change of a letter becomes "rivet," than I am in a symbolic relationship like Hart Crane's [*The Bridge*], in which the river gets related to the bridge or something like that. It's formulated, in that you fill it in with the proper words. But at the same time, underlying that, the bridge is built by rivets, so I'm really interested in the constructive aspect of language: the minute-to-minute, second-to-second building up of a structure which therefore can (and often does) "bridge" something.

MP: In inventing such puns, are you concerned sometimes that the reader may not be able to follow your play of mind? Let me give you, as Robert Hass did to Gertrude Stein, a few of your own lines, and I want you to comment on them. Here is the opening of "Causes of the Crack Up" (p. 13):

> A sentence is hard for a sudden   to spin
>   into space.

See the hand perch on to fish out on the limb
    so to speak?
It's not to place but the verge of,
a breath only a comment can clear the way to.

> What are you trying to convey in that passage, and
> how will it come through to the reader?

DM: There are several things. First of all, I write poetry
to please myself; that's the first basis. I challenge
myself and allow all sorts of possibilities in words,
etc. In fact, when I begin a poem I don't understand
where I'm going or moving. I do by the end of the
poem, and I revise and revise and revise until I finally come to a perspective. But beyond that, I am
concerned, especially in this group of poems, about
the reader. I talk about the reader all the time. But
I want to make a challenge for the reader. For me
the worst kind of poem in the world is something
that I can assimilate in about five minutes and that
doesn't give me any kind of experience in process.
It's a nice sentiment or a nice idea that you can simply pick up whenever you want that idea or expression. I find most poetry that simple. I want to make
the reader go back over the lines, to backstep, side-
step, move forward. Sometimes I even build road-
blocks in the reader's way. For instance, often if I
presume, because of a pun or an association that we

would normally make, that the reader would come to it easily, I might rhyme the word instead. Nonetheless, the poem necessarily has specific meaning for me. The next time I read it I may be a little bit vague and not remember exactly where my comprehension had come from the first time, and there are always new meanings. That's exciting to me. I don't want the poem to be boring to me either. Certainly, though, the reader might have some difficulty the first time or second time.

MP: Let's take that first line.

A sentence is hard for a sudden   to spin
        into space.

Is the reader supposed to fill in the blank after "sudden" with a noun?

DM: It's an instant—the sudden, the act. So, "a sentence is hard for" a single instant. I wanted that sudden stop almost to "spin" it "into space." To allow the process of that word to actually break. It's not to fill in the blank; it's to allow the eye to pause for an instant, for a "sudden." One certainly could fill in the blank, with "instant," "moment," "thought," or anything. But the point is that the "sudden" itself becomes both the adjective and the noun in that kind of action. It's that quick transformation of the mind, that "sudden" that "spins into space."

MP: So, literally speaking, it's hard to perceive the sentence?

DM:

> A sentence is hard for a sudden   to spin
>   into space.

In my case the sentence is always two things. It's a pun in that case, but also it's difficult to suddenly spin that into space, to suddenly make meaning and sense of that, to make a sentence so active, to make it have the energy and force that I'm always trying to give it. And then I try to show the reader exactly that process in a very specific way: "See the hand perch out"—and, of course, once you've got the pun in perch—so "fish out on a limb so to speak." "Out on a limb" uses cliché, but it's also the notion of taking chances, of allowing the language to move instantaneously, line by line, almost syllable by syllable, certainly word by word. In these *River to Rivet* poems particularly I was trying to show the logical language of an immediate, every-second level. Every moment along the way I wanted to show the reader how one word came out of another. "See the hand perch on to fish out on a limb *so to speak.*" "So to speak" referring to both the colloquial meaning—and to be able to speak, to communicate.

MP: How do you get to the "cement" of the ending then?

DM: The unsuspected. Masses, it gels; it creates a mass, and collapses itself into a self. I'm talking about a lot of things at that point, including both total collapse and a sort of gelling of the entity. I feel there's a problem in that, too. That the self then becomes too much of an entity, too much of an issue. Then it cements things, hardens things. But at the same time, when it collapses or gels it *becomes* something, becomes a structure, becomes a "cement." Of course, the relationship of "men" to "cement" is a rhyme relationship, but it does also have a meaning.

MP: So you feel that there must be some sort of complexity, that the more complex the better?

DM: Not necessarily. Not for the *sake* of complexity, but for the sake of thought, and the process of thought. Yes, I'll play with words. Like "the distant scars," which is really like "the distant stars," but no, it hurts, it breaks, scars. The distance, both between the reader and the writer, and between one kind of meaning and another.

MP: What year did you start writing in this mode?

DM: I wrote *Dinner on the Lawn* in 1979, and this is the most recent of those first three related books.

But I began writing these fairly early. I tend to write in closely related sequences. These were the first, the *Dinner on the Lawn* poems. When I first found poetry exciting, through Frank O'Hara and John Wieners, I began by trying to imitate them.

MP: Isn't Williams a big influence?

DM: Williams is important in this early book. But in the beginning, before I got to this book, I tried to imitate. Very quickly I was dissatisfied with the results. Then I began working with collage. I began actually cutting out words and pasting them together and trying visual collages with words on the page. I found that this randomness, this accidentalness, sometimes produced very interesting results. More often, however, it was logical and very ordinary—not very interesting at all. I wanted more control over that, so I began to develop a way of scanning material with my eye and creating a collage with that. This first book is very much a collage of everything I was reading at that time. And Williams was one of the largest sources in this book. "Dinner on the Lawn" is an actual collage poem, written by cutting up *National Geographics* and similar sources. But I began that way, and I would revise and revise and revise, so that by the time I got done the collage was wiped out.

MP: Was the John Ashbery of *The Tennis Court Oath* an

influence, or hadn't you read him when you wrote, say, "Amelia Earhart"?

DM: I don't think John Ashbery was a direct influence in any way. I knew Ashbery, but I don't think I knew *The Tennis Court Oath* at that time.

MP: What would you say is the biggest difference in going from the first to the third of your trilogy, from *Dinner on the Lawn* to *River to Rivet*?

DM: *Dinner on the Lawn,* except for the title poem, deals with much more abstract language—abstract in the sense that it doesn't have the richness. It has a strong lyrical bent but its thrust is towards the abstract. In *Some Distance,* the next book I wrote, I dealt much less with concepts and much more with the way things sounded: what syntactically the sound meant instead of what the word meant literally.

> hands flash hard off fish
> borders between roe. they came so close
> blows thin as in
> a planetarium lost into distance
> nets to knots
> bellying down to where the oven held.
>   (From "Dogs," *Some Distance*)

Those are all actions of hostility, anger, fighting.

Yet these emotions are all created not by the literal logic of the word but the sound of the words in relationship to each other. Here's the perfect one:

> a figure is a fist, there she sits
> into conspicuous to rope up a threshold of
>   course
> one does not put one's hat at even into his
>   pocket
> the jaguar under the house (any house)
> driftwood piling like possessions of what
> surprise through sharp apricot teeth,
> a nice kettle of fish on a friendly beach.
> the back is a cucumber.
> the cat enjoys its prerogatives.
>   ("That Night," *Some Distance*)

Against the almost spitting hostility of the "sharp apricot teeth," "The back is a cucumber": it's icy cold, like a cucumber just out of the fridge. It's that kind of playing with the language on a very deep level. I had begun also, in this book, to find a great fascination with puns, although I don't use them as heavily in *Some Distance* as I do in *River to Rivet*. But there are puns here. The pun offered me a possibility of getting two, three, four levels going in different directions at one time and allowing the poem a greater richness of meaning and density.

Almost how it must've been when people started using symbols. I've rediscovered, too, that the symbol's not something I don't use at all; occasionally I do use symbols. But I find it hard to use traditional symbols because it's really finding something that fits, as opposed to coming about it in a natural way. The pun allows me that kind of naturalness. It also allows me to play the way I like to do with sound, and to mishear things, to work sometimes on a private level of knowing my own identity and experiences to come out in a very public way. In *River to Rivet* I decided, almost in reaction to that, to try to find a middle ground for my reader. I tried to tell the reader about my poetics in the process. That's why I wrote *River to Rivet*. It was a very specific work, a manifesto to try to describe the poetry; and the pun, because it's a more public form, also became more dominant.

Then I couldn't get it out of my head. I began almost resenting the pun. In the newest book I've been working on, I have two sets of poems. One in which the pun is still dominant, and another one in which it isn't.

MP: In *Maxims from My Mother's Milk,* pun is certainly very dominant.

DM: Yes, but I think I counteract that a bit by having the maxim, by setting them off against one another.

MP: How do you come up with these maxims? For instance, "'Twas talking asses turned the tables into tales."

DM: I just play around and play around until I hear it and it's right—until it sounds like a good maxim. I have a propensity to do this, I guess.

MP: "The word dictates its meaning to append"—I thought this was very interesting. The word dictates to append its meaning, or its meaning to append, and then up-end. In other words it seems to be quite a natural way for you to think, in terms of verbal play, pun, sound play, echolalia, and so on.

DM: I also love what I call the maxims of Gertrude Stein. It's a "maximistic" kind of writing. Aphorisms, really.

MP: I think Stein's influence on you is very strong, in some ways the strongest. Like Stein, you write what look like absolutely normal sentences, but they don't relate to one another. "Poetry's always seeking something special"—well, anybody might have said that, perhaps. Next sentence—"Two men with leashed dogs lead everyday lives."

DM: It is a natural thing to me. But I don't think it's necessarily a natural way to think. It's something that sounds interesting to me. That's why I mentioned Barthes at the beginning of the book. His comments on the maxim were wonderful, I thought. And he writes maxims, too. I feel very close to Barthes. Then the maxims also have a lot to do with my upbringing. Growing up in the Midwest, my grandmother especially spoke in sayings, or proverbs. They would become reality for me. She said things like, "The darkest time of day is just before the dawn." And having relatives living on a farm, I have a lot of imagery from nature and from those background roots. Although I think I'm about as removed from them—and have been most of my life—as one can be, they have still had an impact on me.

MP: Do you feel that this new manuscript is a major departure from the trilogy?

DM: Not yet, but it's a movement away.

MP: How does it move away?

DM: My goal is to return more to the deep level of language that I had in *Some Distance*. This is a way of purging myself of the pun by using it upfront again, but in a way that plays with the maxim. In *Hymns to Him*, I think you'll see a movement away often and a different level of the language. In the newest poems I've written for a book I've just begun, *Along Without*, I think you see a return to an almost meditational kind of language, as in "May Day (2)," the elegy for Roger Horwitz. Also within the maxims you see different ways of working, like the poem that's after John Donne, "A Vector of the Straddle," which is an entire rhyming of a John Donne poem. That is, taking a poem and rhyming every word, so that it becomes an entirely different poem. That seems to me another way of working, another way of trying to get to a different excitement of language.

MP: It also seems to me that in the most recent ones you're not using, for instance, this device:

    curling into it
    s or crack
    ing

Because the question would be, "Can one overdo this sort of phonetic spelling?"

DM: Yes, one can overdo it. I did it because, for one thing, there's a cleverness. And I'm a poet of wit; I do believe I belong in that tradition. It's odd, because I don't think of myself as a naturally witty person, but it comes out in my poetry, constantly. Sometimes in a corny joke, sometimes in overstatement, etc. I allow that, though, and share it with the reader, because sometimes it produces interesting results and it shows the play of mind that creates a density of language and meaning in the end.

MP: Do you feel you'll be writing more poems like

"May Day (2)"?

DM: Yes. Almost all the poems in *Along Without* move in that direction. Although there are certainly puns, they are not used in the same way. This is a book about death, a looking into death. I've always been doing that; it's not a new issue with me. Sex and death have been two of my biggest themes. But this particularly is a book in which the pun will be pushed back a little bit. In fact there are some poems in the new book that are really quite traditional in some ways.

MP: How do you feel that these relate to the poetry of some of your contemporaries? Let's get to the vexed problem of the language movement. Do you feel these poems derive from Charles Bernstein in any way, or influence *him* in any way? What would the relationship be there?

DM: No, there's not a direct influence there. There is one poet I'm very influenced—actually affected— by in a strong way. It's not Charles, though I relate to his poetry enormously. And I relate to Lyn Hejinian's and to Susan Howe's. The most shared things we have are the attention to language, and the attention to thought through language, and those issues and concerns which tie up with that, and the approach to the poem as something that gets developed in the process. It's not just process-oriented, but it has that element. Something that is an over-attention, a remarkable attention to language ends up showing that process, not just doing it, but showing it as we're writing it. I think that's the general shared thing. We're all radically different poets when it comes down to actually talking about the poetry.

The one poet to whom I do return to time and time again, especially when I can't write and I can't get to work through collage, is Clark Coolidge. There are several reasons why. He has that maximistic kind of quality, but he also has the attention to sound, hearing, and the oral values that I have.

MP: What do you think of the criticisms of Clark Coolidge? For instance, the one Lydia Davis made, part of which, ironically, was put on the dust jacket of one of his books. In fact, what she says, and David Antin implies the same thing, is that this is wonderful sound play but it doesn't say anything. It's not *about* anything.

DM: I totally disagree with that. Let me take a short little poem that I think is a good example. It has only four lines, so it's easy to talk about, but it shows the way Clark Coolidge works for me. First I want to add, in passing, that I think his relationship to jazz, and to what's heard and spoken, is certainly there. But that's not why I'm most interested in Clark

Coolidge; it's his *meaning*.

The poem is called "Setting," from *Own Face*.

The pot has been brought round.
The disappears over a porch, bird.
They blade, couch.
When crystals vanish they spread perfume.

For me that poem has a great deal of significance. There are many different ways you could read it, so to analyze it is like doing a translation. But I want to use it as an example to suggest where it has significance for me.

The title itself is quite obvious, but it's also a pun. It's both the setting of the poem and the setting of the sun after dinner, and also, I don't know if it's true in New England but it's certainly true in the Midwest, that often when you're going to go out and sit on the porch you're going to "set."

So it begins—"the pot has been brought round." This suggests to me both that the food has been passed around the table, and that the bellies have become round because the body has eaten: it's after dinner.

The next line—"The disappears over a porch, bird." First there's the article "the." It's "the" anything; "the" whatever "disappears," because the

sun is setting, it's getting dark, "over the porch"—
you get the idea of them being on the porch. At
the same time you get both the porch, which is a
linear image and, by comma, a bird. You suddenly
have this movement up. I think the bird's coming
to roost in the trees, but the bird also flies "over a
porch." So you have a sense of both of these perspectives. I think Clark often uses "the" as I do:
"the" becomes the archaic "thee." So "the" becomes
"the people," and also "you." In other words, "you
have disappeared over a porch, bird," because of a
notion of the sun setting and the darkness coming
in.

"They blade, couch" is almost a reversal. The
birds become like a blade, cutting through. And
then "couch" returns to the porch—even the
words are similar. But also the idea of "couch" as
encompassing. The night comes in and couches,
settles down.

Then there's the maxim: "When crystals vanish they spread perfume." There's a notion almost
of a scientific statement. But to me it represents
when things vanish, when the world vanishes,
when what is crystallized disappears, we're only left
with the memory, the perfume, the scent of experience. So to me it's a very exciting poem. And it allows you as the reader to participate, even to think,

"This is my particular reading today and I'll probably have another one tomorrow, and anyone else will have another one." Because of their syntactical structure, these words may not seem to make literal sense. But they do if you start exploring them and if you think about them.

MP: Could the pot reference in the first line be also to smoking pot?

DM: It may be. That's not what comes to my mind. I didn't think of that, but that's what I mean: another reader could bring all sorts of possibilities to that poem.

MP: If it can mean all sorts of things, at what point does meaning become so open that it becomes meaningless? After all, this is a charge made against many of the poets you publish and possibly against your own poetry too by those who are hostile to it. Say pot refers to pot-bellies, a pot of food, marijuana—where do we draw the line? Isn't art supposed to be a selection from ordinary language, and aren't the words supposed to cohere?

DM: I don't know who would say it's a selection from *ordinary* language. But for me that poem is a selection. I mean, he could have said anything. What if he had said, "The dinner has been consumed"? That would be very specific, and some people would think it's a much better line. I think it's a boring line. It wouldn't mean as much. I think it's very hard to create meaninglessness, unless you're just babbling.

MP: Don't you think there are some "language" poets whose work is merely incoherent? Isn't there a place where one draws the line?

DM: Not the poets I'm interested in.

MP: So the ones that you like less would be not too meaningless but perhaps too contrived?

DM: No, the ones that I like least—I usually find it as a fault of mine, that I've not been able to understand, I've not been able to fix anything by which I can bring myself into the poem to understand it, to work with it. The poets to whom I'm most attracted, then, are those with whom I have a great rapport, and I do feel that there are many possibilities—not my one reading.

MP: When you come to people you did not include in the "language" anthology, who you don't think are as good, are they not good because they don't have this richness that, say, Clark Coolidge has? Are they not as good because they dribble off into nonsense verse?

DM: I would never claim they weren't as "good." I didn't include people in the anthology for a lot of reasons. In some cases they were poets who hadn't done as much work as the others. In some cases they were poets who I just hadn't been able to relate to as much. Obviously I make judgments, but I wouldn't say I did not include someone because I didn't think he or she was good. I think most of the poets who for one reason or another are called "language" poets—though obviously they're not all equal—write interesting work. There's not one "language" poet that I haven't read interesting poems by, though that doesn't mean that I like everyone equally.

MP: You say "of the 'language' poets." Suppose I send you a manuscript and say, "My name is Joan Smith. I'm a 'language' poet. I hope you'll consider my manuscript, and here are my poems." You might say, "This is awful." After all, as a publisher, you do turn down most manuscripts. What are your values in selecting poems?

DM: It's not that they're "language" poets first. These are poets that I didn't even know were writing "language" poetry when I first read their work. It doesn't go the other way around. I think we've linked up as a group called "language" poets partly because of social reasons and partly because we've found something that we share. But it's not because they're "language" poets that I'm interested in their work. I get manuscripts every day from people saying they write "language" poetry. I don't necessarily recognize it as such, but that isn't what matters. What matters to me is the attention to language, the attention to the thought process, the skill with the words. For instance, most of the poems I receive are really narratives; they're not poems in the way I understand poetry. They don't really concern themselves with that word-to-word, minute-to-minute, second-to-second attention to what all of us share, language.

MP: So the poems are more transparent; they want to convey some emotion?

DM: A lot of the poems have standard notions behind them; they fall into patterns. A lot of them don't have any mind behind them. You don't have any sense of intelligence or thought process going on in there. It's just a pretty image. In most of the poetry I'm rejecting, there's just nothing behind it; there's no "there" there, so to speak. Of course, there's often craft, often other things that are of value.

MP: To get back to the language poets: why do you feel at this moment in culture that the best poets are writing this way? After all, poems that paid attention to language at the time of, say, even Williams are perfectly coherent. One *can* read them on one level rather simply, and then of course read them on an even more difficult level. But nobody's going to have trouble reading, "An old woman / munching her plums / it tastes good to her / it tastes good to her." Everybody can understand what those words mean; there are no puns or double entendres.

DM: I don't think I have an easy answer. And most of the answers that have come up would sound pretty clichéd, sort of Marshall McLuhanese. But there's no doubt that we live in an age of cinema, of television, of film, of quick changes and cross-cuts, so that our syntax, our language, and our whole way of thinking, certainly in my own poetry, if not in the broader sense, are affected by it. I get bored if I have a long passage which goes on and on when it doesn't need to. Common readers today, especially the younger ones, once they've got one thing, are ready to connect it and allow something new to happen.

So media is a big factor. But I can't say that's the only thing. I also think that it's probably a reaction against a period in which the most exciting poetry, which I would say was of the New York school of poets, was very much caught up in the self and a presentation of that self and that image of self. I think it's partly a reaction against that. Yet it takes some of the best elements of that poetry, some of the ways of using collage and wordplay. It seems to me we've been influenced by that. I invent narrative selves in my own poetry so I'm not against that entire aspect, but on the other hand my self is not what I'm primarily interested in. And I'm not interested in confession at all.

MP: Let's switch over to publishing. How do you feel being a poet relates to being a publisher?

DM: I'm a poet. But being only a poet today doesn't seem possible, recognizing that there's a real economic gap in every kind of way between the large publishers and what's really happening. It's not possible to be a concerned poet and not want to review other people, and also, if you have the ability and the desire, to want to find some way to bring these books to readers. My development as a publisher was almost by chance. It came through the magazine, and it came because I realized that my colleagues in the university were saying, "There isn't any exciting writing being done. That's why we're all turning to theory." At the same time the larger publishers were saying, "We can't do that because it's too weird or far-out. Readers don't read poetry anymore, and don't even read fiction." It gets worse and worse. So on the one hand, because of the economic situation, big corporations didn't have the space anymore for something that didn't make as much money as something else. At the same time, at the university, there was this other reaction of people turning to theory and increasingly saying there was nothing interesting happening. There's a gap there that's got to be filled, and that was my direct involvement. I wasn't and haven't been the only one to try in some way, at least I hope not. But I came about it because I was first interested in poetry and writers, not because I had this goal and then decided I would be a writer, too.

MP: You wear these three different hats: a poet's, a critic's, and a publisher's. The day has only 24 hours. How can you reconcile these things? When you get very busy with the publishing end, the practical end, the shipping and the invoices and all that, how can you keep your poetic sanity, so to speak, and your critical sanity?

DM: I don't write criticism at all anymore, so that answers that. I do miss it. I'd like to find a new critical language with concerns that are very close to me. As for my poetry, it does suffer. I have three slim volumes and now a fourth volume. That's not a large output. But I'm not the kind of person to go away on retreat and just start writing; I don't function that way. I'm trained in certain ways. I make time, especially when I feel there's more writing in me. On those evenings I'll go to a bar in the neighborhood, and sit and write, and order dinner very slowly, and do it that way. I have very little time for writing because I do think the other has become a more important contribution at the moment—although I'd like to think that my poetry is an important contribution, too. But one has to make certain decisions.

MP: Do you feel the same kinds of mental habits are used in writing the poetry as in selecting the manuscripts?

DM: The critical perspective is the same, but I also play in and out of that all the time when I'm writing. You're intensely involved with the experience and language of the moment, don't know why you're writing it, and so you sort of back off and say, "What does this mean?" I feel they're very interrelated; they're not entirely separate. Although I've become something I've never been before: a businessman. It's a very different lifestyle and life activity from being primarily a poet.

MP: But isn't the pleasure there to feel you're really writing what's being read, and certainly what's being published, that you're making a real impact on the literary world?

DM: The excitement is knowing that I'm a missionary in that cause. It's exciting for me to know I'm having an effect—not personally, but speaking for all the poets I publish. Obviously I can't publish everybody that I want to or everybody who's interesting but the poets whom I do take on are changing the scene of contemporary poetics.

MP: Who specifically has changed the scene?

DM: Charles Bernstein has certainly had a major impact on contemporary poetics, as has Clark Coolidge. In terms of poetry, since I'm much more of a purist in that area, I'm very specific in the kinds of books I publish, though there are exceptions to that. I also think in fiction, my New American Fiction series has had a real impact in general because it stands for a kind of fiction that isn't always novel-centered or centered on plot and character. It plays with a lot of different genres and has opened up the possibilities of fiction. That's done in many different ways. Each book has had a different effect. It can be anybody from Marianne Hauser, who's a bit more traditional in her writing style, to Paul Auster, who uses the detective genre, to Russell Banks, or to a much more difficult and radical writer like Steve Katz, and other young writers. All of these together stand as something that will help change the shape of American fiction as well.

MP: Which of those writers do you feel you've discovered personally, that weren't published without your help?

DM: I have a lot of writers coming up. Wendy Walker is one who's coming up right away. Wendy Walker is a writer of fiction whom I met through Charles.

She lives in New York and has never published a book. She's doing a book of short stories, and then a big novel that's written in 17th-century style. It's called *The Secret Service*. It's a very metaphysical book. The major characters have all been transformed into the dinnerware at the king's table. They hear all the secrets. It goes into great specificity as to how this metaphysical occasion was possible and how they could transform themselves. It's absolutely 17th century: it's 500 pages, first of all. No other publisher in the country would publish something like that. The book of short stories we're doing is like rediscovering the Brothers Grimm rewritten by Rimbaud (that's how I describe it) or Emily Dickinson. They're absolutely fascinating—fairy tales for adults—just remarkable, beautiful.

There are lots of other young writers with forthcoming work who I've pretty much discovered or uncovered, or if nothing else I've given them their first opportunity in a larger audience. Like Tom Ahern, who has published a lot in small presses but hasn't had that larger audience.

There are other writers I feel are making new things, like Steve Katz or Ronald Sukenick, who have done a certain kind of postmodern fiction and have now developed into mature writers.

MP: What do you think the hardest things are about

being an avant-garde publisher—aside from the economic problem?

DM: The hardest problems I've had to learn are simple problems that every publisher must have daily. As soon as you get known you find strange people come out of the woodwork. Your agent in Germany is suddenly behaving in a very odd way, and the next day somebody else claims that a book you're distributing is slanderous toward him and he's going to sue you. Those kinds of problems which you don't even imagine when you begin are just daily problems that any publisher faces. And there are the problems of losing writers, getting out books on time (though that is probably economic), and all the logistics that go into publishing.

MP: How much space are you going to continue to devote to the reviving of earlier work, like that of Djuna Barnes?

DM: That's been a big issue—actually we're doing a larger number there than we were originally planning. My fear when I began (and it still is a fear) is that it's very tempting, and we all know there are classics we'd love to see back in print. We're very much interested in that. I don't think *just* our time is the most interesting. I think there are plenty of important books of the past that need to be republished, but my fear is that you begin to do just what the university does, and the big presses, and, say, Ecco Press or to a certain extent North Point Press. Your emphasis falls off the contemporary aspect. I think it's crucial that somebody remain in there all the time, saying, "I'm doing young and contemporary writers—writers of our time." I'll be old in a few years, and then I won't be doing contemporary writers either. I think all presses have lives. I don't think you can continue to be young unless you constantly get a young staff or find someone equally able who can take over. But you really can't. Eventually you say, "These are the writers I stand by. This is what I've developed my press on. I can't equally see young writers because they'll begin to look different, maybe even radically different from where I started." But I think that while you've "got it," while you're at your most important time, you *owe* it to contemporary writers.

MP: What about translations of important new writing from other countries?

DM: That I can't yet offer. I can do the classics because I know they will sell to a certain audience. But if I tried also to do translations of contemporary writing it would mean so much cost. By the time you've paid readers and translators, and gone through all the steps, you're spending so much money on it. I think there's too much good American writing not being published for me to serve that role as well.

MP: Where do you think the experimental writing is now going, if you had to predict, in both poetry and fiction? Let's begin with poetry. The language movement is on the one hand coming in for a lot of kudos and at the same time is coming in for a lot of nasty criticism from various quarters. Where do you feel this movement is going, if you had to predict five years down the line?

DM: I don't know how I would do that. I don't know what will ultimately happen—I wish I did. In my own work I do see things that once were a complete bafflement to me. Without abandoning what I've been working for and aiming at, I find ways to explore and experiment, sometimes with more traditional forms, sometimes even more radical forms. This new poem I am working on, "Running Scarred," is about evil. The only thing about it that's not traditional is, again, the attention to the lines, the line breaks giving attention to certain words. But I didn't set out to write a poem about evil. What I did was play with rhyme in this poem, and work with internal rhyme. Rhyme itself determines certain word choices, which then created, I think, a much more traditionally sounding poem.

MP: What about other kinds of writing? Do you want to write plays?

DM: I've always wanted to write plays. And I've been working on a fiction for ages. I'd like to work on a dialogue if I had the time. But I find myself most clearly expressed in poetry. With such little time other writing takes away from my poetry, and I begin to feel the poem take over again. So that's why my fiction, which I think is really good fiction, has taken me 10-15 years, and it will probably take another 10-15 years before I get it done.

MP: In fiction, it seems contemporary writers have gone beyond the stage of self-reflection. Where do you think that's now going?

DM: I think it's finding ways, not to react against, but to maturely recognize where modernism and earlier forms had something to offer. It's not an "anything goes" attitude, but a maturing of style and awareness. It's not an abandoning of that excitement and dynamism. We recognize the power of high modernism, and that post-modernism relates back to modernism and other forms. Though I don't think any of us are going to sit down and write Symbolist novels, or go back to the style of Cleanth Brooks or Robert Penn Warren.

MP: This is my last question. Are you interested in doing inter-art things yourself? Verbal-visual works, sound texts, visual poems?

DM: I'm interested in them. I've certainly encouraged

them in my poetry as much as I can, without getting into all the materials involved, such as tapes and video equipment. I do have a commitment to the book. I've worked with performances, and theater things which involve that, in my own work. But I've just never realized them, and they haven't been completely successful. I guess it's not natural for me. They all seem very exciting, but don't work out in my own aesthetic.

MP: What are your future writing plans?

DM: I'd like to finish my long fiction.

MP: Who is going to publish this manuscript?

DM: That's been a big issue and debate for me. I thought I should have another press do it. Then it seemed silly, since I have one of the best distributions of contemporary poetry in the country right now. It seemed illogical to send it off elsewhere. So I'll do it. I tell a lot of poets now who can't find places to publish their work to self-publish. I'll even help distribute in some cases!

Reprinted from *Aerial*, No. 4 (1988).

Experiment and Traditional Forms in Contemporary Literature

ONE GENERALLY DOES not associate contemporary literature and art with the use of forms, either traditional or newly invented. Within the context of the high-spirited eclecticism of the writing and visual art that has come to be described as Postmodern, the contemporary arts patently represent a renunciation of formalist principles—whether they be those of Clement Greenberg or of Robert Penn Warren and Cleanth Brooks. After all, if Modernism often demanded "pure" expression and absolutist thinking, its antithesis (if Postmodernism *is* its antithesis) obliges the artist to be self-consciously syncretic. Contemporary literary works such as those by Bruce Andrews, Charles Bernstein, Ray DiPalma, Steve McCaffery, and Ron Silliman (who collaboratively composed *Legend*), in their mix of poetry, prose, linguistic games, and babble, are anything—perhaps *everything*—but formal. Rather, they dramatize a tendency in contemporary literature towards what Jonathan Culler has described as the "non-generic," writings so eclectic in their sources and styles that they transcend or evade generic classification.[1] By contrast, poetic forms and genres bring to mind the concerns of many Moderns, and their continuing dominance in the academy, effected, in part, by critics such as Donald Davie and Harold Bloom, whose theories and criticism are grounded in writers of traditional forms such as Emerson, Hardy, and Frost. And, accordingly, for a great many less academically-oriented writers and readers, an interest in issues of form and prosody suggests a kind of nostalgia, a longing to return to the formal systems so apparent in the works of Hardy, Yeats, Eliot, and Frost, as manifested in the contemporary poetry of Richard Wilbur, Robert Penn Warren, Howard Nemerov, and the early works of Donald Hall and W. S. Merwin.

But, of course, the very definition of form—particularly as it applies to poetry—is a relative matter. Throughout history, one century's poetic forms often have been the previous century's experiments, the constrictions of the next. And in our own accelerated century each literary generation has reused, rejected, or invented new formal systems according to social, political, and personal expedients. Entire genres have risen and fallen in the span of a few decades: the "confessional" mode of poetry of the 1950s and '60s appears not to have survived a third decade; the concretist experiments of the 1960s today look almost like ancient hieroglyphs. And new forms and genres continue to evolve; recently, Ron Silliman has implied that works of his and fellow Californians Barrett Watten, Bob Perelman, Carla Harryman, Lyn Hejinian, David Bromige, and Steve Benson function to create a new prose poem genre focused on what he calls "the new sentence," works in which "actual elements of poetic structure" enter "into the interiors of sentence structure itself."[2] In other words, genres and forms really have not disappeared from even the most seemingly "avant-garde" of poetics; it is only that in the context of a protean literature, one may have difficulty in recognizing them.

However, along with this inevitable establishment of new genres by some contemporary poets, and the return to traditional forms by more academically-aligned ones, a substantial number of writers who would have to be described as Postmodern in sensibility[3] consciously use traditional forms in new ways, and/or work in traditional genres that were less suited to Modern ideas of structure. Indeed, these writers' works—in which form or genre often is used as a foundation or base which frees the author to experiment with or even subvert the form itself—may provide one with a clearer picture of contemporary poetics than either the formal strictures of Richard Wilbur's poetry or the emphatic shapelessness of *Legend.

Clearly, the "remaking" or "reconstructing" of forms is nothing revolutionary. In the 20th century, one thinks immediately of Ezra Pound and his employment of traditional forms in his attempt to bring new life to poetry and ultimately to language, to "make it new." Pound's continued interest in forms such as the sestina, villanelle, and ode, in fact, is directly or indirectly reflected in the contemporary experiments with form. For Pound form is less a tool to teach the poet than it is a container within which to create a poem. "The artist should master all known forms and systems of metrics," he argues; and, indeed, "most symmetrical forms" have "certain uses"; but the vast number of subjects, he concludes, cannot be rendered in a formal manner.[4] Pound's idea of a poem obviously is one in which structure is more open: poetry is to be built "tower by tower," "the plan/follow[-ing] the builder's whim."[5] And, in that sense, Pound's theory initiated the constructionist view of poetry that underlies so much of contemporary poetics, the idea that poetry should be a thing of linguistic process as opposed to representing a set of preconceived ideas and images bound to convention. Nonetheless, if such a poem results in a "rag bag" for the modern world to "stuff all its thoughts in," the skein from which it is woven is form itself; if the poet/builder creates his towers according to whim, in Pound's thinking they stand on the solid foundation of formal traditions.[6]

This idea of form as a foundation or base for the poem made its way quite directly into the poetry of the New York writers in the 1950s and early '60s through the influence and poetry of Frank O'Hara. Marjorie Perloff points out in her book, *Frank O'Hara: Poet Among Painters*, that

> One of the special pleasures of reading O'Hara's poetry is to see how the poet reanimates traditional genres. Ode, elegy, pastoral, autobiographical poem, occasional verse, love song, litany—all these turn up in O'Hara's poetry...."[7]

That is not to say that O'Hara's commitment to the tradition is the same as Pound's. Speaking on his "Ode to Lust," O'Hara remarked in 1964: "I wrote it because the ode is so formidable to write. I thought if I call it an ode it will work out."[8] Beyond the facetiousness of such a statement, O'Hara suggests that the genre here is not something which controls his poem, but rather an attitude that helps to shape it; the poem is not written to *be* an ode, but is written with the idea that it will be *called* an ode. Clearly, that incorporates the knowledge of how an ode works, an awareness of its form; and, as Perloff points out, many of O'Hara's *Odes* have "traces of the Greater or Pindaric Ode."[9] And, in that sense, for O'Hara, as for Pound, the genre is not an enclosure but a starting point, a kind of impetus which sets the process of the poem in motion. Nevertheless, O'Hara's statement *is* ironic, and that reveals his basic attitude. Although O'Hara uses forms, as Perloff notes, "his tendency is to parody the model or at least to subvert its 'normal' conventions."[10]

This "subversion of normal conventions" was especially attractive to many writers of the so-called "New York School," in part because of the Dadaist spirit which imbued their work, and, perhaps to a lesser degree, because of their inherent anti-academicism. And at one time or another each of the New York poets has employed traditional genres in parody. However, their self-conscious attitude towards the tradition often has led them to more sustained and serious formal experiments. John Ashbery's several meditations, sestinas, and sonnets, Kenneth Koch's comic epic *Ko*, and Ted Berrigan's *The Sonnets* all exemplify a usage of traditional forms closer to Pound's avowal of the tradition than to O'Hara's subversion of it.

Ted Berrigan's description—in an interview with Barry Alpert—of how he came to write *The Sonnets* summarizes, it seems to me, the attitudes of some of the New York writers, and points to the way in which forms are perceived by many younger poets today.

TB: I was very interested in the sonnet—I had been for a number of years, actually, because it seemed to me like a dynamic and exciting form. I guess I was stimulated by the fact that nobody was writing them. Literally you weren't supposed to write them and everybody was down on them.... So I was very excited by the form yet every time I tried to write one it was true that the form sort of stultified the whole process. Then sometime later after I had gone through Pound very much in my own manner but very extensively and gotten a certain sense of structure that was like form turned inside out...

BA: You mean using the old forms and making them new?

TB: Yeah, but really the way he did it with *The Cantos* rather than when he wrote imitations. But I mean I went through the imitative process— I imitated certain poems of John Ashbery that are in his book *Some Trees*. And one night I was looking at those imitations; I had about six or seven of them. They were a little too stiff and rigid for me. I seemed to be coming close, yet I had a brick wall all around me. I was reading John Cage and Marcel Duchamp and I was familiar with William Burroughs, but it occurred to me to go back through them and take out lines by a sort of automatic process and just be the typist. I had the poems right next to me and I decided to take one line from each page until I had six lines. Then go back through backwards and take one more line from each page until I had six more. That was twelve. By then I could see that I would know what the final couplet would be.[11]

The differences between what Berrigan is saying here and what O'Hara does in his pastorals and odes, although subtle, are important to note. Both, obviously, are using forms very loosely, and neither is interested in remaining faithful to the sentiments that their forms have by tradition expressed. If O'Hara mocks the pastoral notions by locating the action of his poem in the middle of Manhattan, Berrigan utterly ignores the conventional topics of the sonnet through his "automatic" process. And like O'Hara, Berrigan's attraction to the form stems partly from the fact that it is "out of fashion"—what O'Hara meant, one imagines, by saying that the ode was "formidable." In short, the *idea* of the form is more important to both poets than are the actual formal strictures; Berrigan, like O'Hara and Pound, uses the form as a foundation or base upon which to build, upon which to express the process. Nonetheless, in Berrigan's case the form at poem's end has not been parodied or subverted, but has been recreated.

The Sonnets, no matter how different in subject matter from conventional sonnets, are formally sonnets[12]; they do not merely contain traces of the form, they *are*. And, in that respect, Berrigan has *remade* the form, has brought the form new expression. As he puts it, he has turned form "inside out." By beginning with the idea of the form, and yet allowing the poem to create itself, Berrigan has given new dimension to the form; and, in that regard, he has reconstructed it almost as the first sonneteer would have had to construct his sonnet.

Accordingly, in works such as *The Sonnets*, one can observe a gradual shifting away from the use of traditional forms for parodistic purposes towards a serious recreation or reconstruction of the poetic genres. In Michael Palmer's *The Circular Gates*, David Antin's *Meditations*, Peter Frank's *The Travelogues*, Terence Winch's *The Attachment Sonnets*, Robert Long's *The Sonnets*, Bernadette Mayer's many autobiographical poems and sestinas (such as "The Aeschyleans" and "The People Who Like Aeschylus"), Barbara Guest's odes, Anne Waldman's new formally structured poems, and works by many others one witnesses this same "turning of the form inside out," the poet permitting the poem to create the form, rather than the form to create the poem. As Michael Davidson has expressed it, "many recent poets [use] a formal convention as a way to extend and play with its limitations: incurring them, varying them and opening them into the 'genius,' to use Robert Duncan's term, of their complexity."[13]

Between Pound and O'Hara, of course, there were other poets, some of whom I have mentioned, who abjured free verse and the general abandonment of traditional forms. But their reasons for doing so were quite different from those of O'Hara and his contemporaries.[14] If for poets such as Berrigan, Mayer, and Palmer one can say that form is something from which the poem opens out, for poets such as Robert Frost and Richard Wilbur—two modern poets most associated with the use of traditional forms—form is something that closes the poem in, that serves as a boundary, as a protection. In his recent study of Robert Frost, Richard Poirier observes that for Frost (as for William James) "Form is a gratifying act of will and also a protective one in a universe where we are otherwise fully exposed to chaos...."[15] Questioned by John Ciardi regarding his attitude toward the structure of the total poem, Richard Wilbur phrased this idea in a somewhat different manner:

> ...The use of strict poetic forms, traditional or invented, is like the use of framing and composition in painting: both serve to limit the artwork, and to declare its artificiality: they say, "This is not the world, but a pattern imposed upon the world or

found in it; this is a partial and provisional attempt to establish relations between things.[16]

For Frost and Wilbur, in other words, the form is a container, something that encloses or frames the language of the poem, and in so doing, separates and protects writer and reader—momentarily at least—from the flux of life. It is through creating or reading the poem—or involvement in any such creative act—that imagination, that Romantic repository of correspondences, is freed, as Wilbur puts it, to "establish relations between things," the "things" axiomatically being "out there" in "real" life. For the contemporary poets such as Berrigan and Mayer, however, the in/out dichotomy is inoperative. Influenced by the current semiotic and structuralist environment, these writers conceive language to be less a "signature" of reality than a "sign"—a conception akin to what Richard Palmer describes as the pre-modern notion of language as a "man-invented designation which can be changed at will."[17] Thus, the poem no longer holds the world-of-flux at bay. Immediately upon being said or put to paper, the words, concretized as things in space, become as subject to flux—what Frost calls "the chaos"—as all other objects. For the contemporary, as for Wilbur, the poem is "artificial"—is grounded in artifice—but, unlike Wilbur's poem, the contemporary poem does not retain an organic link with what it names. The poem is not a sanctuary, but a "convention" of words that have their own existence in space. The language of the poem does not *correspond* to life because it *is* a reality in its own right. And, in this regard, experiments in traditional forms by poets such as Berrigan, Mayer, and Palmer reflect not only a different methodology, but a changed poetics.

When one suggests, therefore, that living poets such as Wilbur and Warren are nostalgic in their use of forms, it is less a judgment than a distinction that when blurred obscures the fact that contemporary poetry is as involved—one might easily argue it is more involved—with traditional forms as was Modernism.

This is even truer of prose fiction; but, the context here is much different. If a substantial number of Modern poets have continued to practice the traditional poetic genres and forms, few Modern novelists have demonstrated any interest in genres outside of the tradition beginning with Cervantes of the prose romance. And for the majority of Modern fictionists the prose romance has been seen less as a genre with certain strictures than as a stage for intense experimentation. When one thinks of Modern fiction, it is inevitably its experimenters—James, Proust, Woolf, Joyce, Faulkner, Kafka, and Gide—who first come to mind. Certainly there are exceptions: Ivy Compton-Burnett, Ronald

Firbank, Henry Green, and other British narrativists worked in the genre of the dialogue novel, related to the Socratic dialogues; Gertrude Stein, Djuna Barnes, Wyndham Lewis, Aldous Huxley, and Norman Douglas all attempted anatomies or Menippean satires; and Stein, Barnes, Lewis, Joyce, and Williams experimented in genres and modes as diverse as the almanac, monologue, *tableau vivant*, picaresque, travel guide, and encyclopedia. But these forays into other genres generally have been regarded as oddities, viewed in the context of eccentricism. Indeed, fictionists such as Compton-Burnett, Barnes, Firbank, Stein, and Lewis *are* eccentrics—with respect to the prose romance.

However, if the prose romance has long appeared to be a genre with nearly limitless structural potential, the symbolic organicism which most Moderns have required of it has made it as constricting for several younger authors as a Richard Wilbur stanza. From Percy Lubbock's insistence that "The well-made book is the book in which the subject and the form coincide and are indistinguishable—the book in which the matter is all used up in the form, in which the form expresses all the matter,"[18] from Brooks and Warren's claim that "a story is successful—...it has achieved form—when all the elements are functionally related to each other, when each part contributes to the intended effect,"[19] Modern critics and authors in large have argued for the novel what Wilbur and Frost have for poetry: that narrative art requires a closure, a frame which separates—thus allowing a correspondence between—expression and life.

Predictably—in fact contemporaneously with O'Hara's experimentation with poetic forms—several narrativists, most notably Ralph Ellison and John Barth, sought narrative alternatives to the prose romance. Ellison's choice of the picaresque genre for *Invisible Man*, one suspects, was a necessary abandonment of a form so long dominated by white society and its values. But, just as importantly, in such a pseudoautobiographical form wherein a radically undefined hero generally encounters a random and chaotic series of events,[20] Ellison found a near perfect metaphor for the circumstance of the contemporary black. However, in that fact one must presume, at the very least, that Ellison's attitude toward the picaresque as a viable literary form is ambivalent. And one cannot help wondering, if the American black were less subject to social and political oppression, whether Ellison might not have chosen the prose romance. It is likely, in other words, that Ellison's choice of another genre came about more as a stratagem to express his theme than as a genuine interest in the form itself.

Similarly, Barth's imitation of traditional genres in works such as *The Sot-Weed Factor* and *Giles Goat Boy*—which Robert Scholes has described respectively as a "historical novel" and a "mock epic allegory"[21]—and in his recent epistolary work, *Letters*, is less an affirmation of alternative forms than a commentary on the exhaustion of serious fiction in general—including the works themselves. Leslie Fiedler summarizes this attitude:

> We may begin...by thinking that *Giles Goat Boy* is a comic novel, a satire intended to mock everything which comes before it from *Oedipus the King* to the fairy tale of the Three Billy Goats Gruff. But before we are through, we realize it is itself it mocks, along with the writer capable of producing one more example of so obsolescent a form, and especially us who are foolish enough to be reading it. It is as if the Art Novel, aware that it must die, had determined to die laughing.[22]

Barth's repeated emphasis on the "exhaustion of literature"[23] places his use of traditional genres in a context not unlike that of the New York poets, wherein the artist employs forms he perceives to be ridiculously obsolescent in order to mock the works of his predecessors while mocking himself.

However, as with poetry, such a self-consciously defensive stance has led several contemporary fictionists into new rapport with older genres. In his 1958 fiction,

Alfred & Guinevere, James Schuyler began experimenting with the dialogue novel, with which, in *A Nest of Ninnies* (written in collaboration with John Ashbery) and *What's for Dinner?*, he achieves as consummate expression as the fictions in the genre by Henry Green and Anthony Powell—if not those of Compton-Burnett. Schuyler's intentions, like Barth's, are parodistic; in his relinquishment of the greater part of his fiction to the inanities of stereotypical suburban Americans he has given himself little choice. But in that very relinquishment the form opens up; by using the genre as a base rather than a mold for his satire, Schuyler, like Berrigan, accords it different qualities. The wit and intelligence that pervade the British dialogues—inherited from the philosophical cunning of Socrates—in Schuyler's fictions become cliché and near idiocy. Indeed, the conversations of Schulyer and Ashbery's "ninnies" are about as mundane as the discourses of Compton-Burnett's figures are complex; the compelled machinations of Compton-Burnett's figures are little more than whimsical choices for Schuyler's suburbanites. The genre as reconstructed by Schuyler, in short, has been turned inside out: the form is no longer matrix but matter, is no longer a structure which defines the fiction, but one from which the fiction is propelled into new possibilities, into its own life. Nonetheless, the form here remains intact; and in that fact the genre is enriched rather than merely mocked. In Schuyler and Ashbery's hands the dialogue novel suddenly becomes a dynamic expression of the effects of suburban culture on language and thought, which the more realistic presentations of writers such as John Cheever and John Updike—in their careful use of symbols, metaphors, and analogies antithetical to the lives of the characters they present—have been less successful in capturing. The characters of Schuyler's fiction may be fools, but the works themselves are brilliant satires of contemporary American life.

Marvin Cohen is another writer who uses dialogue to probe contemporary thought. But Cohen's model clearly is Plato rather than British, and, accordingly, in works such as "On the Clock's Business and the Cloud's Nature" and "Rain's Influence on Man's Attitude to Art," his dialogues, at least superficially, appear to function as gnomic philosophical encounters. Yet, here too the genre is turned on its head: in Cohen's commentaries rational logic is demolished as interrogator and respondent surrender rational thinking to puns, malapropisms, clichés, corn-ball jokes, and irrelevant questions and answers. If a sort of logic eventually *is* established, it reminds one less of Socrates than of Gertrude Stein.

Stein, in fact, has had the same relationship to the experiments in forms in contemporary fiction as Pound has had to its poetry. As Pound did with poetic forms, Stein began to experiment very early in her career with the constituent elements of narrative form, the sentence and the paragraph, in an attempt to find "a whole thing" "created by something moving as moving is not as moving should be."[24] Stein's idea of narrative form implicitly is not that of the sequence as in counting one, two, three, four, but of the sequence in which each element—be it clause, sentence, or paragraph—is given new potential, as in "counting one and one and one and one."[25] Accordingly, Stein rejects the prose romance—which requires the sequence of addition for its organcism—in favor of older genres such as the anatomy and picaresque, in which narrative is noncumulative, in which count is lost rather than kept. Indeed, beyond the apparent radicalness of her clauses, sentences, and paragraphs, Stein's fictions are generally grounded in traditional genres. *The Making of Americans* and *A Long Gay Book* have close affinities with the anatomy; *Ida* is a picaresque[26]; *Lucy Church Amiably*, as the critic Donald Sutherland indicates, is a pastoral[27]; *The Geographical History of America* is both a treatise on the relationship between history and geography, and a fictional history and geography of American thought[28]; *Brewsie and Willie* contains elements of the dialogue; *To Do* is an alphabetically structured litany of birthdays; and *The Autobiography of Alice B. Toklas* and *Ev-*

erybody's Autobiography are "fictional" autobiographies. In short, like Pound, Stein uses the traditional genres as a base from which language creates a reality influx.

Stein's influence has been far-reaching, and extends beyond the confines of narrative and fiction into poetry, drama, and non-literary modes of expression. But Stein's particular interest in the interrelationship between language, performance, and life has had the greatest impact, perhaps, upon contemporary experiments in traditional genres of narrative. Nearly all of Stein's works are focused on the way in which language creates reality—or, as I expressed it earlier in this essay, the way in which words said or put to paper suddenly become "things" which are subject to the flux of life. However, in several of her works, Stein further explores how those literary expressions affect real life experiences in the lives of reader and creator. What some critics have interpreted as the mythologizing of an egocentrist is arguably an active investigation of the limits of language and the individual. Especially in her portraits, lectures, and autobiographies, Stein, through the personae of others such as Picasso, James, and Toklas, seeks to know whether language (the expression of her personae), rather than merely coexisting in reality, can actually remake the individual's life—whether language defines *a* reality or *all* reality. Thus, in these works language is far more than an "analogue of experience," which William Gass has argued[28]: it is experience itself.

Stein's quest is reflected in many intermedia works of contemporary literature, music, and art. But in terms of the contemporary work in traditional genres, it has had a special impact on performance fictionists such as Norma Jean Deak and Eleanor Antin. Deak also uses the genre of the dialogue as the base of her short "fictions." Her "Dialogues for Women," however, share little in common with either the British dialoguists or Socrates, but are closer to the dialogues of the Middle Ages between body and soul. Just like the body and soul dialogues, Deak's conversations between two women are represented as emanating from the same consciousness; as Deak notes, "The original idea behind the dialogues was to create a theatre of mind. In the performance I wanted to retain this idea."[29] Thus, the women's voices (her voice on tape) are generally neutral in tone; neither is given dominance. But here the analogy seems to end. Deak's conversations seldom contain any apparent "encounter" of ideas or emotions; in fact, extrinsically they communicate very little of anything: a glass of water, a slight tremor, a broken vase—such are the apparent focuses of these works. It is only because one has been trained to see art within a frame, however, that the conversations appear to be so mundane. The real focus of Deak's art is not on the dialogue between the women but on the dialogue between those projections and herself as she performs them. Deak writes of her performances:

> While I was rehearsing, I noticed that I repeated particular gestures—for example, scratching the left side of my head or pushing my hair out of my eyes. I wrote some of these gestures into the stage directions. As a result, what was first perceived to be an unconscious gesture on the part of the performer was later identified as belonging to one of the characters. At other moments I assumed the character of one of the women and made a gesture immediately following its indication in the stage direction. As I made the movement, I said the same text line at the moment it was said by the taped voice.[30]

In other words, as in Stein's portraits and autobiographies, Deak's dialogues present a constant interaction between personae and author, between language and act. In the end these *are* dialogues between body and soul, not as in the literary dialectics of the Middle Ages, but in a more profound sense; underlying each of Deak's performances is an almost palpable tension between her own physical being and the substantiation through language of her intellect. The body and soul encounter is not between two characters, but between what one calls "reality" and what one calls "fiction," between life and the word made flesh.

Similarly, through various media, Eleanor Antin explores the relationship between personae and self. Hers is not a dialogue, however, but a near-complete immersion of self in four personae—the Nurse, the King, the Black Movie Actress, and the Ballerina—each of which manifests itself in what Howard N. Fox has described as work that "is autobiographical in the way that any fantasy or any fiction may be an autobiographical work of art."[31] Yet, of course, these fictions when enacted become historical facts in effect. The whole of Antin's oeuvre, accordingly, is tied up with issues of autobiography and biography. But particularly in *Recollections of My Life with Diaghilev*, the memoirs of the Ballerina, in which the issues of traditional genre, language, performance, and "real" experience are linked, one can observe an inextricable relationship between the self-as-fiction and fiction-as-self.

Real autobiography—that is the genre as it has defined itself—Antin argues, "makes a powerful claim to truth."[32] And, in that sense, Antinova's memoirs are "merely" fiction. Indeed, in that Antinova, as a member of Diaghilev's Ballets Russes, is a university-educated American black, and since throughout the *Recollections* Antin brilliantly mimics the style of late-19th and early-20th century memoirs, one easily might argue that the form is used primarily for parody. But as scholars of autobiography such as Robert F. Sayre have pointed out, although the traditional autobiographer "...is not passing off the imaginary as actual or willfully falsifying important facts," in his very selection of incidents, and in the tone and manner of personality (the masks) in which he presents them, autobiography has far more to do with fiction than one might suspect.[33] If, as Sayre suggests, autobiography is something in which a "life... is made over in a discovery of the present by means of rediscovering the past,"[34] one might question what role memory plays? Can one "mis-remember, make mistakes," even "lie"? Antin asks.[35] The problem is further complicated by desire; desire may not only color the autobiographer's version of reality, Antin implies, it may be so powerful that it surfaces as a major factor in the autobiographer's life.[36] Even if it does not, Antin might argue that no self-examination can afford to ignore the effects of desire and fantasy upon a life.

In this respect, Antin's writings and performances do not undermine the genre, but extend it. Antinova's *Recollections* do not merely reflect a consciousness in the present remaking a past, but, as Antin puts it, "a present trying to produce the past to take possession of the future."[37] Through her readings of the *Recollections* and performances, language does, in fact, remake life—just as Stein suspected. After nearly every reading of her memoirs, David Antin reports, people have naively asked Eleanora when she performed with the

Ballets Russes and/or to share stories of Nijinsky, Diaghilev, and Pavlova.[38] Such improbable belief in Antinova's memoirs (in order for Antin to have performed with the Ballets Russes she would have to be at least 80 years old) is a testament to both the genius of Antin's reconstruction of the autobiographical genre and to the dynamism of language; it represents what Antin describes as the credibility or "credit" that reality requires between word and being, between name and body. In her performance of the ballet *Before the Revolution*, Antinova observes:

> Sometimes there is a space between a person and her name. I can't always reach my name. Between me and Eleanor Antin sometimes there is a space. No, that's not true. Between me and Eleanor Antin there is always a space. I act as if there isn't. I make believe it isn't there. Recently, the Bank of America refused to cash one of my checks. My signature was unreadable, the bank manager said. "It is the signature of an important person," I shouted. "You do not read the signature of an important person, you recognize it." That's as close as I can get to my name. And I was right, too. Because the bank continues to cash my checks. That idiosyncratic and illegible scrawl has credit there. This space between me and my name has to be filled with credit.[39]

In Antinova's *Recollections*, in short, one again observes a traditional fictional genre being utilized as a foundation or ground for a remaking of the genre and of life itself. Not all contemporary fictionists take traditional forms as far as does Antin, but a great many writers employ the autobiography and related genres such as letters, journals, and confessions in an attempt to explore the boundaries of fiction. From Toby Olson's *The Life of Jesus*—which Olson describes as "an autobiographical novel" told in terms of Jesus' life[40]—to Kathy Acker's *Kathy Goes to Haiti*, Lynne Dreyer's letters and journals, and Nathaniel Mackey's epistolary *From a Broken Bottle Traces of Perfume Still Emanate*, contemporary writers have experimented with autobiographically-related genres in an attempt to return what Jean-Luc Nancy describes as the "pure I," the "I who utters myself uttering" *into* [as opposed to *upon* or *beside*] fiction.[41]

Underlying this remaking of the self, moreover, is a reconstructing of the world, of the universe. Accordingly, contemporary fictionists have also been attracted to more inclusive forms such as the travel guide, picaresque, anatomy, and encyclopedia. Before her current involvement with personae, Antin experimented with the travel guide in *100 Boots*, subtitled an "Epistolary Novel," less because of its form than because the travels of the boots were documented as picture postcards, mailed to various art journals, newspapers, and friends. Clearly, the journey of 100 empty boots across the United States belies a parodistic, if not Dadaist spirit. But a true commitment to the travel guide genre as established by Defoe, Sterne, and Swift is evidenced in the fact that, absurd as they are, the boots do undergo a fictional voyage in which the world is revealed as it is remade. The boots' travels are visually depicted in terms of "real" places—Niagara Falls, the Western desert, the Pacific Ocean, indeed, nearly all the typical tourist stops. But Antin's photographs of these places as invaded by boots makes for a new landscape, a new world never seen before.

Such a visual transformation of the world is achieved linguistically in travel guides such as Walter Abish's *Alphabetical Africa*, in which journey and journeyers are generated and deconstructed by alphabetical accretion and subtraction; in Italo Calvino's *Invisible Cities*, in which Marco Polo, through "memory, desire, and signs," tries to describe his several journeys to a disbelieving Kublai Khan—and in my own *Letters from Hanusse*—which, like Antin's early work, uses the letter as a means to relate the nature of a world in the process of being recreated.

Moreover, in Abish's newest fiction, *How German Is It*, and in my own fiction the I and the world are brought together in a structure that bears some resemblance to the picaresque. Neither of these fictions is a true picaresque; in each the consciousness of the narrator controls and shapes the work too strongly to permit it the episodic form of the traditional picaresque. But such works do indicate a tendency in the contemporary fictionist to reconstruct a self and world against the backdrop of an ever-changing time and space. In the hands of a writer like Kathy Acker, indeed, character, scene, and circumstance shift in a kaleidoscopic rapidity that brings to mind the picaresques of Grimmelhausen and Nash. In her fictions such as *The Adult Life of Toulouse Lautrec*, *The Childlike Life of the Black Tarantula*, and *Girl Gangs Take Over the World*, the self and world are not merely transformed, but are continually rebuilt before the reader's eyes. Form and language is in near-perpetual motion as Acker, having raided sources as diverse as detective stories, political tracts, and pornographic novels, opens her tale to the barrage of experience facing any contemporary picaro(a).

Ultimately, this interest in traditional forms as a base from which to remake the self and world is indicative of an interest in restructuring the universe, in reinterpreting and remaking its metaphysics. And if the picaresque combines the self and world in its structure, it is the anatomy, with its mix of prose and poetry, of philosophy, fact, and fiction, of catalogue, monologue, and dialogue, which is most suited for such a discovery.

Two contemporary works stand out as conscious uses of the anatomy genre: *Seeking Air* by Barbara Guest and *Mulligan Stew* by Gilbert Sorrentino.

Guest's work—like Joyce's great anatomy-encyclopedia, *Finnegans Wake*—is focused on the issues of artifice and reality. The central narrator of her work, in fact, begins as merely a literary figure, surrounded by other such figures, several who, like Clarissa Harlowe, make specific references to fictions of the past. What Guest explores through her use of such artifice is whether or not the contemporary author, faced with an inescapable awareness of the literary and art traditions from Swift to Harry Matthews, from Ingres to Tony Smith, can create character that is anything beyond—to steal William Carlos Williams' description of his poems—a "machine of words." Accordingly, the chapters of Guest's fiction represent different strategies, various literary episodes in the history of narrative art. If her character, Morgan Flew, eventually does "find the way," as Guest puts it, to come to life, it is not because the fiction culminates in realism, but because Guest has had such utter faith in the tradition, in the multitude of linguistic experiments of the past. Her character does not come to life as flesh—or what the imagination conjures up as flesh—but as words in space, the very same space in which man breathes his air.

Sorrentino's anatomy also calls up the presence of

Joyce. But while paying homage to Joyce—Joyce even appears as one of the fiction's characters—*Mulligan Stew* is basically a reaction against the whole avant-garde tradition that Joyce and his peers begat. And in his attempt to satirize what he clearly sees as the degenerate condition of contemporary literature, Sorrentino is much closer to Flaubert, who in his anatomy, *Bouvard et Pécuchet*, attacked the *petit bourgeois* attitudes of the whole 19th century.

As in Guest's work, several of Sorrentino's characters bear literary names, and a couple of them, metaphorically speaking, "come to life." But unlike *Seeking Air*, these figures of language remain bound within the confines of *Mulligan Stew* because their creator purportedly is not Sorrentino, but Sorrentino's character, Antony Lament, an author who has little facility with language, and who continually binds his characters to narrative plot. The whole of *Mulligan Stew*, in fact, dissects and analyzes the ways in which 20th-century literature has failed to create a dynamic art. And, in that sense, Sorrentino's anatomy does not really rebuild a self, a world, or a universe, but, rather, takes all three apart. Opposed to this dissection, however, is Sorrentino's own play with language, the countless puns, metaphors, leaps of logic, lists, litanies, imitations, and literary references, all of which impose a linguistic vitality upon what is otherwise reconstructed, collapsed.

Accordingly, Sorrentino becomes his own hero, so to speak. Instead of his fiction coming to life through language, Sorrentino transforms life into fiction through his linguistic energy.

The idea of life transformed into fiction is an ancient one, and has been central to a great many Modern fictions—the works of Proust, Hemingway, Lowry, and Mailer immediately come to mind. But once again contemporary works such as *Mulligan Stew* reflect a far different relationship between lived experience and fiction than one observes in *The Sun Also Rises* or *Under the Volcano*. For the Moderns like Hemingway and Lowry, life experiences as transformed into the prose romance are necessarily objectified because the artifact is conceived as being temporarily static, a frame. The life presented thus becomes a thing of memory, of the past. For Sorrentino, on the other hand, memory has little to do with it; there is no attempt to recall life, only to express it in the action of writing, what Derrida would call *trace*.[42] Thus, there is no objectification of experience in *Mulligan Stew*. Sorrentino directly enters into the fiction through the play of words. His fiction does not present a life as lived, but a life as it is being lived in linguistic presentism.

Many contemporary writers interested in this sort of "deconstruction" of experience through language write what one tentatively would have to call non-fiction. Yet, interestingly enough, these authors also often use traditional forms, especially autobiography, letters, and journals. Here too Stein has been influential; the same autobiographies in which Stein takes on other personae, causing the works to be fictions, simultaneously express what are supposedly "true" events. Therefore, the same techniques are often used in these prose works as in the poetic and narrative experiments in traditional genres. Ray DiPalma's *The Birthday Notations*, for example, ostensibly is a mere collation of passages from actual 18th, 19th, and 20th century journals; however, in the context of these passages, all being dated the same month and day as DiPalma's birthday, they link to create a kind of fiction in which the hero is bibliographer. Hannah Weiner's *Clairvoyant Journal* is made up of what she declares are "real" events, but for the nonbeliever the words she sees, written on objects, on the foreheads of friends, and in the air, might certainly be perceived as fiction. Bernadette Mayer's *Eruditio ex Memoria* appears to be a kind of confession, a "memory of knowledge"; but, in its mix of metaphysical statement and authorial intrusion, the work has similarities with the anatomy: indeed, the work has been described by Mayer as being taken "from random pages of school notebooks at a moment when I had to throw them all away and couldn't bear not to save some kind of part of them"—a description which supports the feeling that one has of this work being a "cutting up," a "dissection."[43] Similarly, Ronald Vance's *Canoe*, a collation of notes and papers that survived a fire, has many parallels with the anatomy and journal. And what David Antin calls "talk poems"—oral works usually centering around his personal experiences and ideas—are structured according to the classical rhetorical strategies of synecdoche, metonymy, antithesis, and hyperbole. In short, it is not that these works have no genre, but that they cross boundaries between prose, poetry, and fiction. And along with more definitively prose works such as John Ashbery's *The Vermont Notebooks*, Lewis Warsh's autobiography, *Earth Angel*, and the letters of friends, *The Maharajah's Son*, Bernadette Mayer's autobiographical novel, *Memory*, Tom Clark's metaphysical speculations, "Some Thoughts on the Subject," and Bill Berkson's epigrammatic "50 Great Essays," these works reflect a contemporary fascination with traditional prose forms.

What one quickly perceives in the light of so much experimentation with older forms and genres is that contemporary literature not only has "continuity with its literary antecedents"—as Robert Alter has argued[44]—but that it represents an active seeking out and utilizing of pre-Modern forms and genres as a ground from which language opens the work to new dimensions. In such a perspective it even may be valuable to question whether what is generally called Modernism is actually "the tradition," or a diversion from it.[45]

1 Jonathan Culler, "Towards a Theory of Non-Genre Literature," in Raymond Federman, ed., *Surfiction: Fiction Now...and Tomorrow* (Chicago: Swallow Press, 1975), pp. 19-33.

2 Ron Silliman, in an interview with Vicki Hudspith, *Poetry Project Newsletter*, no. 72 (February 1980), non-paginated [8].

3 Although several definitions of Postmodernism have been argued for in the last few years, Charles Altieri's "From Symbolist Thought to Immanence: The Ground of Postmodern Poetics," *Boundary 2*, I (Spring 1973), pp. 605-641, is still the most coherent and suggestive. I also refer the reader to my own study of Postmodern fiction, "Modern Postmodern Fiction: Toward a Formal and Historical Understanding of Postmodern Literature," an unpublished dissertation, The University of Maryland, 1979.

4 Ezra Pound, "A Retrospect," in *Literary Essays* (Norfolk, Connecticut: New Directions, 1954), pp. 9-10.

5 Pound, "Three Cantos," *Poetry*, X (June 1917), 113-114.

6 *Ibid.*

7 Marjorie Perloff, *Frank O'Hara: Poet Among Painters* (New York: George Braziller, 1977), p. 139.

8 Frank O'Hara, as quoted in Perloff, pp. 152–153.

9 Perloff, p. 153.

10 *Ibid.*, p. 139.

11 Ted Berrigan and Barry Alpert, "Ted Berrigan—An Interview Conducted by Barry Alpert, Chicago, May 9, 1972," *Vort*, no. 2 (Winter 1972), pp. 39-40.

12 Berrigan's sonnets, however, are generally neither Italian nor English in form.

13 Michael Davidson, "Advancing Measures: Conceptual Quanti-

ties and Open Forms," a paper delivered at the Modern Language Association's Convention in San Francisco, 1979.

14 There are, of course, several exceptions to this generalization. Robert Duncan and Helen Adam, some of whose works fall into this period, used forms more akin to Pound and O'Hara than to Frost and Wilbur.

15 Richard Poirier, *Robert Frost: The Work of Knowing* (New York: Oxford University Press, 1977), p. 24.

16 Richard Wilbur, interviewed by John Ciardi, as quoted in Donald L. Hill, *Richard Wilbur* (New York: Twayne Publishers, 1967), p. 90.

17 Richard Palmer, "Toward a Postmodern Hermeneutics of Performance," in Michel Benamou and Charles Caramello, eds., *Performance in Postmodern Culture* (Milwaukee and Madison: Center for Twentieth Century Studies/Coda Press, 1977), p. 25. This and other distinctions that Palmer makes between Modern and pre-Modern attitudes are based on his reading of Jean Gebser's *Ursprung und Gegenwart*.

18 Percy Lubbock, *The Craft of Fiction* (New York: Viking Press, 1957), p. 40.

19 Cleanth Brooks and Robert Penn Warren, *Understanding Fiction* (New York: Appleton-Century-Crofts, 1959), p. 684.

20 These qualities of the picaresque are taken from those described by Stuart Miller, *The Picaresque Novel* (Cleveland: Case Reserve University Press, 1967), p. 70.

21 Robert Scholes, *Fabulation and Metafiction* (Urbana: University of Illinois Press, 1979), pp. 75 and 207.

22 Leslie Fiedler, "The Death and Rebirth of the Novel," in John Halperin, ed., *The Theory of the Novel* (New York: Oxford University Press, 1974), p. 200.

23 John Barth, "The Literature of Exhaustion," in Raymond Federman, ed., *Surfiction: Fiction Now...and Tomorrow* (Chicago: Swallow Press, 1975), pp. 19-33.

24 Gertrude Stein, "Poetry and Grammar," in *Lectures in America* (New York: Vintage, 1975), p. 225.

25 *Ibid.*, p. 227.

26 See my discussion of *Ida* in "Modern Postmodern Fiction: Toward a Formal and Historical Understanding of Postmodern Literature."

27 Donald Sutherland, *Gertrude Stein: A Biography of Her Work* (New Haven, Connecticut: Yale University Press, 1951), p. 140.

28 William Gass, "Introduction," in Gertrude Stein, *The Geographical History of America or The Relation of Human Nature to the Human Mind* (New York: Vintage, 1973), pp. 24-25.

29 *Ibid.*

30 Norma Jean Deak, "Dialogues for Two Women," *Sun & Moon*, nos. 9/10 (Summer 1980), p. 178.

31 Howard N. Fox, *Directions* (Washington, D.C.: Smithsonian Institution Press, 1979), p. 27.

32 Eleanor Antin, "Some Thoughts on Autobiography," *Sun & Moon*, nos. 6/7 (Winter 1978-79), p. 81.

33 Robert F. Sayre, *The Examined Self: Benjamin Franklin, Henry Adams, Henry James* (Princeton, New Jersey: Princeton University Press, 1964), p. 7. In equating autobiography and memoirs, however, I am glossing over important distinctions between the two made by Sayre and by Roy Pascal in *Design and Truth in Autobiography*. I do so because I am interested less in defining these specific forms than in pointing to their convergence in contemporary literature. Certainly, I encourage the reader to examine those general distinctions made by Pascal and Sayre.

34 *Ibid.*, p. 33.

35 Antin, "Some Thoughts on Autobiography," p. 81.

36 *Ibid.*, p. 82.

37 *Ibid.*, p. 81.

38 From a telephone conversation between David Antin and the author, April 1980.

39 Antin, "Before the Revolution," in *Dialogue /Discourse /Research* (Santa Barbara, California: Santa Barbara Museum of Art, 1979), non-paginated [30].

40 Toby Olson, *The Life of Jesus* (New York: New Directions, 1976), inside front cover.

41 Jean-Luc Nancy, "Mundus est Fabula," *Modern Language Notes*, XCIII (1978), p. 638.

42 Jacques Derrida, *Of Grammatology*, trans, by Gayatri Chakravorty Spivak (Baltimore: Johns Hopkins University Press, 1976).

43 From a letter from Bernadette Mayer to the author, dated April 27, 1979.

44 Robert Alter, "The Self-Conscious Moment: Reflections on the Aftermath of Modernism," *TriQuarterly*, no. 33 (Spring 1975), p. 218.

45 From a letter from Charles Bernstein to the author, dated April 28, 1980. Bernstein is not making a distinction here between Postmodernism and Modernism, nor between poets who use formal structures and those who do not. Rather, his distinction is between writers that use language that "in its syntax & vocabulary controls/mediates/circumscribes what can be thought/seen" and others. Bernstein writes: "I absolutely do believe that 'we' are the tradition—in a sense the 'high modern' poets like Eliot or Lowell or Auden [are] really a diversion from that more central poetic project going back to Dickinson or Thoreau or Blake or whatever overblown list I'd throw out—Campion!"

COLLEGE PARK, MARYLAND (MAY 1980)
Reprinted from *Sun & Moon: A Journal of Literature & Arts*, nos. 9/10 (Summer 1980)
Reprinted in *Pushcart Prize: Best of the Small Presses 1980* (Yonkers, New York: Pushcart Press, 1981)

Leaving Something Behind

AGNÈS VARDA (WRITER AND DIRECTOR) **LES GLA-NEURS ET LA GLANEUSE (THE GLEANERS AND I)** / 2000

PART DOCUMENTARY, TRAVELOGUE, personal meditation, a lecture on ethics, art exhibition, a series of interviews, and, at moments, simply a silly pastiche of film clips, Agnès Varda's *The Gleaners and I* is nearly always entertaining and moving. Like its very subject, the act of gleaning, Varda's film presents itself as a series of shots that come together as a kind of collection, drawing on images in various locations in France and even, for a few moments, pictures from the director's trip to Japan. And in that sense, we can also perceive this work as a kind of demonstration of how a filmmaker—at least this filmmaker—puts together a movie.

Beginning with Jean François Millet's painting of the same name, Varda, mostly alone, sometimes with a small crew, sets out to discover whether there are still gleaners today. Do people still gather up the wheat and

crops left behind after a harvest? Although some former women gleaners—it was once an activity exclusive to women—claim that such behavior is a thing of the past, we soon discover that large groups of men and women, including poor farmers, gypsies, and urban dwellers, still do gather up potatoes, cabbages, figs, apples, and grapes (although such activity in the grape fields is sometimes policed), along with whatever else they find left to rot. In cities, the poor or sometimes ethically-minded individuals gather at the food markets as they close each day to grab up the numerous tossed leftovers.

Others, as we know, even in the US, are dumpster divers, mulling through the trash near grocery stores and restaurants to pick out still edible foods. At one such spot, Varda gathers together several street teens, a store manager who has sprayed his dumpster with bleach, and a judge who has sentenced the teens for vandalizing both store and dumpster after it was sprayed, trying to explain to each the problems with their behavior. The teens needed the free food, the store manager was outraged by the damage they did, and the judge was simply following the law, each presenting reality from their own viewpoints only.

In the wine country in Provence we meet a vintner, Jean Laplanche, who encourages gleaners to follow the grape har-

vesters, gathering up whatever is left behind. The kindly Laplanche, we soon discover, is also a psychoanalyst concentrating on theory.

Back in Paris, Varda meets with an ethically-minded young man who gathers food from dumpsters and markets simply to make a point of the society's waste. Elsewhere, an award-winning chef explains that he uses every part of the animal, including bones for stock, and gleans his own herbs for the tables.

Meanwhile, the film incorporates the filmmaker herself as an aging woman with a fascination with trucks (she frames them again and again through her wrinkled hands as if her hands themselves were a camera lens), art (she visits several museums to view other paintings of gleaners, and talks with artists, such as Louis Pons, who use found objects in their art), and animals. So do we gradually gather up various aspects and collect information on the director herself.

In a small town she speaks to a man who collects

small objects and furniture abandoned on the streets (the town provides a map and dates when such furniture can be left). And Varda, ultimately, gives us views of her own various "collections."

At another point, the director devotes a short episode to the "dance" of an attached camera lens which she has accidentally filmed on her hand-held camera, representing, I suppose, another kind of "found" art.

Surely one of the most touching episodes, in this picaresque of picking things up, is Varda's encounter with a young man at the market who gathers up discarded vegetables, munching on many of them as he moves around. In a conversation with him, she discovers that he has a Master's Degree and was a university assistant, but now cannot find a job. In the suburban charity house in which he lives, he is surrounded mostly by African and Asian migrants, whom, for free, he teaches French every evening. If there was ever an example of ethical behavior, this man most clearly expresses it.

And so too does Varda in her unbiased conversations with the people she meets. Her open humor and

her obvious wonder at the individuals she encounters bring to her pastiche a warmth that, without sentimentality or self-congratulation, sometimes brings tears to the eyes. This film is a non-judgmental work on people who survive or make their living on gathering up what others have left behind. Somewhat like maggots putting a corpse to good use, the "gleaners" are only too happy to take away what so much of the society wastes.

Although I saw this film in early 2014—in connection with a Varda retrospective at the Los Angeles County Museum of Art—I suddenly realized that it captured the very essence of what I had titled the volume about the year 2000, in which the film was made—another example, surely, of the coincidences that have defined my life.

LOS ANGELES, JANUARY 8, 2014
Reprinted from *World Cinema Review* (January 2014).

THREE RENOIR FILMS OF ART AND LIFE

Reel Life

JEAN RENOIR, JACK KIRKLAND, RENZO AVANZO, AND GIULIO MACCHI (WRITERS, BASED ON A PLAY BY PROSPER MÉRIMÉE), JEAN RENOIR (DIRECTOR) **LE CAROSSE D'OR (THE GOLDEN COACH)** / 1952, USA RELEASE 1954

INTO A BACKWATER Peruvian town of the 18th century comes an Italian *commedia dell'arte* troupe, promised a theater and hotel rooms. The local inn has neither and the innkeeper is determined to keep 60% of their profits. Fortunately, they have traveled with their stars, Camilla (Anna Magnani) and her lover Don Antonio (Odoardo Spadaro), who demand and get a fairer share.

Their first performance is a near-failure, as the inattentive audience members—most of whom have not been asked to pay—sell and buy goods, and applaud

and shout at the arrival of the local toreador Ramon (Riccardo Rioli). But by the end of the play, Ramon has also been smitten by Camilla.

Next door Ferdinand, the Viceroy—whose over-dressed mistress and bewigged ministers and servants clearly bore him—overhears the theatergoers applause, which intrigue him enough to invite the theater company to perform in his home, despite his courtiers' disdain.

The same boat that brought the company to town also carried his brand-new golden coach, a display of his wealth and power, which the company has shared as a bedroom.

Meeting the unimpressed and easy-going Camilla in person a few days later, the Viceroy (Duncan Lamont) feels relaxed, even going so far, as the Marquise observes, to "remove his peruke before her." For her part, Camilla reclaims a comb she has left in the golden coach. In short, they literally let down their hair with one another!

Love, of course, follows, with a hilarious series of crisscrossed dalliances, lies, and duels straight out of both *commedia dell'arte* theater and 19th century farce. Throughout, Renoir frames his various theatrical imitations in a rich Technicolor palette of golds, reds, greens, and blues, as his Columbine plays out love and treachery again and again.

The three lovers, in turn, represent three opposing possibilities for Camilla as the wife of an empty-headed and conceited adventurer (the toreador), a wise and wealthy scoundrel (the Viceroy), or an earnest and honest dreamer determined to live life like the natives (Don Antonio). But her heart, the viewer comprehends, is given over to the drama of life rather than reality. She is a born actress despite her complaints, a failure as a lover in the flesh.

As the Viceroy, who has awarded her the golden coach, faces deposition and possible execution for his profligacy, Camilla dramatically saves the day by handing over the coach to the Bishop of Lima, who was to decide the fate of Ferdinand. Her theatrical gesture saves him, but in the process she must give up all reality. Behind a sheer curtain, as the camera pulls away, she is asked, Does she miss real life. "A little," the actress meekly replies, as Renoir's theatrical film comes to a close, leaving his actress locked away in another kind of reel life.

LOS ANGELES, APRIL 18, 2010
Reprinted from *Green Integer Blog* (April 2010).

Recreating the Past

JEAN RENOIR (ADAPTATION, BASED ON AN IDEA
BY ANDRÉ-PAUL ANTOINE), JEAN RENOIR (DIRECTOR)
FRENCH CANCAN / 1954

IT MIGHT BE fascinating some day to compare and contrast the various versions of films centered around Montmartre's famed Moulin Rouge and the various figures involved—from John Houston's 1952 *Moulin Rouge*, focusing on the life of Toulouse-Lautrec, to Renoir's *French Cancan* of two years later; from the 1960 stage-inspired film musical *Can-Can*, to Baz Luhrmann's extravaganza of 2001, also titled *Moulin Rouge*. All of them perhaps have the word *excess* in common. Moreover, it is quite revealing to compare Renoir's love-letter to Parisian bohemian life and Walter Lang's rather insipid movie tribute to a dance: while in the American version, the Can-Can is presented as a revolutionary, scandalous dance being fought against by the forces of moral reform, Renoir treats the same

as a revival of an old-fashioned dance that faces only the obstacles of love and money. For the Americans, accordingly, the Can-Can represents a radical step forward in sexual freedom, while Renoir's *French Cancan* is a recreation of a romanticized past.

In my estimation, however, only Renoir's movie represents truly great filmmaking. Unlike the other versions, fettered by psychological revelations, ridiculous turns of plot, and casts of thousands, *French Cancan* almost entirely dispenses with story in order to present the viewer with a spectacularly colorful image of a bygone era.

Henri Danglard (wonderfully played by Jean

Gabin) is a down-on-his-luck owner of a small club featuring his lover, Lola de Castro de la Fuente de Espramadura, "La Belle Abbesse," a lovely but somewhat talentless belly dancer. One night, slumming it, as we might describe it today, Danglard, "La Belle Abbesse," and friends visit a small Montmartre café where the locals still dance the Can-Can and other peasant-like trots.

Spotting a beautiful young laundress, Nini (Françoise Amoul), in the crowd, Danglard dances with her, angering his lover, who quickly begins a fight, but not before Danglard arranges a meeting with Nini for the next day.

The impresario suddenly has an idea: he will build a new club, the Moulin Rouge, in Montmartre and re-introduce the Can-Can as the *French* Can-Can, attracting just such people as him and his friends to a safe haven in a somewhat rough, down-and-out neighborhood, alluring his customers by hinting, as the Folies Bergère had and later the Ziegfeld Follies would, at sexual licentiousness. From the beginning we know that the place is destined to be a great success!

The only other events that occur are those which center around Lola's jealousness and revenge, the difficulties in raising enough money for the venture, and Danglard's inevitable romancing of Nini, frustrated by her love for her innocent boyfriend and the attentions of Prince Alexandre (Giani Esposito).

We know from the start, however, that eventually things will take care of themselves and that Danglard will have his way: the Moulin Rouge will eventually open; and Renoir speedily takes care of any fragments of the plot so that he can devote the rest of his film to a visual recreation of the theatrical event, not perhaps as dizzyingly over-the-top as Luhrmann's massive choruses of shifting torsos, arms, and legs, but still a splendidly beautiful series of performances of whistling, singing (by the incomparable Edith Piaf), and, after removing the onscreen audience, chairs, and tables, an exuberant Can-Can.

In this, the second of the director's trilogy about love and art, Renoir, not only captures a past world, but seems to call out for a time gone when art was at the center of living, was one of its major avocations. Love may be beautiful, he argues, but it is, even for "La Belle Abbesse" and the randy Danglard, only a past time; art, music, dance, literature, these are the forces that keep one alive! Will Nini find happiness? Will her boyfriend, who has refused to accept her if she sets foot upon the stage, be able to forgive her? In Renoir's nostalgic creation, it doesn't matter, for Nini has had the joy of performing, an act that transforms life. Living is, after all, so much less interesting!

LOS ANGELES, FEBRUARY 23, 2010
Reprinted from *Green Integer Blog* (March 2010).

The Theater of Love

JEAN RENOIR (SCENARIO, ADAPTATION, AND DIA-
LOGUE), JEAN SERGE (ADAPTATION), JEAN RENOIR (DI-
RECTOR) **ELENA ET LES HOMMES** / 1956, USA RELEASE
1957

THE THIRD OF Renoir's trilogies about theatrical life,
is subtitled a "musicale fantastique," and indeed *Elena
et les hommes* plays out, this time using the background
of pre-World War I French politics, as a kind of fantastic series of musical interludes, dominated by a street
song tribute (sung by Marjane) to Paris and French life.

At the center of this farce is a beautiful Polish
Countess, Elena Sokorwska (a stunning Ingrid Bergman), who, despite her poverty, pretends a life of great
wealth. She is about to marry a wealthy boot-manufac-
turer, Martin-Michaud (Pierre Bertin), but a few days
before the event, lured into the streets by the celebration for Général François Rollan (Jean Marais), she
encounters Le Comte Henri de Chevincourt (Mel Fer-

rer) who clearly wins her heart. He, in turn, introduces her to Rollan, whereupon a love triangle is immediately established, continuing a few days later in the country house of Martin-Michaud, whose son, also about to be married, carries on with the servants, while Elena shifts her lovers from room to room—a hilarious series of frames that recalls Renoir's earlier film, *Rules of the Game*. While that satire, however, had serious consequences, *Elena*, although occasionally suggesting the state of the nation is at stake, represents more a theater of the heart than a theater of war; and Renoir seems determined to move entirely out of the realm of realism by ultimately encamping the three in a whorehouse, surrounded by the police, gypsies, and Rollan's adoring

public.

In order to help Rollan escape, Henri must stand in for Elena's lover, as they kiss before a window with the crowds watching below. Elena is, at first, angry with his behavior, but gradually she warms up to his amorous embraces as the crowd is transformed, like beings out of *A Midsummer Night's Dream*, into a kissing and embracing tangle of bodies.

Some critics, particularly *The New York Times'* Bosley Crowther, were outraged by what they saw as an inferior Renoir film. Crowther blamed Warner Brothers executives for having interfered with the cutting: "How this fiasco could have happened is difficult to explain." The work alternated, he declared, between a romantic drama and a slapstick farce. Jack Warner himself had complained that he found Renoir's plot incomprehensible.*

In fact, *Elena et les hommes* is a farce from beginning to end; like the films that came before, it is a work that embraces the love of all things theatrical, of realities larger than life. Accordingly, the film is also movingly romantic; "Was there ever a more sensuous actress in the movies?" asks Roger Ebert of Ingrid Bergman.

Jean Marais as Rollan is a dashing hero, Henri a handsome lover, and the two of them keep the forceful Elena from having to deal intensely with the reality of her existence. Together they help her rush bravely forward into territory where angels fear to tread, and ultimately reward her with a fabulous life of fiction as opposed to a shabby existence with a venal businessman.

Once again, Renoir celebrates romance over the ordinary, the fantastic over the real, sex over frozen commitment.

---

* To give Crowther his due, the version he probably saw was the American editing, *Paris Does Strange Things*, which Renoir disavowed as his own work.

LOS ANGELES, APRIL 29, 2010
Reprinted from *Green Integer Blog* (April 2010).

Early in 1997, the year I began publishing Green Integer, I met Nicholas Frangakis, a kind, unassuming man who in 1961, as a student at Loyola University in Los Angeles, began to organize a film series. Showing major film classics, Frangakis was able to get Mervyn LeRoy to visit the campus for their showing of I am a Fugitive from a Chain Gang, Charles Bracket, *accompanied by Dorothy Parker, for* Sunset Boulevard, *and George Stevens* for their showing of A Place in the Sun.

Finishing his Philosophy studies at Loyola, Frangakis was about to enter the novitiate at the Benedictine community a St. Andrew's Priory in Valyermo, California. But before he left, the Jesuit administration at Loyola asked if he might set up a film event for the following year.

Frangakis searched carefully for whom he might invite. By accident, he was asked to attend a screening of a film about St. Francis of Assisi by Plato Skouras. He sat with three other men, his friend Fr. Martin of St. Andrew's Priory, Skouras, and "a heavy-set man with a shaved head wearing brown corduroys and a blue denim shirt. I thought the man might be some retired member of the electricians' union who had been invited as a courtesy." But when the film was over, the man came forward, congratulating Skouras. After he left, Skouras told his other guests that the seeming interloper was Jean Renoir.

That chance encounter led to an arranged meeting with Renoir:

At Leona Drive, up Benedict Canyon, I was shown

into the living room of Jean Renoir's home. It was un-
believable! Here I was, sitting, waiting to meet Jean
Renoir in a room filled with August Renoir's paint-
ings. There were Cézannes, a Matisse, paintings by
Braque, a sketch by Picasso and statues by Maillol.

Rather than discussing films or Frangakis' planned film
festival, Renoir spoke to the young film enthusiast about
himself, his plan to enter the monastery, his past as an
unsuccessful actor, etc., looking deeply into his eyes. "I am
interested in telling stories," remarked Renoir, "and the
best stories come from people's lives."

The following year, Renoir attended three films
shown at the Loyola festival, The River, Grand Illusion
and Rules of the Game. *The festival itself played to sold-*
out performances. Yet, as Frangakis admits, "despite high
esteem for his films, Hollywood continued to ignore Renoir
as an available director ready and prepared to work."

At the Priory, where Frangakis determined he was
not cut out to be a monk, the young cineaste received visits
from Renoir and his wife, Dido, and when he went on to
make educational films for schools, Renoir would see each
film after it was finished. A deep friendship arose between
the two, and during the last days of Renoir's life Frangakis
was a regular visitor to the Renoir home. "On the day of
his death, February 12, 1979, his wife, Dido, called me
to come to the house to help her make the funeral arrange-

ments. I called the press to release the news to the world."

As Frangakis started to tell me this rich history, I quickly remarked that Renoir was one of my very favorite directors, and his La Règle du Jeu *was among my favorite films (see my comments on that film in* My Year 2006*). After telling me much of the story above, Frangakis suggested I might be interested in publishing an interview with Renoir from April 15, 1970, conducted at the American Film Institute. Reading it, I immediately expressed interest, and in those early, relatively uncomplicated days of the press, the book appeared one year later, in June of 1998, as* Jean Renoir: An Interview.

Years later, with Frangakis, I visited the Renoir collection at the University of California Los Angeles to investigate some of the numerous unpublished film scripts left at the director's death. A great number of projects loomed, and I was quite excited by the trove, but almost completely overwhelmed by the need to read these on site, and type them by hand, if *Green Integer could get permissions. It remains something in the back of my mind.*

MAY 1, 2010

Acting and Perceiving

PETER HANDKE **ON A DARK NIGHT I LEFT MY SILENT HOUSE**, TRANSLATED FROM THE GERMAN BY KRISHNA WINSTON (NEW YORK: FARRAR, STRAUS AND GIROUX, 2000)

THE SMALL VILLAGE of Taxham—on the outskirts of Salzburg, Austria—was constructed early-on in the manner of many villages throughout the world today, with barriers blocking most of its entrances and exits due to the highways, nearby airport, natural boundaries, and old military bases. In short, it is a city unknown almost to all except those who live and work in it.

Peter Handke's most recent novel, *On a Dark Night I Left My Silent House*, centers on one of Taxham's citizens, the local pharmacist, whose life, like that of the village, has been carefully constructed to keep others out and himself locked in. Although he shares his house with his wife, she and he have little communication and live in spaces (real and imaginary) that the other does not inhabit. His major activities, other than the daily pattern of opening and closing the town's pharmacy, are a morning swim, his reading of medieval romances, and his love of nature which is particularly focused on the gathering, tasting, and analyzing of various varieties of mushrooms.

Indeed for the first third of this work, he appears as an unlikely candidate for the fantastic fable that he, the narrator of the work, and Handke himself are about to tell. But one evening, while in the woods, he is apparently attacked and hit severely on the head. The injuries, which at first seem minor, are soon recognized as serious when, at the local airport restaurant, he is unable to speak. There, as if in a dream, he picks up two strangers—a former Olympic sports champion and a poet, both now down on their luck, and travels with them into a strange world, which, although later named as Spain, represents an archetypal city "of the night wind," as surreal as the worlds created by Kafka, Walser, Céline, and other continental fabulists.

They've chosen the city, almost by accident, because the poet recalls that his ex-wife and a child he has never met live there. But upon arriving in the strange

Santa Fe, they perceive the city is celebrating a festival, and the poet can recognize very little. Although they find the house, the poet's wife no longer lives there. Nonetheless, the pharmacist, now described by the other two simply as "the driver," there encounters, once again, the former woman friend of the ski champion in whose house they had spent the previous night, and who had strangely enough entered the pharmacist's room and pummeled him in his bed; and he also recognizes, among the gypsy musicians, his own son, who had abruptly left his family years before after being slapped by his father in the face upon the boy's release from the authorities for a petty theft. And soon after, the poet recognizes his own daughter as the queen of the festivities at the very moment she is arrested and taken off.

In short, the three together vaguely represent aspects of one being, and events in each of their lives recall and newly affect one another. In the days following the first evening of the festival, the town and townspeople gradually take on stranger and stranger qualities as a plague of near-madness begins to affect the citizens, one by one falling into tirades and attacking others, for no apparent reason, often killing them. Upon saving his poet friend from just such a fate, the pharmacist realizes he must leave, and enters the seemingly endless vastness of the surrounding steppes.

Accordingly, Handke sends his character across a near-desert in a kind of pilgrimage into the self, the past, and all that in the bunkered-up village of Taxham the pharmacist has attempted to escape. The surreal voyage across this seemingly desolate and empty space—which we gradually come to see is actually filled with animals, vegetation, and other itinerant voyagers—is a true literary tour-de-force, as Handke's anti-hero both suffers and finds, at times, near ecstasy in the inexplicable search for something different in his life. The vague magnet of this voyage is the skier's friend, the woman described earlier in the book as "a winner," presumably a term applying to her appearance and personality, but growing in the pharmacist's voyage to mean so much more: a winner in life, something like the young skier was, a champion, perhaps a prize.

Handke's hero does ultimately find something of value, his own voice, a reconciliation of sorts with his son (who is seen with the poet's daughter), and the discovery of love with the "winner." But the final section of the book is not a record of fulfillment and rewards, it is a statement of the role and purpose of art. For life has returned to its usual pattern, slightly altered perhaps, but filled with the tedium of daily repetition and workaday acts. The pharmacist, now designated as "the storyteller," has experienced something amazing, but he knows that he must record it; not only "tell" the story, but see it in print, in "black and white." "I want to have my story in writing. From speaking it, orally, nothing comes back to me. In written form, that would be different. And in the end I want to get something out of my story too. Long live the difference between speech and writing. It's what life's all about. I want to see my story written. I see it written. And the story itself wants that." Handke brilliantly points up the differences here between the act of living and the recognition of it, the *reception* of those acts. They are not the same. As in this profound, short work, things simply happen in life. One is pulled, driven through life in a world where the acts themselves often make little sense, often seem to be without meaning; while art records them, reveals them, allows one to observe them, to give them substance.

LOS ANGELES, 2000
Reprinted from *Green Integer Blog* (April 2009).

Bending Time

RAÚL RUIZ AND GILLES TAURAND (SCREENPLAY,
BASED ON PROUST'S *REMEMBRANCE OF THINGS PAST*),
RAÚL RUIZ (DIRECTOR) **LE TEMPS RETROUVÉ (TIME
REGAINED)** / 1999, USA 2000

RAÚL RUIZ'S *Time Regained*, is not, as its title suggests, a film based on the last volume of Marcel Proust's great *Remembrance of Things Past*, but rather a kind of Proustian cut-up of the entire series of books, seen through the eyes of the character Proust (Marcello Mazzarella) in the last days of his life. Through photographs and the associations of the great writer's mind, Ruiz brilliantly deconstructs Proust's fiction, telling a grand story not through chronological events or even through a consistent narrative logic, but presenting us with a series of haunting and beautiful images of a world gone by, a world of floating women dressed in beautiful gowns and well-groomed handsome men haunting and taunting them with their affairs with other women and men.

This gossipy, chattering, vengeful, and often politically blind Parisian society creates a kind of dark symphony—what Proust describes as "a music that keeps coming back"—throughout the film which, with the poignant music of Jorge Arriagada, suggests themes that are embedded, repeated, and forgotten.

At moments the director creates overlapping images which suggest multiple realities overlaying each other. At other times the film repeats itself, slightly altering the flow of occurrences. And there are surrealist images—including a room filled with black top hats each holding a pair of white gloves, a scene in which the partygoers are turned to stone for the child Proust's cinematic entertainment, and a scene in a male bordello that features a sadomasochistic beating of the Baron

Charlus (a beating which dissatisfies him in its timidity) by a young street-boy with Proust voyeuristically peering in on the action from a ceiling window. But mostly Ruiz's camera focuses on the lavish parties and funerals of these wealthy Frenchmen, in which people, along with hundreds of canapés and glasses of champagne, are swallowed up and spit out with sarcastic spite. Beyond it all, we perceive, are the trenches filled with the dead men of World War I, a reality which will soon completely bring this close-minded society to its end. But as in Proust's long work, the figures of his belle-epoch do not have a clue about what lies ahead, and in fact are clueless about anything including the significance of their actions or lack of. Any coherent "meaning" we might glean from Ruiz's stunningly gorgeous piece of cinema can come only from how we ourselves interpret these images, what we make of them. And as the critic J. Hoberman has pointed out, the film almost seems to be about a man who through his words created a kind of cinema himself.

In short, this film is less about "events" than it is about the process of filmmaking or creating a fiction, focusing on how the mind perceives what the eyes see, how it edits/processes those images, and how it puts them together or recalls them. All of Proust's central characters—Odette de Crécy (Catherine Deneuve), Gilberte (Emmanuelle Béart), Le Baron de Charlus

(John Malkovich), Robert Saint-Loup (Pascal Greggory), Albertine (Chiara Mastrioianni), Morel (Vincent Perez), Madame Verdurin (Marie-France Pisier), Madame Cottard (Dominique Labourier), and even, for an instant, Swann (Bernard Pautrat)—are here, but Ruiz focuses little on the continuity of their interactions. Even when it is quite apparent what they are doing behind the scenes—for example Saint-Loup's affair with the actress Rachel (Elsa Zylberstein) or his later sexual infatuation with working-class infantrymen—events never truly coalesce into a "plot." Indeed, Ruiz purposely, at times, mystifies the interrelationships of his figures, merely suggesting the lesbian bondings of some of the women or hinting at the Baron's vicious political views and his pedophile tendencies with regard to the young Marcel. Accordingly, even those who have never set their eyes upon a page of *Remembrance of Things Past* can enjoy this film. Indeed, if one has read the book, although it might help to enlighten certain scenes, it will more likely frustrate the moviegoer, since nothing comes of it. So removed from the action is Ruiz's Proust, as he shyly if debonairly winds his way through these wealthy charlatans, that he seems—as is more concretely revealed in the scene at the gay bordello—more like a voyeur than an actor. Of course, that is  precisely the director's role in filmmaking, to catch his actors "in the act" and mold them into a more coherent reality. But the "reality" here is not as much coherent or orderly as a thing in process. Much like Penelope of the Odysseus myth, Ruiz weaves and unweaves his tapestry again and again, as the various Proustian figures dance around one another as in a grand ball.

The point to all this, quite obviously, is that there can be no one truth, no one way of seeing things, no day, as the voice of Proust asserts at the beginning, when things truly "change." There is no true past: it gets reconstructed through memory and forgetfulness, through perception and distortion. Proust's grand effort to "regain time" is "the frivolity of the dying." Time is something that is meant to be lost, just as the figures of Proust's Paris—of Woolf's England, of O'Neill's seaside Connecticut—would one day suddenly disappear.

In the very last scene of Ruiz's remarkable film, we see the teenage Proust being watched by Proust the elder, while between them the seated figure of the Baron de Charlus looks out at the boy, a demon about to descend upon his victim. We know the result. We see it through the sufferings of the elder Proust in his cork-lined room being cared for by his faithful Céleste. But there is no going back, no fixing of the clock. No matter how much one desires it, time cannot be recaptured nor held back.

LOS ANGELES, MARCH 2, 2014
Reprinted from *World Cinema Review* (March 2014).

Six Stories of São Paulo: The 2ⁿᵈ Night (The Professor of Everything and the Professor of Nothing)

ON THE SECOND day of my first trip to São Paulo, Michael Palmer and I met with Régis Bonvicino for breakfast, and then walked a short ways to a coffee shop to meet the other editor of the Brazilian anthology, Nelson Ascher.

Nelson—although a very different figure from our charming host, Régis—seemed affable enough. And as we began talking, we could see that he was warming to our company.

Of Hungarian background, Nelson was fascinated that I'd read some of the major Hungarian poets in translation, and as I shared my spotty knowledge with him, he filled in the gaps. Before long he was speaking of a great many things, with long disquisitions on all sorts of subjects, all quite coherently presented, but a bit like never-ending lectures that shifted quickly from theme to theme, and were, according-ly, almost impossible to follow.

As lunch approached, we ordered Antarctica beers and a bite to eat, but the conversation, mostly emanating from Nelson, flowed forth, until I suddenly noticed the sun across the dark blue walls of the bar was beginning to set.

Both Michael and I were still suffering from jet-lag, and we were unable to take in much of what Nelson said. At one point I recall Michael asking what Régis and Nelson felt were the most important books of Brazilian literature still needing to be translated into English. Régis quickly mentioned a couple of titles, but Nelson began a new lecture about the whole of Brazilian culture, a conversation that lasted long after I had any ability to coherently listen. We finally had to insist that it was time for us to go.

At first this free flow of information seemed almost comical, somewhat charming. But after the second day of the torrent of subjects pouring from Nelson's mouth, particularly when we were attempting to help our friends with the translations of our poems, his chatter became irritating. My explanation of a single English word would send him on discourse about several languages. That evening, after Nelson had left, Régis joked, "You see, Nelson is the Professor Everything. While I am the Professor of Nothing."

Some months later, when the two of them traveled to the United States to promote the book, those words grew to mean much more. If there had been an unspoken tension between the two editors in Brazil, by the time they reached the United States, Régis had begun to show signs of great impatience with his colleague. Nelson seemed quite oblivious, easily making friends with the American poets because he spoke so openly— and so much; and he quickly won over friends such as Julian Semilian and my companion Howard simply because of his love of jokes. Régis seemed nervous and slightly tortured in Nelson's presence.

Indeed, when the two performed at a reading I had arranged in the Spanish and Portuguese Department of the University of California, Los Angeles, outsiders became aware of their growing enmity, and I had to step in as moderator simply to prevent it from boiling over into the classroom. The Professor of Everything was slowly burying the Professor of Nothing in words.

I held a small party in my office that evening, and told both of them, staying at a nearby motel, that they

 had to be ready and waiting in the lobby by 7:00 the next morning so that we could catch the plane to San Francisco, the next leg of our travels.

At 7:00 I arrived at the motel, where Régis, as promised, stood ready. Nelson evidently was still asleep. I knocked on his door, awakening him, and insisted that he had immediately to get dressed. We would miss the plane. As it turned out, he had not even packed yet. And, as we nervously awaited him, Régis insisted we should leave him behind.

"I can't do that," I proclaimed.

"You'll make the plane if we leave soon," Howard consoled us.

"We should just leave him. He'll find a way up," Régis persisted.

"But he doesn't even know the name of the hotel," I argued. "And I'm responsible for him as well."

Finally Nelson appeared and Howard rushed us to our plane.

It turned out that Nelson was desperately afraid of flying, and he postponed every moment he could before getting onto the aircraft. When we arrived at our seats, I insisted on sitting between the two to prevent any further arguments.

But out of fear, Nelson began to talk, and talk, and talk. He talked first of the Hungarian language, of the roots of certain words and sounds. He talked of the towns and cities on the Danube and Tisza rivers. He talked of his uncles and aunts. I turned to Régis to speak, hoping it would stall his avalanche of information. It did not. Régis sat with teeth clenched.

At several points, as Régis reminds me, Nelson got up from his seat and attempted to make conversation with the stewardess. After about three such occurrences, she brought him back to his seat and demanded that he remain there. "I was just trying to make friends," Nelson insisted.

When we finally reached our destination we rushed to the baggage chute, but stood waiting. Nelson's overlarge suitcase did not arrive! I told the baggage handler our address, and off we rushed to the hotel via taxicab.

On the way, I attempted to share with both of them some of San Francisco's sights, but every time I pointed out a spot, Nelson brought up the Hungarian language and the etymology of certain words. I too was growing very impatient with the Professor of Everything. It was no longer charming or even funny. When I attempted to show him a San Francisco streetcar, he looked the other direction.

"Nelson," I scolded, "I was attempting to show you

something. One of the famed San Francisco streetcars."

Nelson looked at me for a second, and with a totally serious grimace on his face, answered in a deep growl: "I have seen their tracks!"

Régis and I erupted into laughter, as Nelson scowled, seeming to ponder his fate.

When he reached the hotel, he quickly retreated to his room and suggested, via telephone, that perhaps he was not wanted at the party I was planning that night.

"No, Nelson you have to be there! I've put together a huge event and invited all my San Francisco friends. I want them to meet both you and Régis. I'm sorry if I offended you. I just wanted to make sure that you saw a bit of the city while you were here."

Régis had already rushed into the streets to discover the city for himself. Nelson stayed in his hotel room all afternoon, napping.

Nelson attended the evening event, charming, I am certain, a great many of my poet friends. But the next day, instead of returning with us to Los Angeles, he bought a train ticket to New York.

LOS ANGELES, AUGUST 13, 2000
Reprinted from *Sibila* (November 2009), originally published in Portuguese as "Memória: O Lançamento de *Nothing the Sun Could Not Explain*."
Reprinted from *Green Integer Blog* (March 2010).

The Professor of Everything and The Professor of Nothing made another appearance in 2000 in Michael Palmer's poetry collection, The Promises of Glass. *The poem, "São Paulo Sighs," dedicated to Régis Bonvicino, is one of Palmer's "autobiography" poems, but it is not precisely autobiographical. Of course, as we all know, in its metaphorical statements, imagery, and linguistic conceits, poetry is rarely literal, and unreadable when it is so. Michael calls up an exotic world far from Brazil in his lyrics from "As Time Goes By." Perhaps the actress Ingrid Bergman, who asked Sam to play that song in* Casablanca *in 1942, and two years later lived in Rio in the film* Notorious, *is the connecting link. I did not observe most of the images Palmer mentions on our trip there, but we each see what we want to, so I can't fault him on that. The barroom wall of which he writes in the last lines of the poem was, indeed, blue, and the sun certainly* did *not explain anything (just as our anthology proclaimed) since the Professor of Everything was in the midst of one of his interminable talks. But there were not only three, the two professors and the poet, walking and walking through the city, but four, the missing figure being me. In poetry a trinity has more weight perhaps than a quartet.*

Michael and his wife, Kathy Simon—an interna-

*tionally renowned architect whose San Francisco Trans-
bay Transit Center and Tower I might today point out to
tourists such as our Brazilian friends—joined me, Régis,
Nelson, the noted landscaped designer Lorie Olin (who
redesigned Columbus Circle and Bryant Park in New
York and The Frankfurt Central Station), and my editor, Diana Daves at one of my favorite San Francisco restaurants, Campton Place, a small, posh hotel of the same
name, for dinner after the San Francisco party.*

*The party I hosted beforehand also included Lyn
Hejinian, Leslie Scalapino, Cydney Chadwick, Norma
Cole, Roberto Toscano, Stephen Vincent, Barbara Guest,
Jeff Clark, Steve Dickison, the San Francisco Consul for
Brazil, and numerous others.*

LOS ANGELES, OCTOBER 4, 2009

Six Stories of São Paulo: The 3rd Night (The Raw and the Cooked)

ON MY FIRST trip to São Paulo, Brazil, in 1997, when Michael Palmer and I celebrated the publication of the Sun & Moon edition of *Nothing the Sun Could Not Explain: 16 Contemporary Brazilian Poets*, not only were we corralled into a particular neighborhood, but we were kept on a regimen of what we then perceived might be Brazilian cuisine: day after day, our hosts Régis Bonvicino and Nelson Ascher would pick us up and take us to a restaurant where we were served nothing but *bife* or *churrasco*: Churrasco Brochet, Churrasco de Fraudinha, Churrasco a Moda, Bife Amazonas, Bife ou Frango a Milanesco, Bife Abebolado, Bife a Calvo—accompanied always with rice, beans, or fried plantains.

One day, to our surprise, our friends actually introduced a new-sounding concoction to our diet—Picanha na Chapa—which turned out to be grilled sirloin!

While I certainly enjoy a good steak once in a while, dining every night for two weeks on chewy and stringy grilled steaks does tend to separate those who prefer the raw (Michael and me) from those who eat only the cooked (Régis and Nelson). One day while touring the vast region of São Paulo's "Little Japan," Régis turned to us to inquire: "Do you like Japanese food?" I could see Michael's head suddenly snap into gastronomic attention, his eyes growing large with anticipation. I licked my lips. In unison, we replied, "Yes, we do!" Equally in unison, Régis and Nelson rejoined, "We don't."

The next night we were told we were being taken out for a very special dinner. Our treat turned out to be—how might we have imagined anything else—a steak house, the difference being that the meat was slightly more tender and succulent.

So desperate had we become that Michael and I snuck out to an Italian restaurant for lunch. The menu, however, was primarily in Portuguese, with even the Italian words being somewhat "Portuguesized." We both closed our eyes and pointed at our choices, dreaming of fish or chicken at the very least. Beef was served—although in a tomato sauce, with pasta instead of rice.

I must admit that one day, early in our stay, the head of one of our reading venues took us to a Portuguese restaurant, where we dined on a wonderfully spicy shredded cod. For our very last night in São Paulo, moreover, The Professor of Everything and The Professor Nothing (as Régis jokingly defined the differences between Nelson and himself) took us to a traditional Brazilian restaurant where we dined on various versions of Frijoada. But otherwise, there were no exceptions. Beef was king.

When some months later Régis visited me with his wife Darly and daughter Bruna in the United States, I took them out to several trendy Los Angeles restaurants and held a catered event in my own house before I perceived that Régis had not been eating much. Was he all right, I asked with some consternation. He meekly answered, "Could you take us to a place where they serve beans and rice?"

"And beef?" I added.

"Oh, that would be nice," Darly cried out.

When I returned to Brazil in 2000, I refused to be intimidated by Régis' narrow culinary tastes. One day I dined with him at a local fast food eatery, ordering a cutlet of dry, breaded pork. The next night I announced that I was going to the neighborhood Japanese restaurant.

"I don't like Japanese," he predictably replied.

"That's okay," I blithely responded. "Come along with me. You'll eat the rice!"

He laughed and joined me in an absolutely pleasant night.

NEW YORK, BRAZIL GRILL, MAY 5, 2003
Reprinted from *Sibila* (November 2009), originally published in Portuguese as "O cru e o cozido."
Reprinted from *Green Integer Blog* (April 2010).

Six Stories of São Paulo: The 4th Night (Crybaby)

UPON MY SECOND trip to São Paulo in 2000 I was put up in a nicer part of town than where Michael Palmer and I stayed upon our first visit. Régis Bonvicino, our host, had warned us on that earlier visit to not leave the neighborhood, which seriously delimited our free-time activities. One day Michael and I—frustrated with the boundaries we'd been given—ventured into the older and definitely seedier part of the city.

This time, I was given no such limitations. Indeed Régis and fellow poet Horácio Costa took me to the heart of the city for a spectacular view of the São Paulo skyline from a restaurant atop one of the older skyscrapers. Another afternoon Horácio took me to a historical museum near the old city center, and later, at sunset, we wandered the streets where hundreds of poor Indians and others who had migrated from Brazil's provinces gathered on outlaid scarves and worn rugs

displaying whatever deitrus they hoped to sell—pencils, cards, change purses, and, in many cases, seemingly worthless trinkets of what can only be described as junk.

It was a terrifying and eerie experience to wander about these seated and sometimes supine street peddlers, each calling out to the two us to witness their wares. There was something horrifyingly spectacular, as if thousands of starving human beings had suddenly bowed at our feet. Régis—who works as a judge for juveniles—was angered when I told him that Horácio had taken me there. But I was appreciative of the experience of witnessing such vast poverty firsthand, a humbling revelation.

Since I now had been given no limits in my perambulations of the city, I walked long distances, encountering, for the most part, the stylish and sophisticated shops of this vast metropolis.

One still sees things in wealthy São Paulo, however, that one would never witness in Rome, Paris, or New York. Near one of the swankiest shopping centers of the city, a small child, still almost a baby, had been posted to sell what seemed like sets of colored pencils. The child was crying in its evident abandonment. I watched for a few moments in a combination of horror and fascination before turning back to my hotel.

I had walked about a half hour away from the bawling boy, but could not rid myself of the image, finally determining to return to the child. After what seemed like a far longer period of time than my first journey, I reached the babe again.

I knew that they—the delinquent parents or whoever "looked after" this being—had possibly taught him to cry in order to capture the attention of just such people as I. But the tears still poured from the sobbing boy's eyes; there clearly could be no pleasure in such an enactment.

I dropped the equivalent of $50 in Reals into the child's cup, the boy hardly noting my presence.

"At least," I whispered in self-congratulation, "the family will be fed for a few weeks." Yet, at the same moment, I knew that my action might merely lead to a perpetuation of that poor child's position on the sidewalk, indenturing him only to more months of torture. And when I reached my hotel room, I too began to cry.

NEW YORK, MAY 3, 2000

Six Stories of São Paulo:
The 5ᵗʰ Night (Hello, Goodbye)

DURING MY SECOND stay in São Paulo in 2000, my host and friend Régis Bonvicino had arranged for actors to present my new play, *A Dog Tries to Kiss the Sky*, which Régis had translated into Portuguese, along with a book of my poetry.

The performance took place at São Paulo's Museu de Arte Moderna, MAM. We arrived early, meeting executive curator Rejane Cintrão, who walked us through a show of erotic art, a topic that few American art museums would have dared tackle, but given this show's scope and visual force, was a worthy subject of focus.

Soon the actors arrived, two energetic young women, Cristina Mutarelli and Lígia Cortez, who performed the piece in the large commons room, which served as a kind of meeting place/restaurant. A few people sat about quietly talking when suddenly the two women began their performance. They repeated the

same work the next night at my reading, and continued the run of the play for several weeks at MAM, where I was told it had become quite popular.

Their interpretation of my lyrical Midwestern dialogue made the work seem much closer to Ionesco or Beckett than I had intended. They also introduced a kind of *commedia dell'arte* element into the play which further highlighted the work's farcical elements. Some writers and friends had commented that they thought the performance was far too overstated and, in some respects, I agree; but I have always marveled in and celebrated the various interpretations of my work. A later Los Angeles production, moreover, was performed by actors who couldn't seem to comprehend the absurdly funny behavior of its characters. Interestingly enough, although the play was written for two males, the Los Angeles production also featured, on alternate nights, two women. An earlier Los Angeles reading of the play by the theater company Bottom's Dream was nearer to the way I had conceived it.

In any event, I felt honored to have a performance of the work in São Paulo, and later during my stay in

Brazil I wrote another short piece, *The Sorry Play*, which I dedicated to these women, a play written in a tone that I felt matched their acting styles.

Rather than attempting to maneuver the gridlock of São Paulo traffic, Régis and I had taken a taxi to MAM, and, accordingly, the actors agreed to drive us home. Before delivering us up, however, they decided to show me an element of the city which apparently Régis had never before encountered and which I might not otherwise have witnessed. Driving through the Parque do Ibirapuera surrounding the museum, they suddenly turned off into a field where two long rows of facing cars and trucks had been parked. Outside each vehicle stood gangs of young gay men, who had clearly gathered to create a gauntlet of sexual temptations. As we slowly drove down the center of this glorious display of human flesh, my eyes grew large with delight, while Régis' pupils also widened, but in his case, out of sheer wonderment. Régis, who worked as a government judge for adolescents and teenagers, grew near hysterical with the shock of what he was witnessing, and as the women circled for a second drive down this aisle of available flesh, he simply could no longer contain himself, as he fell into a contagious laugh, calling out to the young, half-naked men, "Goodbye, Goodbye!" and waving as we passed.

By this time we were all laughing, not so much because of what we had seen, but because of Régis' nearly uncontrollable response. The women determined, accordingly, to go one step further, showing us yet another scene, this time much closer to Régis' own neighborhood. There were several hotels and quiet neighborhood streets where gay men had also gathered, these men somewhat older and definitely more streetwise than the young men near the museum. Some of these men stood their ground on nearly every corner, while others gathered in small groups near the hotels. They had little of the lusty youthfulness of those outside their trucks and cars, and it was apparent that if one actually dared to take these men home, one gambled with possible disease, robbery, even murder.

Once more, Régis could not believe what he was seeing, and repeated his salutations of dismissal: "Goodbye, Goodbye!"

"No, Régis, we don't want to send them away, we want to invite them. You need to call out 'Hello!' not 'Goodbye!'" I mockingly scolded him, amused by his behavior, but also sensing a real terror within.

"Hello, Goodbye!" Régis called out to each tough as we circled the area a second and a third time. Régis was nearly on the floor, doubled over in laughter, and we all were again laughing in sympathy, for I think the three of us recognized his horror at the event. Over the years I had known him, Régis had become a dear friend, but the fact that I was gay, I now recognized, had truly been something that, if he had not had to "forgive" me, he had been determined to overlook. It was not that he was necessarily prejudiced against homosexuality; he was, after all, a good friend to Horácio Costa, a gay poet. But he was also fascinated by it, transfixed, somewhat scandalized. Despite his significant contributions of poetry and publishing in Brazil, he was still a government official who had every reason to fear such publicly scandalous behavior. And in that sense, in the clarity of his moral position that night, rather than distancing me, it made me love Régis even more.

LOS ANGELES, SEPTEMBER 22, 2000
Reprinted from *Sibila* (November 2009), originally published in Portuguese as "Arte erótica, Cristina Muturelli e Ligia Cortez"

Six Stories of São Paulo:
The 6th Night (Memorial)

ON BOTH MY 1997 and 2000 trips to São Paulo the major literary events were held at architect Oscar Niemeyer's grand hall of 1989, Memorial da América Latina. Both Michael Palmer and I were a bit taken aback and startled by the size and brutality of this huge hall, built originally, so we were told, to parade troops. While from a distance it appeared quite graceful in the cantilevered arches of its roof, one felt dwarfed inside and isolated outside by its cold, concrete surfaces which offered very few spots to sit or to gather. Perhaps individuals were also meant to march through the grounds and troop through its doors. Inside the ceiling showed signs of several leaks.

For all that, it was certainly a memorable place to present contemporary poetry. At both the celebration for the anthology in 1997 and my reading in 2000, the events were well attended with many young poets en-

thused by the possibility of hearing new work.

In 1997, as I mention in *My Year 2003*, Haraldo de Campos attended the panel discussion, in which Régis, Nelson, Michael, and I participated. I immediately realized, as we began to speak of how the anthology, *Nothing the Sun Cannot Explain*, came to be, that this was a truly important publication for Brazilian poets, representing the first English-language translation of the generation that came after the poets presented in Elizabeth Bishop's 1972 *An Anthology of Twentieth-Century Brazilian Poetry*; and suddenly I felt that perhaps I had not played a large enough role in its selection. Obviously, authors whose work primarily stood between these two volumes, such as the de Campos brothers, felt that we had missed vital links from the early Brazilian Modernists to the "post-concrete" writers of the day. Some younger poets, moreover, undoubtedly felt we had missed some important figures of their generation.

No anthology is without is faults, but after reviewing and revising that 1997 anthology in 2003 for Green Integer, I still feel that the choices the editors made were generally correct and certainly revelatory of a large swath of Brazilian poetics.

At the 1997 event, Michael and I also read some of our own poetry, which had been translated by Régis, Nelson, and others into Portuguese. Intelligent questions were asked and the sizable audience seemed to respond with respect and high interest to our writing. As the Brazilian poets with whom we had been speaking over the last days had told us, the poetry scene in Brazil is small but intense. The whole country seemed interested in what they published, and some of them were able to get work into popular newspapers. Would that we might see some of that intensity in the US public.

On my second trip, I read a large selection of my work from the bilingual book of poetry, *primeiras palavras*, translated by Régis and Rio de Janeiro poet Claudia Roquette-Pinto, published by Ateliê Editorial. That book also contained a translation into Portuguese of my (Kier Peters') play, *A Dog Tries to Kiss the Sky*, performed at Memorial by Cristina Mutarelli and Lígia Cortez, of whom I write above.

The day before, I attended a grammar school dedicated to teaching their students in three languages. As an American poet, I read to one class in English, and the rest of the students asked me questions via the internet. They had also read my play—and translated it into Spanish. It's funny how seemingly easy it had been for these children to understand that play, while some American directors had been absolutely baffled. Overall I was impressed and delighted by the attentions of both younger and older readers.

LOS ANGELES, MARCH 28, 2003

Two Beckett Films

Beginning in 2000, Michael Colgan of Dublin's Gate Theatre and the Irish Film Board determined to film 19 of Beckett's plays and monologues, each directed by a different individual. Directors included Karel Reisz, Anthony Minghella, Damien Hirst, David Mamet, and the two I've chosen below as representative, Neil Jordan and Atom Egoyan. Actors included John Gielgud, Jeremy Irons, Milo O'Shea, Timothy Spall, Julianne Moore, and John Hurt, described below. These films were never put into theaters in general release, but several of them were shown in the 2000 Toronto Film Festival.

Mouth on Fire

SAMUEL BECKETT (AUTHOR), NEIL JORDON (DIREC-
TOR) **NOT I** (PART OF THE PROJECT *BECKETT ON FILM*,
PRESENTING 19 BECKETT TEXTS ON FILM, CONCEIVED
MY MICHAEL COLGAN) / 2000, DVD RELEASE 2002

NEIL JORDAN BEGINS his short film *Not I*, based on
the 1972 dramatic text by Samuel Beckett, with a view
of a young woman (Julianne Moore) entering to sit
upon a chair. Perhaps he just couldn't resist showing
off his actor, but this clearly works against Beckett's instructions, wherein he writes:

> *Stage in darkness but for MOUTH, upstage audi-*
> *ence right, about 8 feet above stage level, faintly lit*
> *from close-up and below, rest of face in shadow. Invis-*
> *ible microphone.*

The auditor, covered head to foot in a loose black djel-
laba, is missing from Jordan's film.

From here on, however, Jordan follows the author's

 suggestions, turning the rest of the work into a film of the mouth.

The mouth—or the voice—is, in fact, the subject of this work, which concerns an older woman (70 years of age, we later discover) whose parents, died or disappeared shortly after her birth, leaving her to be brought up without love and basic human communication. Throughout much of her life she has seldom spoken; grocery-shopping, for example, by bringing a black bag and a shopping list to the store, and quietly waiting until the clerk puts the articles into the bag.

But suddenly, one April morning, upon hearing the larks, she falls face-first into the grass and, accompanied by an interminable buzz she hears all about her, she begins to talk without stop. The speech she releases into the world seems to be often incomprehensible to her friends, but, despite the constant interruptions between words, the tumble of language she uses to describe herself in the third person, we do gradually come to comprehend her "story." It is as if all the silence she has previously lived has been let loose as a roar of suffering, a suffering she has not previously felt. In fact, she has felt little, apparently, throughout her life, unable even by the end of her scree to identify herself as a single entity. Like a character in a fiction, she describes herself as a figure "out there," a "not I" with no inward being.

One might read Beckett's short work as a kind of statement of the writer's art, the writer being a silent entity until he is forced, "once or twice a year," to express himself, often without being properly comprehended. And when those words pour out, or the mouth opens to speak, it cannot stop, swallowing up everything, including the self, in the buzz of a created reality.

Moore credibly plays the interruptive mouth, but it is somewhat difficult to watch this mouth in action—despite the three different views the director presents—in such extreme proximity to the camera. In some ways, the busy lips almost become abstract, so focused is the camera upon them. In the theater, where an unspeaking Auditor also stands in the shadows, there is more to distract the audience, even if it is hidden in the shadows. While I was watching this DVD, the movie was appropriately accompanied by a buzzing, a saw in my neighbor's apartment from their attempts at renovation.

Although I like the theatricality of the moving lips, the gasps, pursings, and poutings of them against the actor's white teeth, I often felt the need to turn away briefly to relieve myself of the apparent pain they express.

LOS ANGELES, JANUARY 26, 2011

Be Again

SAMUEL BECKETT (WRITER), ATOM EGOYAN (DIRECTOR) **KRAPP'S LAST TAPE** (PART OF THE PROJECT *BECKETT ON FILM*, PRESENTING 19 BECKETT TEXTS ON FILM, CONCEIVED MY MICHAEL COLGAN) / 2000, DVD RELEASE 2002

ACTOR JOHN HURT'S portrayal of Krapp in Beckett's 1958 play put to film is absolutely brilliant, despite his and director Egoyan's small changes to Beckett's text. The realist setting of the play, with the spots of bright white light, gives a grand theatricality to Krapp's world, a world in which, under the light, he feels safe while being surrounded by darkness wherein, as Beckett himself described it, "Old Nick" or death awaits. On his 69th birthday, Krapp, yet again, forces himself to interact with a younger incarnation.

Krapp clearly has a fixation with his former selves. For years he has recorded tapes describing his life's events, most of them quite meaningless, but some of

269

them expressing great poetry and sensibility. The tape Krapp chooses on this particular rainy night is "Box 3, Spool 5," the day Krapp turned 39.

Yet Egoyan reveals that what leads up to his playing the tape is as important in some senses as what is actually on the tape. The ritualistic acts, Krapp's continual checking of the time, his strange way of eating a banana—he puts the entire banana into his mouth holding it there for a while before biting it off, clearly a bow to the fruit's sexual suggestions—including his nearly falling on the banana peel he has tossed into the dark, and several of his other actions, reveal him as a kind of eccentric fool—in short, the typical Beckett figure. As his name suggests, he is "full of shit."

Hurt presents Krapp with a kind of valor despite Krapp's obvious distancing of himself from the human race. Clearly Krapp's mother has been a monster, living for years in a world of "viduity"—the condition of being or remaining a widow. The small things he describes are both comical and life-affirming: playing ball with a dog as his mother dies, awarding the ball to the dog as he hears of his mother's death, attending a vesper service as a child, falling off the pew.

Krapp is an everyday man with romantic aspirations, or at least he was, it is apparent, at age 39, the time when we all have arrived in the prime of life. Krapp at 39 is a smug bore:

> Spiritually a year of profound gloom and indulgence until that memorable night in March at the end of the jetty, in the howling wind, never to be forgotten, when suddenly I saw the whole thing. The vision, at last. This fancy is what I have chiefly to record this evening, against the day when my work will be done and perhaps no place left in my memory, warm or cold, for the miracle that…(hesitates)…for the fire that set it alight. What I suddenly saw then was this, that the belief I had been going on all my life, namely—(Krapp switches off impatiently, winds tape forward, switches on again)—

He will not regret any decision of his life. He is also a man amazingly come alive through the love of a woman whom he describes lovingly in a scene where the two lie in a small punt as it floats to shore through the reeds.

The older Krapp, who realizes that his younger self could not imagine the loneliness and emptiness of the life ahead, has no patience at times with his past. His new tape, which he begins after impatiently winding the older tape ahead to escape his previous self's blindness, is filled with bitterness and anger for a failed life:

> Nothing to say, not a squeak. What's a year now?
> The sour cud and the iron stool. (Pause.) Reveled
> in the word spool. (With relish.) Spooool! Happi-
> est moment of the past half million. (Pause.) Sev-
> enteen copies sold, of which eleven at trade price to
> free circulating libraries beyond the seas. Getting
> known. (Pause.)

He has failed, obviously, even in his writing career. Unlike his younger self, so unregretful of his past, the old
Krapp is filled with the detritus of his life, all those materials left over from his disintegration. If the younger
Krapp declares himself to be only moving forward, the
elder would "Be again!"

> Be again in the dingle on a Christmas Eve, gath-
> ering holly, the red-berried. (Pause.) Be again on
> Croghan on a Sunday morning, in the haze, with
> the bitch, stop and listen to the bells. (Pause.) And
> so on. (Pause.) Be again, be again. (Pause.) All that
> old misery. (Pause.) Once wasn't enough for you.
> (Pause.) Lie down across her.

He gives up this, his last tape (or perhaps simply his
latest), to listen again to his former self describing his
sexual moment with the woman in the punt.

Director Egoyan represents these last scenes, nearly 20 minutes in length, with a full shot, where the viewer cannot escape the shaft of reality penetrating the darkness around Krapp. Hurt so painfully suffers and loves his former self that one can almost hear his heart crack.

LOS ANGELES, JANUARY 29, 2011
Both essays reprinted from *Green Integer Blog* (January 2011).

Poet to Painter

RAFAEL ALBERTI **TO PAINTING**, TRANSLATED FROM THE SPANISH BY CAROLYN L. TIPTON (EVANSTON, ILLINOIS: NORTHWESTERN UNIVERSITY PRESS / HYDRA BOOKS, 1997)

RAFAEL ALBERTI **CONCERNING THE ANGELS**, TRANSLATED FROM THE SPANISH BY CHRISTOPHER SAWYER-LAUÇANNO (SAN FRANCISCO: CITY LIGHTS BOOKS, 1995)

BORN IN 1902 in Puerto de Santa María in the south of Spain, Rafael Alberti is one of the preeminent poets of the 20th century, and, perhaps, also that century's most representative poet—in part because he outlived so many others. As Carolyn L. Tipton writes in her intelligent and informative introduction to *To Painting*, "Rafael Alberti and the 20th century progressed together; born in its infancy, he experienced the excitement and novelty of all the artistic movements of the 1920s in his youth—Cubism, Cinematic Imagism, Surrealism; participated as an adult in the political upheaval of the

1930s, working ardently for a more equitable society; and then, having suffered war and exile, finally reached a place of quiet at the end of the 1940s, a place of maturity out of which he created—and would continue to create for years to come—with insight and a profound nostalgia for the world of his youth." Part of the great renaissance of Spanish poetry of the late 1920s—the Generation of '27, which included notables such as Federico García Lorca, Pedro Salinas, Jorge Guillén, and Vicente Aleixandre—Alberti has produced over 47 volumes of poetry. Yet, until the publication of this book, Americans knew him primarily for one work only, the great *Sobre los ángeles* (*Concerning the Angels*) from 1929, most recently reissued in an excellent new translation by City Lights in 1995.

Accordingly, it is a joy simply to hold in one's hands another volume of poetry by this important artist, particularly when it is so beautifully produced as this one. *To Painting* is a watershed work of Alberti's *oeuvre*, a work shedding his angry and often sardonic lyrics of the 1930s. With its 1945 publication in Buenos Aires, to where he had exiled himself, Alberti signaled a return to aesthetic issues, combining his deep love of painting—he himself began as a painter and continued painting throughout his life—with his poetry. As Tipton explains, the book consists of three different types of poems: poems dedicated to colors (which most often take the form of numbered lists of the uses, shades, hues in nature, or associations); traditional sonnets, presented almost as "toasts" to various subjects of art; and poems dedicated to artists—to Giotto, Botticelli, Raphael, Titian, Tintoretto, Bosch, Dürer, Rubens, Goya, Cézanne, Van Gogh, Picasso, and others. These three types, in turn, are structured by theme, chronology, and other issues, and then interrelated by color and artist and numerous other "pairings."

Given what the translator has described as a meticulous structuring, it is a bit strange to be told that she has excised from the original six sonnets and seven poems to painters because "I think that most of them tend not to be as strong as the other poems, and I felt that their inclusion would weaken the whole." Even within the selection we are presented there are certainly poems of less interest than the best of them, so one feels some sympathy with Tipton's decision. But it would have been better, I believe, to have the whole of the original volume, and to let time and readers determine its strengths and weaknesses.

Personally, I find many of the sonnets, in part because of their traditional form, uninteresting. The debate continues whether translators should keep the original rhyme and meter or attempt to bring the poems into a more suitable American-English form by using internal and slant rhymes or subtly suggesting the original rhyme in other ways. Tipton has chosen to retain the end rhyme, and she almost gets away with it:

To Perspective

To you, the perfect hoax, through whom the eye,
like a reaching hand, extends its view,
moving to what is far from what's close by,
to paler amethyst from deepest blue.

To you, feigner of depth & endless space,
giving to flat planes profundity,
through whom, beyond the balcony's iron lace,
we think that we can just make out the sea.

To you, value prized above all others,
hazy diminution of the colors,
architecture, music of the spheres.

On you, pictorial space lays its foundation.
Line & number sing your celebration.
To you, the tiller by which Painting steers.

The form, however, cannot escape the feeling of stiltedness in the American ear—at least this American ear.

Fortunately, many of the other poems are brilliant, and make this book an important one. The lists of colors are often truly inventive, and read, in the vaguely associational connections, a bit like the lists of New York School poets, albeit without the flat, seeming disinterest of those poems. Alberti, clearly, is an enthusiast—of art, of living. His colors represent catalogues of heightened experience.

10

Hosannas in the blacks of Titian.

11

Blacks wet & green
—Tintoretto—rising,
toppling suddenly
in storm.

12

The black of Spain, all
five senses black:
black sight,

black sound,
black smell,
black taste,
the Spanish painter's touch.

(from "Black")

My favorite poems of this volume are among Alberti's very best, and represent to me the importance of this poet. "Goya," for example, mixes narrative and magic incantation to conjure up a world of dark horror:

Your eye: I keep it in the fire.
Your head: I nibble on it.
Your humerus: I crackle it. Your harrying
inner ear: I suck its snail.
Your legs: I bury you up to them
in mud.
          One leg.
          Another.
                    Flailing.

Run away! But stay
to witness, to die
without dying.

And Alberti's "Bosch" is a true masterpiece of poetry and translation. Just a short piece of it conveys little of its energy, but the entire poem is a marvel of image and wordplay:

....

Mandrake, mandrake
The devil has a crooked stake.

> Cock-a-doddle-do!
> I ride and I crow,
> go mounted on a doe
> & on a porcupine,
> on a camel, on a lion,
> on a burro, on a bear,
> on a horse, on a hare,
> and on a bugler.

Cork, cork,
The devil has a small pitchfork.

To Painting will be a necessary volume in anyone's collection of important 20th century poetry.

LOS ANGELES, 1997

A year after the publication of the Alberti book, the translator, Carolyn Tipton, read at a Sun & Moon Press salon held on September 26, 1998. Among the attendees were the usual friends, Will Alexander, Thérèse Bachand, Luigi Ballerini, Diana Daves, Peter Frank, Dennis Phillips (with his wife Courtney and his baby daughter Sophia), and Paul Vangelisti. Soon after that event, Alberti was awarded the America Award of 1998 for being an outstanding writer of world literature. Alberti died in October 1999.

LOS ANGELES, JANUARY 1, 2000

The Emperor is an Emperor is an Emperor

DANIELA FISCHEROVÁ **FINGERS POINTING SOME-
WHERE ELSE**, TRANSLATED FROM THE CZECH BY NEIL
BERMEL (NORTH HAVEN, CONNECTICUT: CATBIRD
PRESS, 2000)

DANIELA FISCHEROVÁ, one of the most accomplished
contemporary Czech writers, composes stories with a
quiet and subtle intensity, some of which have recently
been collected and translated into English as *Fingers
Pointing Somewhere Else*. In "My Conversations with
Aunt Marie," we are presented, from the viewpoint of
a young girl, her and her mother's relations with her
Aunt Marie, an incredibly romantic and independent
woman who is clearly at odds with the child's mother
over issues of love (it's suggested that, perhaps, both
were in love with the same man, now the young girl's
father), behavior, and politics. Marie, it is apparent,
was also in love with a German soldier during World

War II, and was stoned by the citizens of her small village after the war; the aunt has refused to leave her property since that time. But within the small space of the house and yard, the aunt weaves miraculous tales of beauty and love, and engages the child in fantasies that include her being transformed into a beautiful young woman. The mother, who dresses her like a boy, obviously disapproves, and when authorities enter the aunt's isolated world to vaccinate all within, the aunt's world once more comes crashing down on the child's head, ending their enchanted relationship.

"A Letter for President Eisenhower" is also told through the eyes of a young girl, in this case a young imaginative schoolgirl, who is chosen for the honor to write a letter from her school to President Eisenhower asking for world peace. Her young friend, Hana—excellent in penmanship—is chosen to actually pen the letter, and the two go ahead with the activities with conspiratorial delight. Hana's mother, however, finds the whole concept ridiculous on political grounds, and the young narrator of the story, so proud of her achievement, is forced to come to terms with reality when she overhears the mother laughing about the letter's content and, later, is made to understand that the letter was never actually sent. Needless to say, her relationship with Hana is destroyed and the new relationship she undertakes with Sasha, is a dramatization of frustrated love.

"Dhum" tells the tale of a mental clinic doctor who has created a highly structured system of points for awards and punishments for his women patients. His own voyage to a swami in India ends in an enlightenment he could not have expected. And "Two Revolts in One Family" centers upon a dreadfully domineering mother and a rebelling daughter, the latter of whom eventually discovers through her brother (who as a young man attempted and failed to escape their home) that it is not the mother who controls things, but the father who has arranged and allowed for the mother to imagine that she does.

These stories are all well written, narratively well-structured, and (as is evident in Neil Bermel's excellent translations) crafted with superb linguistic skills. With such talent, however, one feels nonetheless a bit disappointed, and wishes that the author would take more chances, would abandon the carefully-wrought, slightly old-fashioned tales she has spun in favor of more adventuresome matters.

It is almost in answer to these feelings that one

encounters, as the last tale in the book, what might be read as the author's definitive answer to just such responses to her work. For "The Thirty-Sixth Chicken of Master Wu" is indeed about a battle between tradition and originality. Cook to the Chinese Emperor and Empress, Wu is asked every year to prepare a new chicken dish in honor of the Emperor's birthday. This year, however, he is clearly having difficulty in coming up with something new, and the visit of his poet-nephew, who rails against the court poets and their inane comparisons of the emperor with elephants, only adds to his agitations. Over the course of the story we discover that, although the chef has little respect for poetry, it was the intervention of the court censor (and esteemed poet) that took Wu from his position as an uneducated, unfeeling boy to the sensitive artisan he has become. When his nephew, after composing what is seen as a blasphemous poem (*The Emperor / is an emperor / is an emperor / is an emperor* goes the first stanza in Gertrude Stein-like fashion), is in danger of being condemned to death, the censor queries Wu to discover the motives for the boy's poetic offering, and when the boy's concern for language becomes evident, the young poet is allowed to escape. Wu meanwhile creates his new chicken dish to great acclaim; only he discerns that the taste is that of the common vegetable radish. Who is the more original creator in this story? What does originality mean? These and other such questions that cling to Fischerová's delicious tale take us to the very heart of her art, and while the tale may not answer the questions it calls up nor entirely explain her art, it and the other tales of this volume certainly reveal a fully comprehending intelligence at work. One only hopes to see more works of this quality by this talented Czech writer in the future.

LOS ANGELES, 2000
Reprinted from *Green Integer Blog* (December 2009).

Why Does the Concubine Have to Die?

BIK-WA LEI AND WEI LU (WRITERS), PIK WAH LI (AS
LILLIAN LEE, SCREENPLAY AND NOVEL), KAIGE CHEN
(DIRECTOR) **BA WANG BIE JI** (**FAREWELL MY CONCU-
BINE**) / 1993

ALTHOUGH KAIGE CHEN'S 1993 film *Farewell My
Concubine* won the Cannes Festival's Palme d'Or (tying
with Jane Campion's *The Piano*), and received generally favorable press in the US, some film commentators,
even today, dismiss the work as overlong, psychologi-
cally vague, and for not having a story that can match
the epic structure of the whole.

To me this seems to be a kind of blindness that
arises out of a miscomprehension of Chinese cultural
values and storytelling procedures. A film historian
such as David Thomson, for example, may be literally
correct in saying that "the characters are not truly revealed," but that presupposes that the characters of this

work have fully developed psychological beings, whereas the writers have gone out of their way to indicate that the students of the Beijing Opera had all psychological identity driven from them in their childhood and youth. The whole method of these opera performances, moreover, is about type and form rather than individuation and psychologically-motivated action. As master Yuan (You Ge) makes clear after seeing a performance starring the two central figures of this work—Cheny Dieyi, nicknamed Douzi (Leslie Cheung), and Duan Xiaolou, nicknamed Shitou (Fengyi Zhang)—the proper way to perform the General's role as he leaves his concubine is to take seven steps away, not three as Duan Xiaolou has done. It is a work of tradition, in which there is no room for experiment.

The entire film, in fact, is a statement about the loss of identity, both gender and cultural. The individual is driven out of the unfortunate group of children studying with Master Guan (Qi Lü) with insistent violence in the form of beatings, whippings and tortures more severe even than those Charles Dickens might have cooked up. When Douzi's prostitute mother first attempts to get her son into the opera school, she is immediately turned down when it is discovered that Douzi has an extra digit on one of his hands. Unable to keep the child in the brothel, she has no choice but to take up a cleaver and cut off the child's offending finger. It is the first of several acts that seems to reify the major platitude of the culture: "You can't fight fate."

Once Douzi has been permitted to join the company, he is beaten endlessly, primarily because he refuses to define himself as a girl—the operatic role his superiors have determined is best for this feminine-looking boy. The child stubbornly and emphatically refuses to say, "By nature I am a girl," but ultimately has no choice as the tortures escalate, making him fear even for his life. He is forced to literally *become* a woman in order to survive, required to change his gender. After his first successful performance of the role, he is taken away to be raped.

It is no surprise, accordingly, that as he grows into adulthood, his relationship with Shitou is not only that of concubine to the other's General, but is that of a tortured lover to his/her best friend, the couple having been advised to "Stick together until you die."

Parallel to these personal dilemmas is the broader cultural picture, in which identity is determined time and again by the political scene. First, it is the war with Japan that requires any citizen of China to shun anything Japanese, disallowing Douzi and Shitou to perform for the enemy. When Shitou is arrested by the Japanese, Douzi has no choice, so he feels, but to attempt to save him by performing at the Japanese general's home. He/she saves Shitou, but his friend is outraged that he has given into the Japanese demands; and throughout the rest of his life, as the country's perpetual revolutions alter the political scene, Douzi will continually be branded a traitor.

So too does Shitou betray him by marrying, almost on a whim, a local prostitute, and creating a wedge between their performative and personal lives. Shitou may be able to separate the two; but as a man living in China performing as a woman and daily living as a homosexual, the beautiful Douzi cannot readily make that separation. He has, after all, been reconstructed by the culture long before the scenes in the film when Madame Mao's Cultural Revolution attempts to do the same to every Chinese citizen.

Li Gong's performance of that prostitute, Juxian— who, as one of the company members whispers, is a true "dragon lady"—is one of the great joys of this film, as she, little by little, binds her husband to her, eventually even forcing him to give up his career as an opera performer. Yet Douzi, in most respects, is her equal, a haughty and regal manipulator, a nasty and campy wit whose very glance (as he remains throughout much of the film in costume, with eyes radically made up to demonstrate the concubine's exaggerated sense of survival and power) withers those around him/her. Inevitably, the two, battling over Shitou, are drawn together as outside political forces overwhelm even the former opera member, and threaten to  make Shitou also into another being. At one point, as we watch Douzi voyeuristically peering into their home while the couple make love, we come to understand just how he is wound up in the couple's life, fascinated as he is by this powerful woman who has stolen his friend.

For his part, Shitou continues to care for and help his former partner, going so far as to spend hours with Douzi to help in his horrific attempts to overcome opium addiction. But as the Cultural Revolution threatens its severe punishments, Shitou again betrays, this time both of his lovers, Juxian and Douzi, by revealing her past as a prostitute and Douzi's involvement with the Japanese. The betrayal is truly unforgiveable, and both the "females" are quite explicably devastated by his acts. Although we do not know specifically how this has affected them, we can gather its force by the final scenes of Chen Kaige's masterpiece.

The film begins and ends with a final performance of *Farewell My Concubine*, in which, in an act of both revenge and redemption, Douzi uses a real sword to kill his character at the end of the opera, thus ending his own bondage to a world that has stolen the being that he might have become, while answering his life-long question, "Why does the concubine have to die?"

LOS ANGELES, JUNE 9, 2011
Reprinted from *World Cinema Review* (June 2011).

Cataloguing Evil

JENS BJØRNEBOE **THE BIRD LOVERS**, TRANSLATED
FROM THE NORWEGIAN BY FREDERICK WASSER (LOS
ANGELES: SUN & MOON PRESS, 1994)
JENS BJØRNEBOE **SEMMELWEIS**, TRANSLATED FROM
THE NORWEGIAN BY JOE MARTIN (LOS ANGELES: SUN &
MOON PRESS, 1998)

AS I MENTION in *My Year 2007*, in the 1990s I published two plays by the noted Norwegian writer Jens
Bjørneboe, *The Bird Lovers* in 1994, and four years later, *Semmelweis*. Both works are "didactic" in the sense
that the writer is determined to convey to his audience
large, banner-like themes. In the early 1960s Bjørneboe
stayed for a time with the Berliner Ensemble, working
through a kind of apprenticeship with many of the major figures of Brechtian theater, and these plays, both
of which contain songs that point up dramatic events,
show the influences of the German playwright.

Yet, as Joe Martin points out in his introduction to

Semmelweis, Bjørneboe's theatrical "alienation," similar as his views are to Brecht's, takes his plays in very different directions from the master. Indeed, both of these plays work nicely with Bjørneboe's more complex late trilogy, *The History of Bestiality* (1966-1973), of which I wrote (through the example of *Kruttårnet* [*Powderhouse*]) in my 2007 essay. In these fictions, as well as in the two plays, Bjørneboe is primarily interested in cataloguing evil rather than assigning it or even creating solutions which might prevent it.

In *The Bird Lovers*, a small group of working Italians, who served together in the war and were imprisoned by the Germans, gathers regularly at a bar to talk and to eat; they are particularly fond of serving up the small game birds in the region. Enter Mrs. Director Stahlmann, a bird lover who is determined to stop the practice of killing birds in the village and, with the support of the National Society for Animals Rights, plans to bring new tourists to the region by establishing it as a bird sanctuary. The various verbal volleys between the two groups are predictable and mostly comic, with the locals clearly getting the better of the situation.

To this town also comes Huldreich von und zu Greifenklau—a German judge determined to enjoy the local songbirds for their music—and his servile friend, Johannes Schulze, both of whom are immediately recognized by the cafe regulars as men who tortured them and killed their friend in prison. Despite the protests of one of the men's wives, the group is bent on kidnapping the two from the local hotel and putting them on trial for murder.

The mock trial reveals the horrible evils of Greifenklau's past, and the group is ready to hang both him and Schulze until the defendant's assigned lawyer, Father Piccolino, points out that the evil these men have perpetuated came as much from their superiors. Piccolino argues (despite his belief in their guilt) that they were merely doing their duty like many other Nazis during World War II. But Piccolino also argues from another point of view, that of the executioners, pointing out to them that if they proceed with the hanging, they too will be guilty, just as Americans who strung blacks up in trees, as Turks who drove the Armenians into the desert, as the English who shot and hung the Irish, and the French who electrocuted the Algerians. The theme, highly reminiscent of Bjørneboe's listings and descriptions of punishment in *Powderhouse*, turns the tables, so to speak. Gradually, one by one, the men see the folly of their acts, and "sell out" by accepting the Germans' promises to financially help them when the city becomes a tourist spot.

In short, as translator Frederick Wasser points out, Bjørneboe does not attempt to answer what to do *about* evil, but merely wants to recognize it in all of us. It is as if Bjørneboe, despite his hatred for all the tortures of individuals by human beings and institutions, does not comprehend a way to end it—except through comedy and, of course, death. We are a race unforgivably cursed by our past.

So too is the great Hungarian doctor Ignaz Semmelweis, mocked by all those around him for his theories about handwashing before operations. The doctors and students he calls "murderers" are just that, men who because they refuse to see the truth do not take the proper precautions and kill every year hundreds of their patients—particularly women during childbirth. One of the comic frustrations of this drama is the outlandish scientific belief of the day that child-bed fever is not contagious but is brought on by the sexual enjoyment of women of the lower class. These and other such notions would be merely comical except for the fact that they cover up any truth, and the other doctors use these beliefs, moreover, as tools to ruin Semmelweis.

But as in *The Bird Lovers*, Bjørneboe's "heroes," Semmelweis and Kolletschka, are also fools. Semmelweis is a kind of mad innocent, a man so devoted to his beliefs that he has no notion of how to make any compromise that might cause his theories to be practiced. Despite his seeming purity of purpose, Semmelweis drowns his sorrows in sentimentality, wine, and whores, ultimately dying of a kind of slow suicide. Kolletschka dies, ironically, of the very disease which he once proclaimed was not contagious.

Bjørneboe's play centers less on individuals than on the institutions, the universities, the hospitals, and other organizations which, while supposedly searching for truth, fight any possibility of discovering it. The reality of these organizations is that if the teachers, students, and doctors were to admit to being wrong they would be crushed by the very thing they believe they are promoting. Accordingly, truth is the last thing that such institutions can permit. The playwright makes this even more ironic by encasing his play in a student protest which ends with one student insisting that such protests have been the "forerunners of fundamental change"; meanwhile the students within the play are often the most resistant to Semmelweis' dictums.

Once again Bjørneboe makes it clear that evil is so prevalent that everyone can share in its curse. The students of 1968 may have been admirable for their refusal "to allow [themselves] to be used for oppression and genocide," but we know that the students of just a few years later would become the powers behind new atrocities.

LOS ANGELES, MARCH 27, 2010
Reprinted from *Green Integer Blog* (March 2010).

Saving the Drowned

ROD LURIE (WRITER AND DIRECTOR) **THE CON-TENDER** / 2000

I FIRST SAW Rod Lurie's political film, *The Contender*, when it originally appeared in 2000, a period in which I was not yet writing film reviews. Seeing it again the other day on the TV Sundance channel I was faced once more with both its pleasures and failures. When the film first appeared in late October 2000, a great many reviewers saw the movie as a contender for the Academy Awards, and two of its stars, Jeff Bridges and Joan Allen, were nominated for acting awards. But in retrospect, it seems clear that the movie was not destined for greatness.

Certainly the film begins well enough, with the sudden plunge of a car into the waters near where Governor Jack Hathaway (William Petersen), a Democrat from Virginia, is fishing with a male assistant. The Governor miraculously escapes the car, attempting—

but alas failing—to save its occupant, a woman friend who has accompanied him on the trip.

His valiant attempt to save the woman has made him a kind of hero in the eyes of many, and he is a shoo-in, so some claim, to be President Evans' (Jeff Bridges) Vice Presidential appointment to replace his former Vice President, who has apparently died in office. When called to the White House, we can see Hathaway almost drooling with anticipation for his appointment; yet, somewhat inexplicably, Evans deflates the governor, explaining that he plans to extend his legacy in his second term by choosing a woman, Republican-turned-Democrat Senator Laine Billings Hanson (Joan Allen) of Ohio.

So far, so good, the film having interestingly mined two major political events for its subject matter: Kennedy's accident at Chappaquiddick and Presidential Candidate Walter Mondale's choice of Geraldine Ferraro as his running mate.

Writer-director Lurie immediately takes these somewhat historical events into new territory, however, when those who oppose Hanson's appointment,

 notably Republican Representative Sheldon Runyon (Gary Oldman) and Democratic Representative Reginald Webster (Christian Slater), investigate Hanson's background and come up with seemingly shocking pictures, revealing that, as a college Freshman, Hanson had participated in an orgy, willingly, so it appears, servicing several young frat boys. Although she has long been married and has a charming son, her sexual openness is apparently reconfirmed by her having begun an affair with her husband while he was still married to her best friend.

With a kind of cold passivity that is not only slightly unbelievable but helps to make Allen's character almost unbearable, Hanson, under the scrutiny of the House Judiciary Committee, determines to take the high road, refusing to discuss her private sexual life in any form, insisting that she will only answer political questions, which the sleazy Runyon and associates cleverly refrain from asking while insinuating that she has taken money for those sexual acts, opening her up to a charge of prostitution.

The issue is an important one, particularly since Lurie's script ties Runyon to Joe McCarthy-like tactics—

even if that is a far reach, since McCarthy destroyed numerous careers and lives, while Runyon is only attempting to squelch one contender, much in the same manner—conservatives will claim—that Democrats attempted to end Clarence Thomas' judicial career. Yet it is hard to believe, given the visual and testimonial evidence against Hanson which Runyon and his group have already leaked to the press, that any president, no manner how highly-principled—a quality which this fictional President seems not to have—would so calmly continue to support his nominee. Lurie's script insists that were Hanson a male candidate, her long-ago indiscretions would be utterly ignored; but we know, given the derailed careers of several congressional and gubernatorial candidates (Edwards and Weiners* immediately come to mind, although, admittedly, their behavior occurred during their campaigns instead of years previous to it; even the not-so-saintly fictional Hanson votes to impeach Clinton, we discover mid-film, because of his "responsibility" for his sexual behavior), that sex is still a potent factor within the American consciousness. Lurie might have done better to explore that very fact: why is it that Americans are still so puritanical when it comes to their public figures' sexual behaviors?

Unfortunately, Lurie drops the whole issue by revealing that Hanson, despite her refusals to deny or admit her past sexual "deviancy," was, in fact, innocent.

Expected by her sorority sisters to participate in the orgiastic celebrations, she had refused to go along, leaving the event even before it began. The pictures held by Runyon and, now, by the media are of another woman; and the rumors about Hanson's own participation are, as she puts, "urban legend."

Not only is this a cop-out, I would argue, but it renders Evans' moment of rising to greatness by refusing Hanson's resignation quite meaningless, particularly since he has also discovered, through his own back-street investigations, that Runyon's favorite, Hathaway, had paid his woman companion to drive into the lake so that he might be able to save her—an action that has turned him from a potential hero into an obvious criminal.

Runyon is politically outed in front of the entire legislative body, and, presumably, goodness and wisdom has been revealed to all. Not even Capra's *Mr. Smith Goes to Washington* provided such a lame example of political majesty.

What if, a little voice in my head keeps asking, the Vice Presidential candidate had really participated in and enjoyed the orgy in which she was wrongly purported to have been involved? What if she had actually committed adultery? Would that have meant that she was any less of a significant candidate, politically speaking, for the job? We all know, of course, that such actions would have led to the contender's immediate dismissal and, likely, the end of her career. Certainly, the uplifting message of Lurie's fable would have become impossible. Just as Runyon perpetually twists truth throughout this tale, so too do the writer and director, who have made it easy for us to buy into this contender's right to be a winner. Even Gore Vidal's President in the creaky stage drama *The Best Man* was forced to make a compromise. However, Lurie's complacent Evans becomes an immediate hero by saving the woman who, politically-speaking, nearly drowned. That nagging voice, however, will not go away: is Evans really any different from Hathaway? Well, yes, the writer has made it far easier for him to save the gal and win the public adulation which all politicians obviously seek out. And so too has Lurie pretended to create a feminist hero only so that he, like a macho-hero, can save her from drowning.

*New York Democratic Representative Anthony Weiner was forced to resign from Congress after texting a suggestive photo of himself to a woman following him on Twitter. Another controversy erupted when he "sexted" to another woman during his New York mayoral race.

Former Senator from North Carolina and Vice Presidential running mate for John Kerry, John Edwards was found to be having an extramarital affair during his 2008 Senatorial campaign.

At almost the very moment that I completed this review-essay, I opened *The New York Times Magazine* of September 21, 2014 to find a cover article by Matt Bai, "Legend of the Fall," on precisely the same kind of situation in which the Vice Presidential nominee finds herself in *The Contender*. Recounting the downfall of the 1987 Democratic candidate for President, Gary Hart—not only the likely Presidential candidate but a man far ahead of George H. W. Bush in the pre-convention polls—Bai suggests that the press' treatment of Hart, coming as it did on the heels of the Nixon cover-ups as reported by Bob Woodward and Carl Bernstein, represented a new shift in journalism. Prior to this period, journalists focused on the campaign issues of their subjects, emphatically steering clear of their private lives (Theodore White is quoted as being reasonably sure that, of all the candidates he covered, only three—Harry Truman, George Romney, and Jimmy Carter—"hadn't enjoyed the pleasure of 'casual partners'"). But suddenly in the wake of the Woodward-Bernstein revelations about the private persona of a troubled President, reporters sought out all information about their subjects, permitting the public to determine whether or not the information they uncovered had any value in terms of their competency as a politician. Hart was, like Kennedy one might argue, clandestinely involved with several women other than his wife, with whom he had had a troubled relationship. In this case he was literally tracked down and, as Bai makes clear, stalked by reporters from the *Miami Herald*, who, confronting Hart in an alley outside his home, demonstrated the candidate's difficulty in handling questions about his affair with Donna Rice. Like Hanson in Lurie's film, Hart also attempted to argue that his private life was no business of the press. But with a photograph and other evidence in the hands of the press, there was no way he might possibly escape published accusations, and he was soon forced to abandon any Presidential aspirations. Bai, highly sympathetic to Hart's moral dilemmas, quotes former senator Bob Kerrey: "We're not the worst thing we've ever done in our lives, and there's a tendency to think that we are." And the sad thing, suggests Bai, is that ever since Hart's campaign, in protection of their personal lives, candidates have been terrified to speak out about their personal viewpoints, refusing to reveal any aspect of their inner being that might be interpreted by some element of the public as morally reprehensible. Given what Bai describes of Hart and the numerous downfalls of political candidates ever since, it is inconceivable that Lurie's fictional nominee could win out, even with Presidential support, over the lurid details exposed in the press. The sad thing is that Hart most certainly would have been a better President than his opponent and would have saved numerous American lives.

LOS ANGELES, SEPTEMBER 21, 2014
Reprinted from *World Cinema Review* (September 2014).

Performers

WHILE THE DIRECTOR has called his 2000 documentary *Musicians*, I would suggest that, although many of the figures in this film are indeed musicians, Askarian displays as much interest in "performance"—particularly dance and high-wire movements (which often mimic dance)—as he does in musical sound. And, at times, even when he does focus on musicians, the interest of their performance has less to do with musical sound than with other things in which they engage.

The several scenes filmed in dance clubs and dive bars in his homeland, Armenia, have far less to do with music—although we do hear recorded music of pieces that seemingly have not been performed in the US—and more to do with the dancing which animates his figures. Perceiving this, Askarian uses stop-frame and strobe lighting to great effect, representing the emo-

tional feelings of the young dancers he is portraying.

In one long scene, a small musical group, with unbelievably beat-up horns and a long worn-out drum, arrive at their destination against a rotting wall in the city, occasionally blaring a note or two before they sit down acround the overturned drum to dine on tomatoes, bread, a stew, cured meats and, most importantly, slightly diluted vodka, before they are willing to take up their instruments again. Their brief performance sounds as if it might just as well have been played by a group in Sicily as in the mountainous country north of Turkey and Iran. But soon the players have put down their instruments again to drink more vodka, and it is clear that despite the director's urging for them to return in their concert, they are perhaps too drunk to continue with the music. Yet their whole performance, such as it is, is one of the most joyous, even comical moments, of Askarian's film.

Another "musical" performance involves a funeral ritual at a cemetery. A young boy burns something over the grave, before anointing the spot with oil, and serving drinks to the two men who then play a brief piece upon their flute-like reed instruments. But the ceremony is far more important, and im- pressive, than the mu-  sic with which they close the event.

One of the longest scenes involves a brilliant tight-rope walker performing before the ancient monastery of Khor-Virap. With only a balancing pole, the walk-er not only gracefully crosses the metal rope which is nearly invisible against the landscape, but walks blindly, his entire body covered in a black robe, across the same space, climbs small ladders balanced upon the wire, and dances in leaps and bounds across the same space as if he were flying in mid-air. True, this performance is also accompanied by music, but it is the wire ballet that is truly awe-inspiring.

When musicians are the subject of Askarian's documentary—a drummer, two accordion players, and players performing on string instruments that seem re-lated to the lute—they are generally placed in covered pathways, alleys, the halls of Yerevan dwellings, and other odd locations where the camera focuses not only on their performances, but on the comings and goings of passersby, young boys, girls, old men and women who live their lives, apparently, as much on the street as inside their houses. Throughout the strange and soaring music these musicians' performances are played out against a world of decay—walls, buildings, gates, and other objects peeling away and in near collapse. Even the men who perform these pieces are nearly destroyed: one accordionist—who plays what appear to be improvised pieces—is missing a leg; another displays a large portrait of himself in his youth, in almost painful testimony to the old, toothless man he has become.

That is, obviously, Askarian's major point. As he writes of this film:

> What happens after the empire? All know and expect it in the advance, only one thing they don't know: despite the destruction, the disintegration, the betrayal...despite the annihilation of all bases of the life, the music sounds, and how it sounds! Higher and higher, over the human sorrow and over the pain! It is also one, daily practiced mental attitude, stand and exercise, that awakens a hope in the abandoned and in those, who already have lost the last hope.

I would argue, however, it isn't just the music that represents this but the positions, the movements these

figures make, their insistence upon performing whatever it is they have left to display. The old women who stare out the windows, those who stand upon the streets with a kind of defiance, the young club dancers throwing themselves into the act of movement, even the careful ritual of dining in an open street with the drum standing in for their table, certainly the amazing high-wire leaps of the ropewalker reveal a kind of graceful opposition to the world which they inhabit, a world in which they survive through their performances, through these very personal acts of art.

We enter an institution of art in this film only once, where we see two men wearing the same costume, ritualistically battling it out with the other, wrestling with and tossing over and over the other and his own body. Askarian views the scene from the top, a spiral staircase spinning out below the camera. Is this his statement about spiraling down, the inevitable need to wrestle with oneself to express a vision, in short, a failure, of formal art? As a noted filmmaker, Askarian clearly has known that struggle throughout his life. The folk artists whom he primarily observes have no such dilemmas; their performances are simply part and parcel of the greater community, as natural as breathing in and breathing out.

LOS ANGELES, OCTOBER 21, 2011
Reprinted from *World Cinema Review* (October 2011).

In 2003, I arranged to meet Don Askarian to discuss the possibility of publishing one of his screenplays, In Noraduz. *Since I was in Frankfurt in October for the Frankfurt Bookfair, and Askarian was either on his way home from Armenia to Berlin or going in the opposite direction, we met at a cafe at the Frankfurt Airport. We briefly talked over coffee, discussing possibilities, him showing me a large, beautifully produced book presenting scenes from his films in color.*

Soon after my return to the US, his assistant, Achim Berheide, wrote me, enclosing several manuscripts, including a film Askarian was hoping to make, Avetik's Diary. *Berheide also wanted my non-profit organization, The Contemporary Arts Educational Project, to invite Askarian and Nune Hovhannisian to the US so that they might arrange a retrospective of his films at the Los Angeles County Museum of Art. I believe they were hoping to get a grant to achieve this. But the whole project sounded* rather poorly thought out, and I was afraid, without an actual agreement with the County Museum or grant in hand, I might end up having to pay the travel and hotels myself.

After demurring, I heard no further from them. The screenplay, although a fascinating story, was poorly written in English, all action being described in the past tense. Accordingly, it might have needed a great deal of work on my part. So, obviously, no book ever grew out of our meeting, although I would have loved to have done something with him.

OCTOBER 30, 2011

SHALL WE DANCE?: SOME
MASTERPIECES OF FILM DANCE

AS A LOVER of dance, I have been wanting for some time now to write about my favorite film dance numbers. I began this project rather innocently, without imagining just how extensive my list might ultimately become. I little expected the problems about this genre that I discovered.

From the start, I determined not to include balletic performances transcribed to the screen. I also, somewhat arbitrarily, decided not to include filmed music videos, which also meant that I had to ignore wonderful dances on film such as those by Michael Jackson; but I felt that I was more interested in dance that interrelated with the story, the music, and other elements of film than a promotional effort to sell music.

With perhaps even more regret, I decided to exclude ice dancing (by energetic performers such as Sonja Henie) and water dancing (by graceful beauties such as Esther Williams). In some ways these two dancing genres seem more related to sports to me than to the numerous elements of cinematography, even though they often make for dramatic cinematic images.

Finally, and here, so to speak, is where I may be skating on the thinnest of ice, the reader will note that I have included no films after 1968. That is not to say, obviously, that there have been no interesting dancers and dance performances in films after that date. But something notably changed. The majority of the musicals and films after that period did not responsibly represent their dancers; by cutting every few seconds, portraying the dance through focuses on various body parts instead of the entire body, directors seemed more interested in the illusion of dancing than in a portrayal of the actual dance. Some performers in these films were clearly professional dancers, but it would be hard to know that without prior information. In a work like *Footloose*, for example, or *Grease*, or, most particularly, in *Chicago*, the camera cannot rest on a figure long enough to represent a real dance. The actors may be dancing, but their dances are made up of a thousand cuts that cannot allow anyone to perceive if they are really dancing or moving into various positions that give the illusion of dance.

Certainly there were tricks of the trade among even dancers I have included, and I mention some of these in passing. But when one can no longer determine whether or not a dancer, trained or otherwise, can really dance, I feel it demeans the whole event. How can I point to a great dancer or a great moment of film dance when it may be all an illusion of the camera? The best of the early dancers, Astaire, Kelly, etc. went out of their way to show their talents, often insisting that their directors portray their work in long, one-shot sequences. Most of these directors also understood the importance of seeing the entire body as opposed to torsos, thighs, and feet segmented from the whole.

Accordingly, it is not dancers that have disappeared, but directors who might properly represent their talents.

Finally, I am sure that each reader will find several of their favorite films and dance numbers missing. I plead guilty of excising many of my own favorites, simply because I determined not to have more than a few devoted to each performer. I might have selected 15 or 20 of Fred Astaire and Gene Kelly works alone! But I felt that would not reveal the richness of the genre. I am certain also that I may have simply overlooked numerous worthy dancers and films. Someday I may return with a second installment.

LOS ANGELES, SEPTEMBER 9, 2011

Groucho Marx

GEORGE S. KAUFMAN, MORRIE RYSKIND, BERT KAL-
MAR AND HARRY RUBY (SCREENPLAY), BERT KALMAR
AND HARRY RUBY (MUSIC AND LYRICS), VICTOR HEER-
MAN (DIRECTOR) **ANIMAL CRACKERS** / 1930

LOOKING BACK NOW on Groucho Marx's dance near the end of "Hello, I Must Be Going," we recognize just how physical the Brothers were. In many of their films, Groucho danced, in *Duck Soup* with two women at a time, alternating between a waltz, a rumba, a mad tango, and, finally, something like a Charleston—all of them containing dozens of other smaller steps that seem almost impossible to negotiate within the larger whole, including darting through the crowds from the arms of Margaret Dumont to the *other* woman.

In *Animal Crackers*, however, the dance is pure Groucho as the rubber-legged comedian first does a Michael Jackson-like "Moonwalk," moving laterally across the floor in two directions without lifting his

feet. A moment later he kicks, his riding boots set against his white safari pants, in an up and backward movement as if he had no joints. From there he simply joyously sets out on a series of leaping kicks, sideways and forward, that add fun to the ridiculous lyrics:

SPAULDING:
>Hello, I must be going,
>I cannot stay, I came to say, I must be going.
>I'm glad I came, but just the same I must be
>   going.
>La La.

MRS. RITTENHOUSE:
>For my sake you must stay.
>If you should go away,
>You'd spoil this party I am throwing.

SPAULDING:
>I'll stay a week or two,
>I'll stay the summer thru,
>But I am telling you,
>I must be going.

Groucho is a kind of naif dancer, a bit like the role Grandma Moses played in the world of art—except, of course, Marx is completely in the know, spoofing the very gracefulness of dance.

LOS ANGELES, MARCH 11, 2011

Bill Robinson

EDGAR DORWELL, PORTER GRAINGER, AND JOE JORDON (ORIGINAL MUSIC), IRWYN FRANKLIN (WRITER AND DIRECTOR) **HARLEM IS HEAVEN** / 1932

FRANKLIN'S ALL-BLACK 1932 movie *Harlem is Heaven* is a disaster of story and acting, with an absolutely remarkable cast, nonetheless, of musicians and dancers, including Bill "Bojangles" Robinson and Eubie Blake and his Orchestra. Robinson is at the center of this piece and does numerous numbers throughout, all of them brilliant. But the best dance, the "Stair Dance," stands out as one of the most memorable dances of all time.

In some respects Robinson repeated this dance, or at least elements of it, three years later, as he strutted up and down a set of stairs with Shirley Temple in *The Little Colonel*, but in the original the simple set consisting of a small staircase of five steps up and five steps down better reveals his amazing footwork, and stunningly

points up his simple but graceful dancing. And unlike the second "Stair Dance," he does not have to play an old "darky" to get the opportunity to strut his stuff.

The dance begins with a simple multiple tap as he learns forward, exploring the steps as if he were perhaps afraid of undertaking the moves he is about to make. Then he goes up the first step upon which he gently taps out a rhythm, before moving to the second and so on, until he reaches the fifth, retreating back down the five stairs. But soon he is at the top again, this time moving rhythmically down the other side (skipping one step going down by twos, etc.) back and forth in an incredible pattern of taps that surprises us with its simple variety of ascent and descent.

Robinson displays little of the athleticism of the marvelous Nicolas Brothers, but his grace and lithe moves cannot be matched. It's as if this energized movement were a simple warm-up for something else—a leap across drums as he performs in the "Drum Dance" or the slip and slides of the marvelous sand dance of *Stormy Weather*. But there is something so abstract and pure about his "Stair Dance" that, in my estimation, it can't be matched.

LOS ANGELES, APRIL 2, 2011

Fred Astaire and Ginger Rogers

ERWIN S. GELSEY, H. W. HANEMANN AND CYRIL
HUME (WRITERS, BASED ON A STORY BY LOU BROCK
AND A PLAY BY ANNE CALDWELL), THORNTON FREE-
LAND (DIRECTOR) **FLYING DOWN TO RIO** / 1933

THIS FILM, Astaire's and Rogers' first pairing, would be
hardly worth writing about were it not for some of the
brilliant dance numbers by the famed duo, particularly
in one of their first encounters in the Brazilian capitol,
Rio de Janeiro. At a hotel nightclub the couple experience, for the first time, the local dance craze, the Carioca, "not a fox trot or a polka," where the couples dance
forehead to forehead while rhythmically moving their
feet in time to the nine-note line, repeated before ending with eight off-beats. Of course, after watching for
a while, the American couple, both dressed elegantly
in black, have to give it a try. The floor is cleared for
their wonderful variations, at times—with foreheads
locked—catching the off-beats of music, while at other

times dancing stunningly in sync with the rhythm before Rogers spins off into a circle around her partner.

It's all lovely to watch until the couple, banging foreheads together, stagger off in opposite directions as they comically mock the dizziness they suffer (a trick Astaire would use brilliantly as a drunk years later in *Holiday Inn)*. As they make their ways back to their table, a whole chorus of dancers, choreographed by dance director Dave Gould and his assistant Hermes Pan, follows in the style of Busby Berkeley, uniformly dancing in identical costumes and movements up and down the stairway while Etta Moten warbles out the song's lyrics: "I'll dance the Carioca 'til the break of day."

LOS ANGLES, FEBRUARY 28, 2011

Fred Astaire and Ginger Rogers (2)

ALLAN SCOTT AND DWIGHT TAYLOR (SCREENPLAY, BASED ON A PLAY BY SÁNDOR FARAGÓ, ALADA LASZLO, AND KÁROLY NÓTI), IRVING BERLIN AND MAX STEINER (MUSIC), MARK SANDRICH (DIRECTOR) **TOP HAT** / 1935

WITH GREAT SONG and dance numbers such as "Isn't This a Lovely Day," "Fancy Free," "The Piccolino," and "Top Hat, White Tie and Tails," it seems almost impossible to select just one dance! But of all Astaire's and Rogers' performances throughout their years as a duo, the most memorable of all may be their brilliant "Cheek to Cheek."

In terms of the plot, the number might never have happened. Dale Tremont (Ginger Rogers) is furious with Jerry Travers (Fred Astaire), whom she believes to be her good friend Madge Hardwick's husband, Horace. Travers has flirted with Tremont, but Madge seemingly doesn't care, for, in reality, she is trying to marry

off Travers, suggesting Tremont as the perfect match. It is with due hesitation, accordingly, that Tremont accepts his offer to dance. As he begins the love song, moreover, she turns several times to Madge, pondering what to do, but Madge merely motions that they should get closer together.

The dance begins as a simple waltz, with Travers (Astaire) stopping several times to sing the famous lyrics ("Heaven, I'm in Heaven / And my heart beats so loudly I can hardly speak / And I seem to find the happiness I seek / When we're out together dancing cheek to cheek"). After each stop they dance for a while, until suddenly, at the music's crescendo, they swing upstairs, she spinning before laterally jumping, Astaire moving into a soft tap. Both leap, moving backwards, then forwards, until in a final *pas de deux*, Rogers being gently lifted before Astaire lets her down, the two spin, returning to the quiet waltz.

Perhaps the most notable thing about this dance is Rogers' beautiful white feathered dress (at least it appears white on the screen; the lining, so I have read, in reality was blue) that is so absolutely breathtaking a costume that we might forgive them, he in his tuxedo and she in the gown, if they merely stood there talking. Yet their graceful dancing equally transports us into "Heaven."

Astaire and the director had tried to dissuade Rogers from wearing the dress, and as she began to dance, just as they feared, the feathers flew off every time she made a move. Astaire described it as something akin to "a chicken being attacked by a coyote." You can still see some feathers floating through the air at scene's end. And after this event, Rogers' nickname became "feathers."

LOS ANGELES, APRIL 16, 2011

Eleanor Powell and Fred Astaire

MOSS HART (STORY), JACK MCGOWAN AND SID SILVERS (SCREENPLAY), HARRY W. CONN (ADDITIONAL DIALOGUE), ROY DEL RUTH (DIRECTOR) **BROADWAY MELODY OF 1936** / 1935

JACK MCGOWAN AND DORE SCHARY (STORY), LEON GORDON AND GEORGE OPPENHEIMER (SCREENPLAY, WITH UNCREDITED WRITING BY WALTER DELEON, VINCENT LAWRENCE, ALBERT MANNHEIMER, EDDIE MORAN, THOMAS PHIPPS, SID SILVERS, AND PRESTON STURGES), NORMAN TAUROG (DIRECTOR) **BROADWAY MELODY OF 1940** / 1940

WATCHING ELEANOR POWELL'S last number in her first starring film role, *Broadway Melody of 1936*, it is difficult to not be completely dazzled by her movements, while in the same instant perceiving those movements as somehow a bit clunky or, at least, executed with too much intention and force. It's partly her body—she appears taller and lankier than most dancers—and partly her costume—dressed as she is in long striped satin pants and shirt with a rhinestone coat whose tails come down seemingly lower than her knees, all topped off with a rhinestone-covered hat. The Yankee Doodle Dandy look gives her a sense of being  even taller than she probably was, which helps to make her hips even more central to her physique. Yet, moving through "Got to Dance," how she can tap, bend her body backwards nearly to the floor, and spin and spin and spin as she were on ice instead of a gravity-pulling stage. If she hits each tap a little too forcefully, we are still stunned by the impact. It is little wonder that Ann Miller describes Powell as being the major influence upon her entering that career.

Fred Astaire perhaps said it best: "She 'put 'em down like a man,' no ricky-ticky-sissy stuff with Ellie. She really knocked out a tap dance in a class by herself." There *is* something almost manly about her technique, and that is perhaps what makes her taps seem, at times, so emphatic.

Yet when she dances Cole Porter's "Begin the Beguine" with Fred Astaire in *Broadway Melody of 1940*,

we see another, slightly softer side of her. This time dressed in a flowing thin white skirt and a halter trimmed with spangles, Powell seems completely to move with the flow of the Latin rhythm that is often used contrapuntally against the song's tune. Dancing across a black marble floor against a black backspace upon which small pin lights reflect what appear to be stars, Powell matches Astaire nearly perfectly step by step with a grace that seemed to elude her in that earlier number. Together they seem the perfect match.

LOS ANGELES, JULY 19, 2011

Ray Bolger and Judy Garland

NOEL LANGLEY, FLORENCE RYERSON, EDGAR ALLAN WOLF (SCREENPLAY, BASED ON THE BOOK BY L. FRANK BAUM), IRVING BREACHER, WILLLIAM H. CANNON, HERBERT FIELDS, ARTHUR FREED, JACK HALEY, E. Y. HARBURG, SAMUEL HOFFENSTEIN, BERT LAHR, JOHN LEE MAHIN, HERMAN J. MANKEWICZ, JACK MINTZ, OGDEN NASH, ROBERT PIROSH, GEORGE SEATON, AND SID SILVERS (CREDITED AND UNCREDITED DIALOGUE), HAROLD ARLEN AND E. Y. HARBURG (SONGS), VICTOR FLEMING, GEORGE CUKOR [UNCREDITED], AND MERVYN LEROY [UNCREDITED] (DIRECTORS) **THE WIZARD OF OZ** / 1939

IT SEEMS AS IF everyone in Hollywood was, in one way or another, involved in the writing and directing of the great film classic *The Wizard of Oz*. But the enduring song "If I Only Had a Brain" had only a composer and a lyricist, the incomparable Harold Arlen and E. Y. Harburg. Originally written for the 1937 Broadway musical, *Hooray for What!*, it was cut from that production.

Writing new lyrics, Harburg featured it in his great score as a perfect song for the movie's talking, dancing scarecrow.

Dancing as if he were a straw-stuffed puppet whose strings were pulled from somewhere on high, Bolger, always an entertaining and comical dancer, outdoes himself with the lightness of his feet. At times his entire body seems almost to float, as if he really were stuffed with hay instead of bones and gristle. Yet, as a straw man, each attempt to fly off into dance ends, sadly, with gravity's pull, and his body's collapse.

The song he sings also seems to float in its whimsicality, making his poignant desire to "have a brain" even more magical, since we realize immediately that anyone who can think of what to do with a brain like he can is near to genius:

> I could wile away the hours
> Conferrin' with the flowers
> Consultin' with the rain
> And my head I'd be scratchin'
> While my thoughts were busy hatchin'
> If I only had a brain.

He and Dorothy (Judy Garland) end this wonderful dance number in their memorable skip-to-my-lou down the yellow brick road, which also demonstrates the dancing talents of the young Garland. Garland, while not a *great* dancer has certainly shone in several dance numbers. Her pairing with Fred Astaire in "We're a Couple of Swells" in *Easter Parade* and her memorable struts in "Get Happy" in the musical film *Summertime* immediately come to mind. But in her gingham dress and red ruby shoes, she is unforgettable. Even the dog, Toto, trots along on cue.

LOS ANGELES, MARCH 1, 2011

James Cagney

ROBERT BUCKNER AND EDMUND JOSEPH (SCREEN-PLAY, BASED ON A STORY BY ROBERT BUCKNER), JULIUS J. EPSTEIN AND PHILIP G. EPSTEIN (WRITERS, UNCRED-ITED), GEORGE M. COHAN (SONGS), MICHAEL CURTIZ (DIRECTOR) **YANKEE DOODLE DANDY** / 1942

FOR THOSE WHO have only seen Cagney in his gang-ster films such as *Little Ceasar, The Public Enemy,* and *G Men*, it will come as a surprise, I am sure, that he was also—if almost accidentally—one of Hollywood's greatest dancers. Playing George M. Cohan and per-forming in one of his musicals as a jockey who has been accused of fixing a race, Cagney awaits a signal from a nearby ship to tell him of the decision of the jury: he has been acquited and his dance to the tune of "Yan-kee Doodle Dandy" is a joyfully nervous tapping out of absolute delight that is so original in its combina-tions of straight tap, turns, spins, and occasional leaps that it is clearly something that he has created himself,

outside of the more conventional dance numbers of the film choreographed by Seymour Felix and LeRoy Prinz.

Cagney's whole body is so naturally jumpy that he seems like a marionette strings, as others have described him; but unlike Ray Bolger's puppet-like Straw Man, described above, Cagney's legs, hands, and shoulders appear never to come to rest, as they dangle at the very moment his torso seems to rise. Instead of being pulled back to earth by gravity, Cagney seems unable to come to rest, his feet nervously tapping away something like the horses this jockey might have raced. Given the heaviness of most of his verbal roles, we are understandably stunned by his lightness of foot. And he can even sing!

LOS ANGELES, MARCH 2, 2011

The Nicholas Brothers, Katherine Dunham, and Company

FREDERICK J. JACKSON AND TED KOEHLER (SCREEN-
PLAY, BASED ON A STORY BY JERRY HORWIN, AND
ADAPTED BY H. S. KRAFT AND SEYMOUR B. ROBINSON),
HAROLD ARLEN (MUSIC), ANDEW L. STONE (DIRECTOR)
STORMY WEATHER / 1943

ONE OF TWO major studio movies with all black casts
(the other being Vicente Minelli's *Cabin in the Sky*),
Stormy Weather was packed with great performances
by Lena Horne, Dooley Wilson, Cab Calloway, Fats
Waller, and the great dancer Bill "Bojangles" Robinson. But nothing in this heady concoction of music
and dance can quite match the legwork of Fayard and
Harold Nicholas. The two not only tap dance up and
down stairs in near-perfect unison, but work as a linked
duo, mirroring each other's movements in reverse, be-

fore jumping into the orchestra to leap from oval to oval (which recalls Robinson's "Drum Dance" elsewhere in the film), the seemingly gigantic music stands for the musicians.

Soon the tuxedoed duo hoist themselves up upon a piano, looking perfectly at home there, before they tap up a double staircase, and, in a series of leapfrogs that land them each time in perfect leg splits, they again reach the bottom, coming together only to tap up the staircase once more, this time taking a slide down to the floor. The audience can only be wowed, and wonder how their torsos have endured their acrobatic maneuvers.

Fred Astaire has been quoted as describing this performance as "the greatest dance number ever filmed." Enough said.

Although Lena Horne's sultry rendition of the song "Stormy Weather" is at the center of this film, Katherine Dunham's dance with her company to the same song is worth viewing again and again. The dance begins in a rainy street scene where couples soon begin to jive; Dunham, however, seeming to be somewhere between a streetwalker and sleepwalker, conjures

 up a balletic version, wherein she is quickly joined, in her dreamy imagination, by a whole company of men who lift the women in rapturous grasps before laterally holding their partners and returning them to the floor. The most notable aspect of this dance is the constant flow of the wind machine, which makes the silky costumes seem to be in eternal motion, which Dunham reflects time and again through the movement of her hands and fingers.

There is something a bit ridiculous with this, reminding one a little of the song "They're Doing Choreography" in *White Christmas*, but Dunham manages to take some Martha Graham-like gestures into the realm of sensuality.

LOS ANGELES, MARCH 2, 2011

Carmen Miranda

NANCY WINTER, GEORGE ROOT, JR., AND TOM
BRIDGES (STORY), WALTER BULLOCK (SCREENPLAY),
LEO ROBIN AND HARRY WARREN (MUSIC AND LYRICS),
BUSBY BERKELEY (CHOREOGRAPHER AND DIRECTOR)
THE GANG'S ALL HERE / 1943

AT FIRST GLANCE, it may be hard to even imagine Carmen Miranda's performance of "The Lady in the Tutti Frutti Hat" as being described as a dance. Although Miranda had long before proven that she could dance—or at least smartly wave her hips—in pieces such as "Chica Chica Boom Chic" from *A Night in Rio*, in *The Gang's All Here*'s "Tutti Frutti Hat" we see her mostly from the knees up, and the movements she makes are almost all in her hands and eyes. The piece might best be described as a kind of choreographed performance, yet that doesn't really do justice to Busby Berkeley's giddily absurd number, which *TV Guide* once described as "a male hairdresser's acid trip." And, in the end, I feel that if this isn't dance—which the *Random House Abridged Dictionary* defines, in its first definition, as "to move one's feet or hands, or both, rhythmically in time to music"—I don't know what we might call it. As ridiculous, moreover, as this particular dance may be, it is certainly one of the most strange and original dances ever performed on the screen.

Berkeley has always defined his choeography as being made up of numerous of the same things, usually beautiful chorus girls, moving in visual patterns, which this piece demonstrates fully. Supposedly performed on a nightclub stage, "Tutti Frutti" begins with the arrival of an organ grinder and monkey, who pass through the audience of the club (representing the audience as well in the movie theater). The monkey jumps to the top of a banana tree, whereupon we discover several other matching monkeys and banana trees. Beyond the trees is an island strewn with the bodies of chorus girls lying in a vague pattern of banana-like curves. A cart approaches upon which Dorita (Carmen Miranda) sits, singing about her propensity to wear high hats, which she will not remove for anyone, including the many men whom she meets. The hat, made up of bananas and other fruits, is truly "tutti frutti" in all the meanings of that word, and, as if to carry the metaphor into its fullest realization, the women bring forth a series of other banana- and fruit-laced "things," including a xy-

lophone made up of bananas, upon which Dorita performs, along with obviously oversized bananas, which they wave up and down in patterns that suggest not just the ocean but, you guessed it, sex itself.

In case the audience misses this obvious reference, the girls put their own bodies, shot from Berkeley's famed crane shots, on the line, linking them into kaleidoscopic patterns of delicious flesh and fruits. As Dorita turns to go, the girls again run to the edge of the island to wave their monstrous bananas in slow motion (censors insisted they could only hold their bananas flat across the waist, not jutting out at the hip).

Panning away, the camera returns us to the audi-

ence, wherein a long row of organ grinders now re-
trieves the several monkeys, disappearing from sight.

The whole event is so hilariously gay, in all senses of
that word (part of Miranda's song reads, "Some people
say I dress too gay, / But ev'ry day, I feel so gay; / And
when I'm gay, I dress that way, / Is something wrong
with that?") that it clearly defined the "camp" sensibility long before Susan Sontag even began to write.

LOS ANGELES, JUNE 8, 2011

Ann Miller

SIDNEY SHELDON, FRANCES GOODRICH, AND AL-BERT HACKETT (SCREENPLAY), IRVING BERLIN (SONGS AND MUSIC), CHARLES WALTERS (DIRECTOR), **EASTER PARADE** / 1948

CLAD IN A YELLOW DRESS cutaway in front—so that all can keep their eyes peeled on her long, shapely legs—with a longer, knee-high train in back, Ann Miller, hands in the air, smile frozen upon her face, is kept busy "Shaking the Blues Away" in *Easter Parade*. The cascades of her coiled hair on the top of her head echo her frilly black bustier and the drapes behind her, all intimating something so close to kitsch that it is hard to take her seriously. Yet how can she dance, tapping her feet out as fast as a speed typist. Reputedly, the taps were fabricated by the sound man in most of her films, but she moves her gams so well that we are certain that her toes perfectly match those clicks.

Throughout the film she is mad at Don Hewes

(Fred Astaire) and jealous of his attentions to his new partner, Hannah Brown (Judy Garland). So that jackhammer of a performance might almost be interpreted as nails driven into his coffin (Hewes sits in the audience), or, at least, a kind of passionate dance of revenge. But then, Miller always seems to be giving her all, if a little ungainly at times, stirring a storm up to the rafters.

LOS ANGELES, FEBRUARY 28, 2011

Moira Shearer, Robert Helpmann, and Léonide Massine

MICHAEL POWELL, EMERIC PRESSBURGER, AND KEITH WINTER (SCRIPT, BASED ON A STORY BY HANS CHRISTIAN ANDERSEN), MICHAEL POWELL AND EMERIC PRESSBURGER (DIRECTORS) **THE RED SHOES** / 1948

WHEN I FIRST conceived of this series of short essays, I determined that, since I was most interested in how dance was used in film, I would not include cinematic representations of ballet. It would be as if I were to explore singing in film, and choose to include the many operas that have been committed to screen. Ballet transcription to film may be an interesting topic, but it is not the one at hand.

The more I wrote about the subject, however, I realized that I could not exclude Powell's and Pressburger's masterful *The Red Shoes* simply because it included

real ballet dancers and had, at its center, a "real" ballet. The ballet, in this case, is completely integrated into the film, and the dancers are credible actors as well.

Moreover, even though the great "Red Shoes Ballet" is a theatrical work that might just as easily have been performed onstage, so too is the whole a masterful piece of film-making, as Powell and Pressburger conjure up their highly artificed cinematic style, filled with lush and vibrant colors that parallel, at times, the works of Nicolas Ray and Douglas Sirk. Like those later films, *The Red Shoes* most definitely suggests what one has to admit is an exaggerated aesthetic that may or may not be related to ballet. In any case, *The Red Shoes* works as a piece of cinematic art before it serves to represent anything about dance.

Having said that, the ballet, choreographed by Robert Helpmann and danced by three professional ballet dancers—Helpmann, Moira Shearer, and Léonide Massine—is surely the most traditionally choreographed of my selections. But who can dismiss a work based on a tale in which, once the dancer has put her slippers on, she must dance in a frenzy unto death?

The theme of the ballet is the same as that of the movie: despite her desire to live a normal life with composer Julian Craster (Marius Goring),  Vicky Page (Shearer) cannot escape the imprisonment of Boris Lermontov's ballet except through death.

At times sentimental, overly melodramatic, and fraught with a desire to mean more than it does, *The Red Shoes* is filled with brilliant dancing, costumes, and sets.

LOS ANGELES, SEPTEMBER 9, 2011

Fred Astaire: The Ceiling Dance

ALAN JAY LERNER (STORY AND SCREENPLAY), STAN-
LEY DONEN (DIRECTOR) **ROYAL WEDDING** / 1951

PERHAPS THE MOST famous of all film dances, the so-
called "Ceiling Dance" of *Royal Wedding,* is less a spectacular feat of dancing—although Astaire performs
with his usual panache—than it is a technical wonder;
so well is it achieved by both dancer and designers that
it is, at first, difficult to even conceive how the overjoyed Tom Bowen (Astaire), could move from the flat
floor of his hotel room up the wall and onto the ceiling, to gradually dance back down again, and up once
more, balancing his body on paintings, wall-hangings,
and even the chandeliers.

In reality what we are seeing is a room enclosed in a
framed wheel that is gradually turned, with the dancer
timing his leaps within the slow movement of the rect-

 angular room. The furniture and other trappings are clearly attached into position and, accordingly, are unable to move, allowing Astaire to pretend to balance his head on the back of a chair, climb the desk up the wall, etc.

Some claim the idea was Lerner's, others insist it was Astaire's. But the fact is that it could not have been achieved without Donen's near-flawless direction and Astaire's perfect timing, appearing to leap as brilliantly as Spider Man might today. But Spider Man, after all, has his webs to help him, ropes and pulleys. Astaire had only a machine which created an illusion within which he tapped, twirled, jumped, and turned through the motions of his legs.

LOS ANGELES, SEPTEMBER 7, 2011

Donald O'Connor and Gene Kelly

BETTY COMDEN AND ADOLPH GREEN (WRITERS),
NACIO HERB BROWN (MUSIC), ARTHUR FREED (LYRICS),
STANLEY DONEN AND GENE KELLY (DIRECTORS) **SING-
ING IN THE RAIN** / 1952

I HAVE TO admit that, perhaps because of the fact I saw so many *Francis* and *The Talking Mule* movies in the early 1950s, I had never given Donald O'Connor, the actor in these silly caprices, a thought until as a college student I saw a tape of *Singing in the Rain*. His burlesque-like humor still, from time to time, makes

me cringe, but what a remarkable dancer he was, particularly in comic numbers such as "Make 'Em Laugh!" Based on Cole Porter's "Be a Clown!," Nacio Herb

Brown's and Arthur Freed's joyful anthem to humor is perfect for the rubber-faced O'Connor, who uses everything in the room as a prop. With his bright blue eyes, hat on head, O'Connor dances across couches, chairs, walls and, after fighting a battle with a headless dummy that might remind some viewers of the Surrealist artist Hans Bellmer's dolls, O'Connor spins in a circle upon the floor like a Samuel Beckett figure, unable to stand. His final series of backward leaps off walls painted to look like vast perspectives, and his last dive into a thin veneer of wood truly do bring smiles to all faces, both out of wonder for his rhythmic energy and his ability just to survive.

Little need be said of one the greatest of all film dances, "Singing in the Rain," by the matchless Gene Kelly. With a broad smile upon his face, Kelly doodles down the street in a rainstorm before embracing a lightpost from which he hangs in midair, spinning his umbrella like a top, and, in a blue, rain-soaked suit and red shoes, splashing his way through the puddles as a joyful child might. The lively tap number quite literally plays out its lyrics in his body movements, revealing physically that despite the natural elements and all they symbolize, everything can be conquered through the inner joy of love.

LOS ANGELES, FEBRUARY 27, 2011

Tommy Rall, Bob Fosse, Ann Miller, Carol Haney, and Jeanne Coyne

DOROTHY KINGSLEY (SCREENPLAY, BASED ON THE BOOK BY SAM AND BELLA SPEWACK), COLE PORTER (MUSIC AND LYRICS), GEORGE SIDNEY (DIRECTOR) **KISS ME, KATE** / 1953

I HAVE ALWAYS felt that the film version of *Kiss Me, Kate* was a sort of mixed bag. The introduction of Cole Porter into the film as he tries out a couple numbers in Fred Graham's living room, and the abandonment of the great show opener, "Another Op'nin' of Another Show," framed the work like too many other film musicals, and missed the opportunity to display the open theatricality of the original. But then, there is something contradictory in the original as well, where the onstage personalities of the leads (in this case Katherine Grayson and Howard Keel) seem in their operatic style of singing and action in opposition to the other figures. Porter's songs for them, as well, songs like "Wunderbar" and "So in Love" appear to be worlds

away from the more sprightly numbers such as "Why Can't You Behave?" and "From This Moment On."

Accordingly, the musical and film both seem almost divided in two, with a Shakespeare-coated operetta at one end, and a jazzy series of dances choreographed by Hermes Pan and Bob Fosse at the other. Although most of the songs are wonderful, the story and its structure seem almost to break the piece in two.

But the dances are all so good that I might have chosen four great dance moments from this film instead of the two I've selected, the other two being Miller's tap performance of "Too Darn Hot" and Miller's and the chorus' rendition of "Tom, Dick, and Harry."

However, it is hard to match the dancing wonder of Ann Miller's and Tommy Rall's "Why Can't You Behave?" in which she lovingly chastises him for his reckless behavior, while all the while he jokingly mocks her. The rooftop location of this scene, which literally flirts with "a loss of gravity," is perfect, for the character clearly has no sense of *gravitas*. Indeed, when Miller reaches the roof she cannot, at first, locate her lover until he slides in from above, down a pole which he has evidently previously shimmied up. It is the first of his gravity-defying feats, as, the moment she finishes singing, he skips away, she tapping along, as he spins like an ice skater before somersaulting and cartwheeling off. A short rhumba between the two in which she plays out her frustrations in mock punches, butt kicks, and feet stomping only sets him into a more irresponsible state as Rall dizzily dances at the very edge of the roof, imitating a near deathly fall before he leaps back to safety, catapulting himself up again and again (presumably with the help of a hidden trampoline), spreading his legs, and returning to the floor on his knees. Given Rall's amazing acrobatic leaps one might almost be able to believe that he is propelling himself with his own leg power, instead of a piece of stretched fabric to help him spring back, except that had he truly fallen back to earth from the heights he reaches, he would surely have broken his knees. As it is, he makes a final leap onto another small construction before closing the piece in a balletic spin that seems for a few seconds it may never cease.

If the first dance belongs to Rall, the second, "From this Moment On," belongs to Fosse, who choreographed part of it. The dance is a celebratory one af-

 ter the news of Kate's marriage, which means her younger sister Bianca can now pick between one of her three suitors. The male dancers don't seem to care as much about pairing with the women (danced by Carol Haney and Jeanne Coyle), as they do about the joy of the occasion. Using the Roman arches repeated throughout the set, the couples dance out separately or together several times, moving in lateral parallel patterns before shifting from front to back. After several of these arrivals and exits, however, Carol Haney dances out as the song changes rhythm from a zippy, upbeat song of new beginnings to a jazz-infused rhythm that works perfectly for Fosse's moves.

After a few seconds of Haney moving across the stage, Fosse suddenly leaps out through the arch seemingly from the sky instead of the floor. As he catches up with the surprised Haney, he leaps to the small ledge of a post, allowing his face and arms to go limp in what would become a signature Fosse pose. Haney crawls toward him in a prone position before they join up again, alternating between leaps and sweeps upon their knees as they move forward to close the piece.

Pan is a great choreographer, but by allowing Fosse to direct his first dance in the film, he truly makes the piece fresh, and we absolutely do believe something has changed in all the characters' lives.

LOS ANGELES, APRIL 12, 2011

Cyd Charisse and Gene Kelly

ALAN JAY LERNER (SCREENPLAY AND LYRICS), FRED-
ERICK LOEWE (MUSIC), VICENTE MINNELLI (DIRECTOR)
BRIGADOON / 1954

ALTHOUGH CYD CHARISSE was brilliant as the gambler's dancing moll in the long "Gotta Dance" routine
in Kelly's *Singing in the Rain*, she is even more exciting
as the restrained Scottish elder sister, Fiona, in Minnelli's *Brigadoon*, where she again pairs up with Gene Kelly.

Particularly in "The Heather on the Hill," where
Kelly first sings the song's lyrics before the two break
out into dance, we can sense Fiona's growing sexuality
in the gracefulness of the long-legged Charisse's moves.
The couple begin their duet as a tease, pulling on the
basket in which she gathers heather (which actually
was purple spray-painted sumac) and spinning like in-
nocents before she begins her gentle run higher and
higher up the hill.

We perceive even through their costumes—Kelly's

beautiful ensemble of an emerald green silk shirt underneath which he wears an orange T-shirt, matched by his stockings, and Charisse's pearl-white dress with an underlining of orange—that they are a perfect match. The dance itself soon tells us that, as he seemingly effortlessly lifts her time and again; and after running forward and backward in reversing patterns, each gracefully lifts their entire bodies, one after the other, onto the bough of a nearby tree.

There is a shyness about Charisse's balletic movements that perfectly fits her character and allows us to take in the scenery, loch, and heather-covered hills below where they dance. Minnelli and others wanted to film the scene on location in Scotland, but the studio insisted they do the entire shoot on the lot, which led some critics to later criticize it for its slightly staged, artificial look. Yet, so film-lore goes, the set was so realistically painted that several birds attempted to fly into it. Certainly the dance is magical enough that viewers may want to join them, leaping through the screen.

LOS ANGELES, FEBRUARY 27, 2011

Vera-Ellen and Danny Kaye

NORMAN KRASNA, NORMAN PANAMA, AND MELVIN FRANK (WRITERS), IRVING BERLIN (MUSIC AND LYR-ICS), MICHAEL CURTIZ (DIRECTOR) **WHITE CHRISTMAS** /1954

I AM A PARTICULAR FAN of Vera-Ellen, in part because she worked in some of the best musicals of film over just two decades before withdrawing from public life. But in the second major song of *White Christmas*, "The Best Things Happen While You're Dancing," it's Danny Kaye, dressed in a blue-slate suit and matching slate suede shoes, who truly shines.

The dance begins just as another ends. Leaving the dance floor for the outside, the couple gradually move from the waltz to the fox trot as Kaye finishes the song's lyrics, and, crossing a small bridge whipped up, obviously, just for this piece, they use its metal posts for acrobatic swings, she moving out and around while he swoops higher over her petite body. An upside-down canoe is the perfect place for the couple to tap out the fox trot beat, a short tap-dance version of the jazzy rhythms, before they execute—the music accelerating—a series of spins, lifts,  and falls, Vera-Ellen (playing Judy Haynes) ending with her body draped across Kaye's lap, just as sister Betty Haynes (Rosemary Clooney), wondering where they have gotten to, exits the inside dance floor to discover them.

If Danny Kaye is usually goofy, his whole body awkwardly lurching forward and backward like a heap of jello, in this dance he is expertly solid and graceful, a Romeo who has moved suddenly from the comic to romance. As he sings, "Even guys with two left feet come out all right if the girl is sweet." He seldom got other chances to so clearly display his dancing talents.

LOS ANGELES, FEBRUARY 28, 2011

Bob Fosse and Tommy Rall

BLAKE EDWARDS AND RICHARD QUINE (SCREEN-PLAY, BASED ON A PLAY BY JOSEPH FIELDS AND JEROME CHODOROV, AND STORIES BY RUTH MCKENNEY), JULE STYNE AND LEO ROBIN (SONGS AND LYRICS), GEORGE DUNING (ORIGINAL MUSIC), RICHARD QUINE (DIREC-TOR) **MY SISTER EILEEN** / 1955

IT IS HARD to imagine a more endearing dance couple than Bob Fosse and Tommy Rall. In *My Sister Eileen*—overall a weak film when compared with Leonard Bernstein's theatrical version of the same materials in *Wonderful Town*—the two become rivals, each trying to outdo the other in an attempt to woo Eileen (Janet Leigh). Fosse, playing Frank Lippincott, is the count-erman at the local Walgreen's diner, while Rall plays Chick Clark, a newspaper journalist. Their short dance together is an all-male ritual to see who's the fittest, like two rams butting heads or gorillas thumping chests.

The compact and lean Fosse has the edge, simply

because of his ability to deliver sharp spins and turns, moving along an arc like a sliver of moon, hat in hand, a movement for which he has become well known.

Rall, a taller and just as lean dancer, occasionally appears a bit gangly in comparison, but for my taste his dancing, even more athletic because of his height, is more brilliant. His spins are perfect, with more rotation than Fosse gets. And his huge outstretched legs, in his leap from one of the boxes in the alley where they wait for Eileen to return from an audition, are absolutely stunning.

There is no winner, of course, in this dance rivalry.

Both are simply brilliant in their competitive moves. But while Fosse, mostly through his role as a choreographer, has become internationally famous, Rall has crept, undeservedly, into the background, despite his appearances in *Kiss Me, Kate* (along with Fosse), *Seven Brides for Seven Brothers*, *Pennies from Heaven*, and, onstage, *Milk and Honey*. Strangely, he is not even listed as a character in the credits for the DVD of *My Sister Eileen*, as if his role was played by a ghost. My film guides have repeated the error, wiping his name from the production. But one only need watch this scene to see how brilliant of a dancer he was.

LOS ANGELES, FEBRUARY 23, 2011

Gene Kelly, Dan Dailey, and Michael Kidd

BETTY COMDEN AND ADOLPH GREEN (SCREENPLAY, MUSIC AND LYRICS), ANDRÉ PREVIN (MUSIC), STANLEY DONEN AND GENE KELLY (DIRECTORS) IT'S ALWAYS FAIR WEATHER / 1955

ONE OF THE most under estimated film musicals of all time, *It's Always Fair Weather* concerns the return home of three soldiers, their last night on the town in New York, and their reunion 10 years later in the same city. Predictably they have grown apart in the interim, having taken on vastly different careers, with Ted (Gene Kelly) ending up as a down-on-his-luck boxing promoter, Doug (Dan Dailey) as an ulcer-ridden advertising man, and Angie (Michael Kidd) as the owner of a hamburger stand. Like Sondheim's *Follies* showgirls they now all seem to live diminished lives from what they had imagined might be facing them that joyous night a decade earlier.

When Ted meets a girl, Jackie (Cyd Charisse), he falls in love, and behind his back she arranges for the three to appear on a television show together.

Audiences of 1955, many fixated each night on their television sets, also did not like the bleak message of the script. But today the film seems to have a depth of meaning that many successes of the era do not. The film is also helped by several great song and dance numbers, two of which I believe are among the best of film dances.

The first, "The Binge," danced by Kelly, the often overlooked Dan Dailey, and Michael Kidd (known best as a choreographer of films like *Guys and Dolls* and *The Band Wagon*), is an explosion of athletic movement, as the three soldiers, having left a bar drunk, take to the street. At first they are all so drunk they can hardly stand, as Dailey, in particular, manipulates his legs into a series of positions that makes him look more like a rubber Gumby than a man with ball-sockets. Kelly kicks Dailey, Dailey momentarily steps upon Kelly's ass, before Kidd is swept up upon Dailey's shoulders as Dailey-Kidd dance a quick rumba with Kelly and move to their street routines.

Stopping a taxi, the three move in and out, through doors, windows, and ceiling, joining up each time before returning to the endless intricacies of taxi hopping. No sooner do they finish that breathless scenario than they leap down the street, each attaching a trash can lid to his left foot, and performing a seemingly impossible tap with it, a stunning terpsichorean feat!

Finally, the three dance off down the street once more, reentering the dive to dance across tables and onto the bar itself before ordering up two more drinks.

Later, discovering that his new girlfriend, Jackie, likes him, Ted decides that he "likes himself" ("I Like Myself"), and decked out with a pair of roller skates (he has just exited a skating parlor) he skates through the streets as he croons the song. Before long, a crowd has gathered. He begins to tap, gradually with greater and greater ferocity, alternating between curb and gutter, then closing with higher leaps in the center of the street and posing with Kelly's usual smiling face, hands out for the cheers of the audience. Pure hokum, brilliantly done.

LOS ANGELES, APRIL 14, 2011

Marge and Gower Champion

EDWARD HOPE AND LEONARD STERN (SCREEN-
PLAY, BASED ON W. SOMERSET MAUGHAM'S *TWO MANY
HUSBANDS*), GEORGE DUNING (MUSIC), H. C. POTTER
(DIRECTOR) **THREE FOR THE SHOW** / 1955

ONLY MUSICAL FANATICS like myself would ever remember this mediocre musical, a film made to bring
Betty Grable, through the choreography of Jack Cole,
more into the musical mainstream, hoping to give her
the kind of boost Cole delivered by teaching Marilyn
Monroe her moves in *Gentlemen Prefer Blondes* and
Some Like It Hot. I'm not, however, convinced of Grable's dancing skills.

Far more interesting to me is Marge and Gower
Champion's more ballroom dancing style in the lovely,
almost non-musical performance of George and Ira
Gershwin's "Someone to Watch Over Me." It begins
as a practice session, in which Marge is talking about a
date she has that night, and wondering what color dress
to wear. The two patter back and forth as they make the

 notable spins, parallel parts, and lifts that might be said to define the Champions' dancing style.

One lift, however, seems to be different, as the couple's lips come close to each other. Still talking up a blue-storm, they try it again. Gower proclaims, "It is different!" as we perceive that, for the first time, he has noticed her as someone more than just a dancing partner.

Marge continues the conversation and the two carry out the requisite turns, lifts, and balletic runs—that is until suddenly they reach the staircase, the song which has quietly begun in the background crescendoing while the two take off in a beautifully realized dance that basically defines their work. Evidently Jack Cole choreographed the number, even though Gower would serve that position in most of their pieces before and after.

I might have also chosen their wonderful, more jazzy, "Casbah" piece in *Everything I Have Is Yours* of 1952, if it weren't that the movie is so awful that I wouldn't dare send anyone to see it just for the sake of that dance, even if they might find the disc.

LOS ANGELES, APRIL 14, 2011

Gene Nelson, Charlotte Greenwood, and Chorus

SONY LEVIEN AND WILLIAM LUDWIG (SCREENPLAY, ADAPTED FROM THE MUSICAL BY RICHARD RODGERS AND OSCAR HAMMERSTEIN II AND BASED ON THE PLAY BY LYNN RIGGS), FRED ZINNEMANN (DIRECTOR) **OKLAHOMA!** / 1955

ONE OF MY favorite childhood musical memories is the exuberant "Everything's Up to Date in Kansas City" early on in *Oklahoma!*. What begins merely as a comic number, with Will Parker (Gene Nelson) recounting his small-town hick reactions to the big city, Kansas City, gradually is transformed into a statement of joy, camaraderie, and community through Nelson's and Greenwood's great dancing and Agnes de Milles' skill as a choreographer.

Much of the "action" of the scene lies dormant in its hunkering cowboys, Will among them. But as he recounts the wonders of Kansas City, it is clear that he cannot for long remain still, particularly when he's seen a building seven stories high and a dancing girl who has revealed that everything she  had was absolutely real. The actual dance begins, innocently enough, with Will executing a two-step that has taken his world by surprise, supplanting the waltz! Although Eller (the long-legged, high-kicking Charlotte Greenwood) joins in for a few minutes, the cowboys don't like it.

When a few minutes later, Will taps out the first few steps of Ragtime, they like it even less. But the women are smitten, particularly two younger girls, and before you know it, they are cautiously attempting to join in. His cowboy friends, however, are still not convinced, and Will, accordingly, returns to the hunker, before, one by one, the men pick up the rhythms and try out the dance. Suddenly everyone is up and dancing, moving forward and away, backs to the camera, as Aunt Eller holds out her hands in an iconic de Mille movement that suggests that the community sensibility has prevailed. Soon there is a whole chorus of ragtiming, tap-dancing cowboys, which so thrills Will that he takes out his lasso, skillfully stepping in and out of

the symbolic circle it creates. In his ecstasy of the shared experience, he leaps upon a railroad car just as the train takes off. As in any good western, his horse comes to his rescue, whereupon he is returned to his comrades and friends.

LOS ANGELES, MARCH 2, 2011

Yul Brynner and Deborah Kerr

ERNEST LEHMAN (SCREENPLAY, BASED ON THE MU-
SICAL BY OSCAR HAMMERSTEIN II AND RICHARD ROD-
GERS, BASED ON THE BOOK BY MARGARET LANGDON),
WALTER LANG (DIRECTOR) **THE KING AND I** / 1956

I'VE SEEN the film musical *The King and I* dozens of times, and I still don't know whether Yul Brynner and Deborah Kerr can actually dance, but in the case of "Shall We Dance?" does it matter? If this isn't a great dance number, I have no way of defining the genre.

Dressed absolutely beautifully, he in a royal red open coat and matching jodhpur-like pants, all woven through with gold braids, she in a beautiful silk gown with many underlays of bustle and skirts, the two begin the dance with what has almost become a subgenre of dance numbers: one teaching the other how to do it (think of Barbra Streisand in *Hello, Dolly!* or the lesson in how to Cha-cha-cha given by July Holiday's two friends in *Bells Are Ringing*). But it quickly shifts,

 as Brynner recognizes there is something different in their positions from the other waltzers he has observed.

With that shift the couple spin away on an exhilarating "1-2-3 and" rhythm that takes them around the huge palace room again and again until they literally run out breath, only to have the King announce: again!

Over the years in amateur and professional productions of this work, I have seen dresses slip to the floor and the dancers nearly stumble, but never did I think it ridiculous or have I ever laughed. The joyful sense of liberation this performance gives to both the dancers and viewers is at the heart of why dance is such a profound experience.

LOS ANGELES, APRIL 16, 2011

Carol Haney

GEORGE ABBOTT AND RICHARD BISSELL (SCREEN-PLAY), RICHARD ADLER AND JERRY ROSS (MUSIC AND LYRICS), GEORGE ABBOTT AND STANLEY DONEN (DIRECTORS) **THE PAJAMA GAME** / 1957

ALTHOUGH CAROL HANEY worked with Gene Kelly on the dance numbers in both of his great films *Singing in the Rain* and *An American in Paris*, and danced in the chorus of *Kiss Me, Kate*, her only starring role on film, as a dancer and actor, was in *The Pajama Game*. Sadly, her early death at the age of 39 did not permit her to show her skills in other roles.

In *The Pajama Game*'s "This is My Once a Year Day" and particularly in "Steam Heat" we recognize Haney's immense talents. Dancing with two male dancers, Haney performs the latter number of hissing S's with the controlled lateral slide and cool frenzy that parallel the lyrics. Fingers spread and shaking somewhat like a tambourine—a familiar Bob Fosse trope—

the three reveal that "steam heat" is not enough to keep
them hot, even when they pour more coals on the boil-
er. In their jerky motions they uniformly suggest their
shivering desperation for love. Lifting their hats up and
down, the trio gives the sense of a moving train constantly changing in perspective as they slip to right and
left. Near the end of this almost jittery dance, the two
men collapse, skittering across the floor toward Haney
as if they have finally blown their tops or boiled over.

LOS ANGELES, APRIL 11, 2011

Gwen Verdon

GEORGE ABBOTT (SCREENPLAY, BASED ON A NOVEL BY DOUGLAS WALLOP), RICHARD ADLER AND JERRY ROSS (MUSIC AND LYRICS), GEORGE ABBOTT AND STANLEY DONEN (DIRECTORS) **DAMN YANKEES** / 1958

IT IS SAD that the extremely gifted Gwen Verdon did not get to show her dancing talents in more films. On Broadway, she performed in some of the best dancing roles of her time, including *Can-Can*, *Damn Yankees*, *Redhead*, *Sweet Charity*, and, later in her life, *Chicago*. But the former wife of choreographer and dancer Bob Fosse is absolutely memorable in her role as Lola in the film version of *Damn Yankees*, even if the film often leaves one with the feeling that something is missing. And her memorable "Whatever Lola Wants" dance and song has to be recognized as one of the great sexual numbers of film history.

There is something absolutely ridiculous about Lola, formerly the ugliest woman in Providence,

Rhode Island, whom the Devil has transformed into a Cuban trollop, determined to get what she wants from every man she (and the Devil) desires to corrupt. Mock striping, as she dances, Lola writhes over the stolid body of ball player Joe Hardy (hilariously rendered by gay actor Tab Hunter), using his persevering figure as something close to a pole against, through, and across which she traverses, attacking him like a bull, waving her black negligee and clicking fanny to negotiate what she presumes is the inevitable—his abandonment of moral values into absolute lust. The dance is almost an old-fashioned hoochie-coochie, but so sparklingly satiric in its conception that we can only watch in wonderment.

Of course, it doesn't work: Hardy is in love with his wife, and the actor in love with men. But if ever anyone might have shaken up the opposite sex, it would have been Verdon as Lola; and later, in the lovely song and dance number "Two Lost Souls"—almost as good as Verdon's siren song—she nearly succeeds in unfreezing him.

LOS ANGELES, APRIL 4, 2011

Rita Moreno, George Chakiris, Yvonne Wilder, Tucker Smith, Eliot Feld, Tony Mordante, and Choruses

ERNEST LEHMAN (SCREENPLAY, BASED ON THE LIBRETTO BY ARTHUR LAURENTS, CONCEIVED BY JEROME ROBBINS), JEROME ROBBINS AND ROBERT WISE (DIRECTORS) **WEST SIDE STORY** / 1961

I MIGHT ARGUE that *West Side Story* is the best film musical ever made. It's far tougher and thematically more challenging than two other favorites, *Singing in the Rain* and *An American in Paris*, and its music, singing, and dancing is at a level that is near impossible to compare.

When I say this, however, I always flinch a bit because the three major actors (Nathalie Wood, Richard Beymer, and Russ Tamblyn) are not up to the quality

of the film overall. Wood is a brittle Maria, even with Marni Nixon's golden voice to back her up; and at moments it is entirely impossible to believe she has even heard of Puerto Rico. Richard Beymer (later an acquaintance of mine) is a handsome lead, but there's something slightly gangly about his performance, and although he seems at times to be a fresh and energetic force, his overall acting is somewhat lethargic and even a bit effeminate. Russ Tamblyn, despite his dancing pedigree, is a tumbler, not a dancer; and his acting is difficult to endure.

For all that, the film is something of a miracle— what with two directors, the imperious Jerome Robbins and the far more accommodating Robert Wise. What tensions there must have been on the set do not show up in the film. The brilliant opening sequence moves from a seemingly abstract set of lines to a helicopter-pan of the city of Manhattan, before settling down in the deteriorated streets (actually the location of what is now Lincoln Center, which delayed its construction until the film had finished shooting). Through a neighborhood basketball court, the finger-clicking Jets pass

on their way to the street where Tony Mordante (Action)—in what has to be one of the most difficult beginning dance movements of all time—releases some of his pent-up energy in a dance move that ultimately affects the entire gang. That sudden transformation from a realistic series of actions to a group of dancing men signifies the powerful pulls in this film between utter realism and theatrical fantasy, which propel this "musical" into a new dimension. Even street-hardened young boys had to admit that Robbins' dancers were different from any other kind of screen-dancing of the day.

West Side Story has a multitude of such wonderful dance moments, but two numbers, in particular, are unforgettable. The first might not have even happened, it appears, if Stephen Sondheim had not convinced Robbins to restore the song to its original intentions in the story. Laurents, Bernstein, and Sondheim had originally intended "America" to be what it appears on film, an argument between Bernardo and Anita, between the male dancers and the female, in order to establish relationships that had not been explored in the libretto. In the stage version, however, Robbins saw it as an opportunity for a female dance number, so it was performed by women only, a new character, Rosalia, being invented to take over Bernardo's role. A couple of years ago, in Laurents' Broadway revival of the musical, I saw it performed as it had been originally, and it had little of the dynamism and magic of the film version.

"America" spins out of an argument between Anita and Bernardo, quickly moving, with the haunting rhythms of Bernstein's *huapango* and through Sondheim's witty dialogue, into a battle between the five shark males and their five women. Suddenly Chakiris and two other males switch from their mock-battling antics, into a hand-clapping fandago-like movement straight toward the camera, a few minutes later followed by Moreno and her five friends. Shooting from below foot level, the camera watches them on the move horizontally toward it, as if in their kicks and whoops they were a descending army—and they are!—as again and again the two sides move toward one another, before the other breaks up and runs. It is a game, but it also a real war, not only between ideas—a commitment to America and a nostalgic longing for what has been lost—but between presence and absence, faith and defeat, reiterated in the final four last lines of the lyrics:

BERNARDO: I think I go back to San Juan.
ANITA: I know a boat you can get on. [*The women jeer, "Bye, bye!"*]
BERNARDO: Everyone there will give big cheer!
ANITA: Everyone there will have moved here.

Although Anita and her female companions win out in the battle of wit and dance, absence and defeat will be the substance of the events of the rest of the musical.

The second dance number, "Cool," strangely enough, had a similar transformation from stage to film as "America." In the stage version, the song was almost lost, as it was sung near the end of the first act in the back of Doc's drugstore, as a way for Riff to defuse the rising tensions of the Jets. Once again, onstage, the dance is unimpressive and almost meaningless, coming so early before the actual battles. Sondheim, so he reports in his voluminous *Finishing the Hat*, suggested that it be moved to the second act, after the rumble, replacing the more comic post-rumble number, "Gee, Officer Krupke." Robbins declared that he had no time to restage it, particularly since the sets had been determined. Fortunately (although Sondheim still has doubts about his own suggestion), in the film Robbins took the lyricist's advice. Sung, as it is, in a darkened garage with a low metal ceiling, the entire number takes on a completely different character, the set and location reinforcing the pent-up emotions of the gang.

Since Riff is now dead in the story, Robbins was able to feature the brilliant dancer Tucker Smith (Ice) as the lead. Tall and rugged, Smith literally towers over the other figures as he pulls them into the garage, demanding that they "get cool." The bright lights of the truck and car headlights against the darkness make for a perfect backdrop to the series of leaps, spins, punches, floor crawls, and pirouettes that the Jets perform to the jazz refrains of the saxophone/trumpet/xylophone combo. Mordante and Feld are particularly excellent, but all, including the three female dancers, create a near frenzy of motion before settling into the "cool" frieze at dance's end.

Both of these dance numbers are spectacular, and show what a great choreographer like Robbins can do for a filmed musical. Just as importantly, both numbers still appear fresh and innovative today.

LOS ANGELES, JULY 27, 2011

Robert Preston, Shirley Jones, and Chorus

MEREDITH WILLSON AND FRANKLIN LACEY (BOOK),
MARION HARGROVE (SCREENPLAY), MORTON DACOSTA
(DIRECTOR) **THE MUSIC MAN** / 1962

WHEN I FIRST began this project, I determined I would only include exceptional dancers, and not concern myself with actors carefully trained to make the right moves. But in four films I've chosen, although the actors are not natural dancers, the final pieces are so joyful that it would be unfair, and perhaps unrepresentative, not to include them.

The third of these beautifully choreographed works is Oona White's stunningly performed dance sung to "Marian, the Librarian" by the leads Robert Preston, Shirley Jones, and the chorus in the small Madison Library in Iowa.

The moment Preston, as the charming con-man Professor Harold Hill, enters the hallowed space, where

 "talking out loud" is not allowed, we are utterly entranced by his tender assault on the beautiful librarian. But the question remains, how to get Marian to participate in the event. He threatens to drop a bag of marbles upon the floor, gradually wooing her by his moaning lament with the cleverly outlandish rhymes of "Marian," "librarian," and "carrion."

White's choreography sweeps up the librarian into dance by employing the entire male chorus as her partner in a long lateral traipse up and down the winding staircase, through the stacks, and into the central reading room, Harold Hill in chase. Peevishness alternates with joy, as little by little, the community envelops Marian into the dance that at its apogee includes a whole library of moving bodies, pandemonium truly breaking loose in the city's major sanctuary to silence. Whatever lack of dancing skills Preston and Jones may have is totally disguised by the chorus' acrobatic prances and taps. Even the film's marvelous dance number "Shipoopi," a more standard set dance piece, cannot match the brilliance of this achievement.

LOS ANGELES, APRIL 12, 2011

Ron Moody and Boy Chorus

VERNON HARRIS (SCREENPLAY, BASED ON THE
MUSICAL BY LIONEL BART, LOOSELY ADAPTED FROM
CHARLES DICKENS), CAROL REED (DIRECTOR) **OLIVER**
/ 1968

THE DANCING in *Oliver,* like that of *The Music Man,*
is an example of the coming together of a talented chorus and a gifted choreographer, again Oona White.
The almost frenetic dance number, "Consider Your-

self," centered upon
the youthful talents
of Jack Wild playing
The Artful Dodger,
is something to be
remembered in the
dance world. But,
for me, the far better
piece is "You've Got
to Pick a Pocket or

Two," where the young boys, strutting in the awkward poses of White's choreography, work together with the light-legged and quick moving Ron Moody as Fagin.

Perhaps, except for Wild, none of them are great dancers, but together their antics create a kind of comic mayhem that relates back to my comments on Groucho Marx; and Mark Lester's seemingly uninhibited laughter is one of the few times that Oliver, the character, comes alive.

LOS ANGELES, SEPTEMBER 9, 2011

Difficult Dances

BARBARA TURNER (SCREENPLAY, BASED ON A
STORY BY TURNER AND NEVE CAMPBELL), ROBERT ALT-
MAN (DIRECTOR) **THE COMPANY** / 2003

ROGER EBERT describes Robert Altman's penultimate film, *The Company* as, strangely enough, an autobiographical film—even though when the director was first presented with the script by former dancer Barbara Turner, he responded, "Barbara, I read your script and I don't get it. I don't understand. I don't know what it is. I'm just the wrong guy for this."

Yet, he was clearly not the "wrong" guy, perceiving that the ensemble performative elements of the Robert Joffrey ballet company and the persona of Gerald Arpino, renamed in this work Alberto Antonelli (Malcolm McDowell), did, in fact, have a great deal in common with his directorial activities: both Mr. A's (Altman and Arpino) had always to deal with the large egos of their performers and the impossible costs of mounting such

exuberant and often experimental works.

Ballet stars, however, are paid, as this film makes clear, far less than their Hollywood counterparts, often having to work extra jobs just to pay the rent, or, even worse, like the balletic star of this film, Neve Campbell, having to camp out on the floors of other ballet members' small apartments. Although the vicious hierarchal star system of Diaghilev's Ballets Russes as represented in Michael Powell's and Eric Pressburger's *The Red Shoes* may have been obliterated by the shifting casting of the Joffrey company, the various shifts of plum roles still riffle long-time company members. And the serious commitments these endlessly-working performers must make to their career clearly interfere with any possibilities of their love-lives.

Although Campbell (playing a character named Loretta 'Ry' Ryan) falls in love with the seemingly perfect young man, a young chef, played by James Franco, she fails to show up on time for his lovely late-night meal. How she possibly maintains her daytime dancing career, moreover, and her night-time activities is not entirely explained.

Even more importantly, dancers, unlike the Hollywood actors with 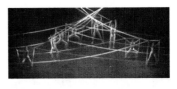 whom Altman works, live in a fragile world not unlike beloved race horses: at any moment the strenuous imposition of legs, feet, and other limbs, forced to disobey the obvious laws of gravity, endangers not only their careers but their lives.

Both the incredible popular dancers Michael Jackson and Prince, one must remember, suffered so much pain that they sought relief in opioids and other drugs. These Joffrey dancers must not only bind their feet—a bit like the ancient Chinese women—but daily suffer pain that, as with the older major dancer of the group, often ends in broken tendons and the end of their career. It is important to remember, also, that Joffrey's own life ended in AIDS, a fact that the Arpino character, Joffrey's real-life companion, memorializes in his comments on the AIDS-related deaths of several of his greatest male dancers. Far more than great sports figures, dancers generally have, for many reasons, extremely short careers. Great dancers are basically lean young men and women who can accomplish incredible acts of bodily movement for a few years at most. Ten years, as one dancer indirectly argues, is a long time to perform with the company, even if her interpretations are no longer respected.

And, finally, even if Joffrey and Arpino were not tyrants in the way that Diaghilev was to Nijinsky and the rest of his corps, Mr. A. can certainly be a difficult and dismissive man, castigating his dancers, whom he perceives as rebellious children, at the very moment he praises them in such a way that they cannot know whether he is serious or not. And guest choreographers, such as Robert Desrosiers, can dismiss central dancers, endangering their careers and certainly deflating their egos, with a flick of his wrist.

Altman, amazingly enough, says all of this while actually stating very little. The actual Joffrey ballet company primarily practices and performs their works with only intermittent staged episodes, engaging primarily the "actors" of his work. Any conclusions we might make about this "company" are presented in small gestures: the crack of a tendon which ends the career of a great ballerina, a voice raised in anger over the contradictory orders of Mr. A, a series of Band-Aids and bandages removed from a ballerina's foot each night, the indignity of having to move to another barre simply to do one's morning exercises, a work-out of an older

ballerina before the
younger ones arrive,
the dancers' mockery
of their ballet masters
at a private Christ-

mas party, a late-night dinner missed. Yet, the director,
through these little gestures, reveals so much that he
doesn't bother to shout.

On top of that, Altman seems genuinely interested
in actually showing ballet. Unlike so many contemporary directors who seem to think dance is something
better left to the camera, Altman moves his camera
back, time and again, to let us actually see the performers in full perspective. Yes, at moments, just like the
HD Met Opera, he pushes in to see the expression of
his performers (Joffrey was an advocate of a very ex-
pressive quality in his dancing, "pretty" dancing "by the
beat" being his self-declared enemy), but Altman generally moves out to let us actually encounter the entire
performances of great works such as Alwin Nikolais'
Tensile Involvement (the film's opening piece), Arpino's *Light Rain, Suite Saint-Saëns* and *Trinity*, Moses
Pendleton's *White Widow*, Lar Lubovitch's *My Funny
Valentine* (performed in an open Chicago park during
a sudden rainstorm), and even Desrosiers' somewhat ridiculous dance drama *The Blue Snake*. Although some
dance critics did not perceive Altman's mastery, anyone

who truly loves dance will want to see this film. And I'd argue that it represents some of the most fortuitous filming of dance history any film ever made.

LOS ANGELES, JULY 4, 2016
Reprinted from *World Cinema Review* (July 2016).

As I've written in a later My Year *volume, I studied at the Joffrey Ballet Company in New York for several months in 1969. Every night I would attend classes that lasted for at least one or two hours at the barre. I knew, even though in those days I was lean and athletic, that I was probably never going to become a dancer, but after several weeks I was encouraged by one instructor when I did a perfect in-line brisé. I, myself, was amazed at my accomplishment. Yet given my equally lean salary from Columbia University, I could no longer afford my lessons, and realizing that I did not truly have a dancer's body, I soon after left my daily regimen.*

It must have been in that period in New York City when I first attended a performance of the company. I can no longer remember the date. It can't have been as early as 1967 when the Joffrey Company first revived Kurt Jooss' The Green Table, *but I remember that evening as including both that performance and Agnes de Mille's* Rodeo. *It certainly made me want to dance.*

Missing the Ball

SUSANNAH GRANT (SCREENPLAY), STEVEN SODER-
BERGH (DIRECTOR) **ERIN BROCKOVICH** / 2000

I AM CERTAIN that I first saw Steven Soderbergh's film
Erin Brockovich when it premiered in 2000; but I have
seen it so many times since that I no longer can recall
my first feelings about it. Certainly it is the kind of com-
mercial movie that I occasionally enjoy watching—a
morally righteous presentation of an underdog. Erin
Brockovich (Julia Roberts, playing, in this case, the
out-of-work, nearly broke, under-educated mother of
three young children) proves her intelligence and com-
petence by going up against a huge, evil business empire (in this instance, Pacific Gas and Electric), working
with sometimes equal frisson with a small-time lawyer,
Ed Mastry (Albert Finney).

Surely a film that fits so nicely into the genre
(which includes films such as *All the President's Men*
and *Three Days of the Condor*) must have immediately

appealed to me, since I have, admittedly, always secretly defined myself as a sort of outsider prophet. Brockovich's amazing pluck, devotion to her cause, and empathetic embracement of those hundreds of individuals who she discovered had been suffering the cancers and other diseases caused by PG&E's callous use of unlined cooling tanks (containing the dread carcinogenic hexavalent chromium 6) make her the kind of unintentional hero who any moral citizen can admire—despite the fact that this very sexual being (with two previous husbands and, suddenly, a current, live-in boyfriend who is somewhat inexplicably devoted to her children), jokingly describes using her cleavage as entry to the division of county records, and later reports to the astonished law firm working with her boss that she was able to obtain the 600-some signatures necessary because she performed "sexual favors":

> KURT POTTER: Wha...how did you do this?
> ERIN BROCKOVICH: Well, um, seeing as how I have no brains or legal expertise, and Ed here was losing all faith in the system, am I right?
> ED MASRY: Oh, yeah, completely. No faith, no faith....
> ERIN BROCKOVICH: I just went out there and performed sexual favors. 634 blow jobs in five days...I'm really quite tired.

The truth—at least the way the movie portrays it—is apparently that Brockovich's casual dress and down-to-earth manner are what help her to communicate with the Hinkley natives in a way that the lawyers cannot. Even the "Deep Throat"-like revelation of a former Pacific Gas and Electric employee, Charles Embry (Tracey Walker), that the company was ordered from headquarters to destroy evidence, is based on what "she looks like," the fact that she looks like a woman to whom you could tell anything—everything.

All of this helps to make the former Miss Wichita (in truth the real Erin Brockovich was crowned the far more glamorous-sounding "Miss Pacific Coast") an even more miraculous and formidable figure, a woman who, thanks to Julia Roberts, seems to have everything: beauty, family, brains—and suddenly a career! How can you not love this astonishing figure?

But this time, watching the film on my home DVD the other night, something else kept pulling at me. While early on in the film Erin describes herself as a very ordinary person—"I just wanna be a good mom, a nice person, a decent citizen. Just wanna take good care of my kids. You know?"—as the film progresses, she becomes fewer and fewer of any of those things she desires. Even though she eventually is earning enough money to pay for daycare for her children, she continues to leave them in the care of her "biker" neighbor, George (Aaron Eckhart). When, understandably frustrated with her lack of personal interest in him, he leaves her, she proceeds to lug them around both to her office and to her homestead visits of potential clients. We have to presume that she just hasn't been able to find the time to get a proper care person or to enter them into nearby schools.

Previously, she has spent so much time away from them that her son, Matthew (Scotty Leavenworth), and her daughter, Katie (Gemmenne de la Peña), show

 signs of strong re-sentment about their mother's absence, anger which she meets with equal frustration instead of the neces-sary sympathy. Her absences have also meant that she has painfully missed important events in her children's lives, including her youngest daughter's first word, reported by George to have been "ball."

If at times Brockovich seems to be taking a slightly feminist position, arguing, for example, that neither of her children's fathers cared about what *she* might think or feel, at other times in this work it is quite appar-ent that the character is still entirely dependent upon men, particularly the kindness and passivity of George. Obviously, one could argue that this paradox is what faces many women with the competing pulls of family and career, and we sympathize, as does the script, with Brockovich's plight.

Yet we cannot quite escape the fact that this wom-an is still a very needy girl, so desperate for recognition of her abilities, and that she is nearly willing to give any-thing for the attention; as she demands of George:

ERIN BROCKOVICH: For the first time in my life, I

got people respecting me. Please, don't ask me
to give it up.

In fact, she does *not* give "it" up, but does in some very
real ways abandon her children, and most definitely
sacrifices George in the bargain.

Susannah Grant's script attempts to ameliorate
this trade-off slightly by having Erin's son read one of
the dispositions about a young girl his age suffering
from cancer because of chemical effects. And in the
final scene, Brockovich takes George with her to visit
one of the suffering families so that he might see what
he made possible by allowing her to work.

Nonetheless, at film's end, as the former Midwestern beauty queen stands in her office with her
two million dollar check in reward for her remarkable
achievements, we can't help but feel that she has somehow missed the ball—that, at the very least, she has left
something behind.

In real life, if there is such a thing, Brockovich married again, raising her children with her new husband
Eric Ellis, a relationship that also ended in divorce. I
have no information on how her children turned out.
But perhaps the film does hint at some of the tensions that would actually recur later in the real hero's
life. Along with one of her ex-husbands, the character
upon whom George was based attempted to sue her

in a bungled con-job, suggesting that she had had an affair with her boss Ed Mastry. Fortunately, neither Brockovich nor Mas-try took the bait. What is clear, however, is that real life can never be as good or bad as a motion picture portrays it—nor as big or small as the figures it represents.

LOS ANGELES, JULY 26, 2014
Reprinted from *World Cinema Review* (July 2014).

Funeral March

CLAUDE CHABROL, CHARLOTTE ARMSTRONG, AND CAROLINE ELIACHEFF (SCREENPLAY, BASED ON ARMSTRONG'S BOOK *THE CHOCOLATE COBWEB*), CLAUDE CHABROL (DIRECTOR) **MERCI POUR LE CHOCOLAT** / 2000

I HAVE RECENTLY grown quite fond of the films of Claude Chabrol, and so I jumped at the possibility of watching *Merci pour le chocolat* in order to include it in *My Year 2000*, a year in which I did not get a chance to see it.

Several critics have noted that Chabrol is less interested in the motives of his often-twisted characters as he is in the playing out of their psychological disorders, almost as in sophisticated boulevard comedies, however without the farce. There is something of Oscar Wilde or even Noel Coward in Chabrol's works, without, strangely enough, their witty dialogue. But what Chabrol presents in its place is his witty and rich cinematography that captures us almost entirely, taking us into the dark corners of his characters' rooms—and into their illogical thinking.

Merci pour le chocolat, after 50 some films, is the latest of this type. The beautiful home, in this case, belongs to Marie-Claire "Mika" Muller (Isabelle Huppert), heir to the great Swiss chocolatiers, and a strong-minded business woman to boot. We see her in her offices only once, at a board meeting, where she goes head to head with her older arch-enemy Dufreigne (Michel Robin), as she startlingly closes the meeting down before literally laughing at him the moment her office door is closed.

Mika has just been remarried to the sublime pianist André Polonski (Jacques Dutronc), to whom she had been briefly married 18 year earlier. Polonski's second marriage to Lisbeth ended one night on the curving road into town as she drove to get her husband some medicine, the potent Benzodiazepine Rohypnol, to help him sleep. Despite the alcohol and drugs found in her system, no one quite seems to know (or care) how they got there. She drank only one cognac each night, and evidently took no drugs.

Polonski is played as a romantic dreamer, pounding away at the piano throughout each day almost the way a young child might play upon a game board; indeed his own disaffected son, Guillaume (Rodolphe Pauly), whose mother was Lisbeth, does precisely that, settling in at a young age as a couch potato.

It is clear that the remarried couple are not particularly in love, but that the marriage serves both of their purposes. As Polonski observes, Mika's father died "before I could disappoint him." Mika tells a friend that she is not at all in love with the pianist, and has waited for his son to become an adult before reentering the union.

For Polonski it is clear the Muller house offers him what he needs for his study of the piano, a large music room with two grand pianos, and the leisurely space in which to disappear. Mika's reasons are less apparent, but as the movie quickly progresses, we understand early on that she is in love with Polonski's son, Guillaume, and appears intent upon seducing or, perhaps, even raping him.

I'll return to that later.

Into this drawing-room world comes a young, independently-minded pianist, Jeanne Pollet (Anna Mouglalis), as exuberant and spirited as Guillaume is broodingly dead. Jeanne has just discovered, by accident, through a dinner discussion with her mother—a forensics doctor—and a friend, that upon her birth she and a male child were temporarily mixed up in the hospital, she being handed over as Polonski's child. The hospital, having run out of baby bracelets, had marked the children with the first letters of their last name, so

that the POL of Polonski was confused with the POL of Pollet. In any event, the matter was quickly straightened up when Lisbeth awoke, asking to see her baby boy.

The very idea that a great pianist might possibly have been Jeanne's father is utterly fascinating to the talented young pianist just beginning her career. And although the mother Louise reassures her that she is her issue, Jeanne cannot escape the intrigue, going so far as to visit Polonski without an invitation.

She is unconditionally told to go away, but barges ahead into the great pianist's music room, blurting out her story. Before you can say Liszt, he is helping her to play "Funérailles," and introducing her to the wonders of new works.

Losing even more of his father's scant attention, Guillaume sulks deeper into the couch, while Mika, with a great mocking show of motherly-like attention, breaks out her thermos of late-night chocolat (the reason that the American title was *Nightcap*). Mika even invites the young girl upstairs to see Lisbeth's photographs, which cannot help but engage the child, since she is a near-lookalike. One of Chabrol's most brilliant cinematic moments is when Jeanne, staring into the photo of a woman who could be her mother, catches the reflection of Mika, who drops her  filled thermos to the floor.

"Why would a woman purposely drop a thermos of chocolate?" muses Jeanne the next day to her boyfriend, Axel, a young apprentice researcher at Jeanne's mother's hospital. "Why indeed?" Although the viewer has not necessarily perceived it as an intentional act, it is Chabrol's way of loading the dice, creating suspicion even when there is none.

The clever Jeanne, having caught some of the mixture on her sweater, even has the savvy to have Axel check out the chocolate mix in his lab. Sure enough, something's up, since it turns out to be none other than the date-rape drug Rohypnol. That chocolate, we recall, was made particularly for Guillaume! And the implications of that suddenly cast this sparkling comedy into a sinister psychological thriller.

Charmed by the beautiful pianist who looks so much like his former wife, how could Polonski not invite her back, and, finally, ask her to stay for a few days so that he can help her win her upcoming competition?

Jeanne is touched, but her choice to go is almost made for her when, at another mother and daughter meeting, Louise (Brigitte Catillon) reveals that Jeanne is her daughter through artificial insemination. "We have been hiding things, haven't we?" responds the young girl.

Back at the Muller mansion, Jeanne reveals to Guillaume what she knows. But his response, like almost all the adult responses in this film, is one of denial. Why would she intentionally spill the chocolate if she were determined to drug him? It is almost as if Chabrol has set up certain situations to see if he can out-smart himself, or perhaps stir the pot just enough so that there can be no easy answers as to what lies within.

In fact, *Merci pour le chocolat* quickly flows in the direction of even further uncertainties, as Mika, brewing up another thermos of chocolate, is caught spiking Jeanne's coffee in the mirror by Guillaume. Oh dear, Polonski has run out of his Rohypnol again! Jeanne's offer to run into town for the drug is absolutely baffling. But when Guillaume demands to go with her, we see perhaps some sense in the act. "Why did you switch our coffee cups?" asks the suddenly clueless girl of Guillaume.

No matter. Without further ado, she begins to feel the drug's effects and ends up crashing into a stone wall!

Meanwhile, Polonski, suddenly waking up it appears, begins to question his wife. What was she doing with his Rohypnol, etc., until it is impossible for the villain Mika to say anything but confess. Suddenly, the reason for Lisbeth's death becomes quite obvious. The couple had spent the night at the Muller house, with Mika in attendance. A quick call to Jeanne's mother sends her and the police to the young couple's rescue. The two are unhurt, but everyone will soon be paying a visit to the Muller estate.

Tears drop from Mika's eyes before she curls up into the fetal position. Any explanations will come, obviously, after the screen goes black. But who could claim he didn't enjoy the trip?

LOS ANGELES, MARCH 9, 2011
Reprinted from *World Cinema Review* (March 2011).

The Marvelously Loony Imagination of Man

J. RODOLFO WILCOCK **THE TEMPLE OF THE ICONO-CLASTS**, TRANSLATED FROM THE ITALIAN WITH AN IN-TRODUCTION BY LAWRENCE VENUTI (SAN FRANCISCO: MERCURY HOUSE, 2000)

BORN AND RAISED in Argentina, Rodolfo Wilcock, the son of an Englishman and an Italian mother, was involved in the 1940s with the innovative writers of Argentina, including Jorge Luis Borges, Adolfo Bioy Casares, and Silvina Ocampo. He contributed to their anthologies of fantastic literature and wrote poetry. His Argentine writer friends affectionately called him "Johnny." But in the late 1940s, Wilcock increasingly grew repulsed by the Perón dictatorship, and in 1954 traveled to England, working as a commentator for the BBC and as a translator. He returned briefly to Argentina, but in 1957 left the country for Italy. There, in Rome, he began to publish works in Italian; in 1962 he moved to Lubriano, north of Rome, and over the next decade produced 15 books in Italian of all genres, including the 1973 homoerotic novel *I due allegri indiani* (A Couple of Gay Indians). His name, now associated with Alberto Moravio, Elsa Morante, Tommaso Landolfi, and Pier Paolo Pasolini, was  made famous in Italy, in part, by the 1972 publication of *The Temple of Iconoclasts*.

This book consists of numerous histories of basically unknown crackpots, theorists, scientists, inventors, and philosophers whose ideas were either absurd or ridiculously out of sync with rational science. These include figures such as André Lebran, the inventor of the pentacycle, or the five-wheeled bicycle; Charles Piazzi-Smyth, who was convinced that the Egyptian pyramids were originally encased in white limestone blocks, "cut so finely as to be virtually seamless," and that the base of the Great Pyramid, divided by the width of a casing stone, equaled exactly the number of days in a year; and Klaus Nachtknecht, who, believing in the healing powers of radium, encouraged the sale of radioactive soap and planned luxury spas to treat his customers to thermal waters and mud baths that were radioactive. John Cleves Symmes, Cyrus Reed Teed, and Marshall B. Gardner all believed, in different ways, that the core of the earth was hollow and not only affected the surface of the earth but internally consisted of beings and plants such as the mammoths discovered in Siberia and The Eskimos, who came from the interior. The book is filled with such ludicrous ideas that one can only wonder at Wilcock's imagination and—when one discovers that some of his figures were based on real beings (Piazzi-Smyth and the Hollow Earth theorists, for example, truly existed)—the marvelously loony imagination of man.

LOS ANGELES, 2000

Swinging at the Swingers

RICHARD BLACKBURN AND PAUL BARTEL (SCREEN-PLAY), PAUL BARTEL (DIRECTOR) **EATING RAOUL** / 1982

MR. AND MRS. BLAND (Mary Woronov and Paul Bartel) are a perfectly happy couple living in a TV-version world of the 1950s in an appropriately bland apartment, decked-out with Paul's mother's 1950s plates, lamps, and other accessories, double-beds with matching bedspreads, and matching pajamas. The couple has equally bland dreams of opening a restaurant to be called Chez Bland or Paul & Mary's Country Kitchen.

The only trouble is that they are living in the hubristic, self-centered culture of Los Angeles of the late 1970s and early 1980s, when booze, swinging sex, and cocaine were served up at nearly every celebratory event. The long-legged, statuesque Mary is sexually accosted not only by the patients she is nursing, but by the bank manager, Mr. Leech (Buck Henry), from whom she attempts to get a loan. Paul is ogled by a bux-

om woman customer in the liquor store where he works. Even taking down the garbage is an ordeal, as Paul is pulled into a party where Doris the Dominatrix (Susan Saiger) immediately attempts to whip him into submission. Swingers pour into their apartment building, seeking out parties, while the clean-living Blands have, as the film begins, recently had their credit cards cancelled; Paul has just lost his job for ordering a case of Château Lafite Rothschild and refusing to sell his customers the rotgut featured by his boss. Although Mary, in particular, attempts to maintain her natural good spirits, both she and Paul realize that life doesn't seem to be fair. All the swingers seem to have wads of cash.

A space just perfect for their restaurant has recently been discovered by their real estate agent James, who's about to join them for dinner, but how are they going to pay for it in the two weeks they've been given to raise the cash? As if this weren't enough, a drunken swinger forces open their apartment door and attempts to rape Mary. When Paul slugs him in the stomach, he retches all over their bland shag rug, in response to which Mary joyfully sprays the entire room with a fragrant carpet deodorant.

413

After being pulled into the bath- room, the drunken delinquent appears to drown himself in the bathroom toilet,  only, soon after, to revive and, once again, try to rape poor Mary. What is the assaulted couple supposed to do? The quick-thinking Paul picks up their ready frying pan and hits the man over the head, this time truly doing him in. In his billfold they discover several hundred dollars, money which will certainly go well toward that down payment for the restaurant location. With their guest at the door, the couple throw the body into a garbage bag and, after the agent leaves, toss the intruder into the apartment garbage compactor. Now, that wasn't so hard, was it? And Los Angeles now has one less "pervert."

Bartel's dark comedy is so very funny because, even though the Blands are imaginatively living in another era, they are as blinded by selfish motives and are just as violent as the world in which they actually live; in short, they are Americans. Like the batty sisters who kindly poison the lonely men they encounter in the comedy *Arsenic and Old Lace*, the Blands quickly decide to become serial killers with all the good intentions of societal redeemers.

Putting an ad in a local newspaper read by all the swingers, they promise to play any fetish or sexual scenario imaginable; and part of the fun in this world of upside-down morality is the fantasies they are forced to play out: a Nazi camp matron (after that "fantasist's" death, Mary quips, "Why don't you go to bed, honey. I'll bag the Nazi and straighten things up around here."), a hippie chick, and a maniacal nurse. As David Ehrenstein, writing in the DVD's accompanying flyer, describes one of Woronov's best scenes, "...in a Minnie Mouse-like outfit and having served up the latest sex maniac to Paul's trusty frying pan, she sits down, exhausted, in a chair and complains about the heat—as if she were a typical wife finding it hard to unwind after a long, hard day." But now, little by little, the money comes in, as they work, like any ordinary couple, to obtain their American Dream.

The only trouble they encounter comes in the form of a handsome Chicano locksmith, the Raoul of the film's title (played by *Zoot Suit* star Robert Beltran). Raoul, while attempting to  rob the couple, discovers their secrets, and offers to help them by disposing of their victims' bodies: selling the dead men's clothes, rings, hats and other accessories, and rendering up their "meat" as dog food. He shares some of the profits with the couple; but what he doesn't tell them is that he also tracks down the victims' cars, selling them at a huge profit.

Such a symbiotic relationship might have worked, nonetheless, had Raoul not determined to also collect further payment in the form of sex with Mary. Plying her with drugs, he awakens her not so very deeply buried libido, resulting in her secret entry into the very world she and her husband are trying to cleanse. After Raoul blackmails her into a deeper relationship, Paul begins to suspect, following their collaborator, only to discover what he's been doing with the bodies, etc.

Desperate to raise enough for their final downpayment, the couple determine to attend a swingers party themselves, where Mary, once again, encounters the sex-obsessed banker; when he tries to force himself upon her, she is forced to kill him and toss him out a

 bathroom window. And when the couple attempt to retrieve the body, the entire naked group of Swingers, having jumped *en masse* into a hot tub, demand they join them. A nearby space heater, which Paul lobs into the tub, results in a mass murder of the gyrating orgy-participants. This time, they themselves sell the wealthy partygoers' cars!

Hearing of their newfound success, Raoul goes in for the kill, determining to take Paul out of the triangle. The film's title says everything; the trusty frying pan is swung once again, as the Blands sit down to dinner for a final meal with their real estate agent, who comments on how tasty Mary's new dish is. This time they can pay him for the restaurant. And we are left wondering whether the new dish, à la *Sweeney Todd*, has actually made it onto their menu.

LOS ANGELES, JANUARY 20, 2016
Reprinted from *World Cinema Review* (January 2016).

Director Paul Bartel died on May 13, 2000. As I mention in My Year 2014, *I met Bartel a few times, occasionally with Paul Mazursky, at a restaurant/bar across the street* from my home and from the Los Angeles County Museum of Art.

I had first been introduced to Mary Woronov several years earlier at a gallery exhibition, and over the years had spoken with her at Otis College of Art + Design, where she also taught, and at a couple of Consortium (my book distributor) gatherings in New York City. I'd also read extensively about her career working with Andy Warhol through playwright Ronald Tavel, with whom I worked on his proposed book, an experience I've described in My Year 2009.

Finally, Bartel's early film, Private Parts (1972), a noted cinema failure, was done for producer Gene Corman, brother of famed director Roger Corman. Gene and his wife Nan were acquaintances through their involvement with the Los Angeles County Museum of Art, and Howard and I visited their Beverly Hills home at least a couple of times. I've never seen Gene in a suit, since he had the habit of wearing the most beautiful (and obviously expensive) sweaters.

WELLMAN'S CROWTET

A Linguistic Fantasia

MAC WELLMAN **A MURDER OF CROWS** / NEW YORK,
PRIMARY STAGES, APRIL 22, 1992

WITHOUT COMPLAINING ABOUT the very thing I've determined to do, I still have to admit I feel a bit daunted about writing on Mac Wellman's unforgettable play, *A Murder of Crows*. Without any true plot, you might describe this work as more of a linguistic fantasia than a drama peopled with interrelating characters. Although family is vaguely at the center of this play, all is more than slightly askew, as the very set suggests, where Nella stands on a porch without a house attached: "We lost the house," suggests Nella (Anne O'Sullivan) glibly tossing out one of the hundreds of American vernacular terms with which this work engages.

I first saw this play at Primary Stages in late April 1992, and I published it, along with the second of Well-

man's so-called "Crowtet," on my Sun & Moon Press two years later; I reprinted those plays through my Green Integer imprint in 2000, adding the second volume, containing the last two "Crowtet" plays, in 2003. So, I obviously have great affection for and intimate knowledge of the play. Yet it has taken me all this time to attempt to write about it, and I still find it more experiential than explicable.

Let me just suggest that although the characters are slightly related—Susannah (Jan Leslie Harding), her mother Nella, and her brother Andy (the handsome Reed Birney, who stands all in gold throughout as a kind of lawn ornament) having come to live with Nella's brother Howard (William Mesnik) and his unbelievably lucky and mean-hearted wife, Georgia (Lauren Hamilton)—it might be best to think of their interrelationships more as a series of monologues that each satirizes various aspects of contemporary American culture.

Wellman's play is set somewhere in the Midwest (he grew up in Ohio) near a vast "hellacious grease pit" and a nearby reactor which makes the rivers "look like bubble baths, and the air's all mustardy." Nella's husband, Raymond (Stephen Mellor), has evidently been drowned in the pit, and all they have is a shoe left. With feet of different sizes and a dislocated face, Nella is clearly a dependent, in need not only of the begrudging housing (in a chicken coop) that her relatives have provided for her and her daughter, but of inspirational reading matter and spiritual help. She is, in short, a representative of all in American life that is hated, a woman who has been bypassed by any element of the "American Dream." Although her brother Howard is somewhat sympathetic, he himself is impatient with his sister, and particularly her dreamy daughter, whose major focus seems to be a "weather change":

SUSANNAH: The weather is changing, the weather
is changing for sure, I can smell it.
The weather has got a whole wheelbarrow
full of surprises up its sleeve for us.

Not only is she pre-
dicting, like a local
Cassandra, a serious
change in the cli-
mate—leading to sig-
nificant implications

in the environmentally ravaged worlds where many
of Wellman's plays take place—but a change of philosophical, spiritual, even metaphysical significance. For
her, "The moment will come. Everything that is vertical will become horizontal," Time will turn inside out.
In part, of course, Susannah's "strangeness," as Howard
describes it, is simply the desire of any young being for
change. But the change she prophesies is also terrifying, particularly for the hidebound gold diggers whom
Howard and his wife represent.

The wife, Georgia, has not only broken the bank
at Monte Carlo, one of the hundreds of clichés Wellman proudly spouts, but wins big weekly at their atten-
dances at the local horse track, from which she brings
home wheelbarrows full of money. If she can be said to
characterize the dream of all Americans, hooked on a
system that promises enormous, accidental, and unde-
served wealth, she, in her xenophobic hostility of anything outside what she finds to be normal, experiences
little happiness. Berating Raymond's shoes and hats, for

example, she snarls:

> ....Grotesque. Perverted
> If it's possible for a hat to be obscene, his
> hats were obscene. I mean. They made you
> think of things no sane person ought to think
> of, ever. They were not good-looking American
> hats, law-and-order type hats, or patriotic,
> military hats, or socially eminent country
> club or corporate hats.

Later in the play Howard and Nella reveal that their own strange attic-stored hats (fezzes) and clothes were a result of their having as children been gypsies (or pretending to be gypsies) and stealing money from German tourists. Their real family name, so they claim, was Babaghanouj, their great grandfather having been a rug merchant from Istanbul named Nebuchadnezzar. It all reminds one, a bit, of the patriotic, right-wing Eleanor Shaw Iselin from *The Manchurian Candidate*, who near film's end is revealed to be a Communist set on taking over the US.

It is almost inevitable, accordingly, that the shining gold statue, Andy, says nothing and does nothing throughout most of the play, since, as he briefly admits, the excitement aroused in him by bombing Iraqi cities has taken him into a higher plain of being than any of the family members can comprehend.

Like most American comedies, Wellman's *Murder of Crows* predictably ends happily as the dead father Raymond reappears, rising from his coffin, having, he admits, been living all these years with the crows. As confused and mysteriously baffled as his daughter, he would go on living with them, he vows, if he weren't allergic to their feathers. Released from her earth-bound bondage by his sudden resurrection, and by her mother's symbolic death as she retreats into the coffin the husband has left, Susannah discovers she is not at all allergic to their wings, and joins up with the busy crows, who, somewhat like the cartoon figures of Heckle and Jeckle, sit apart, at play's end, discussing interminably deep and unanswerable philosophical issues:

> What if we are Type A entities.
> That is, what if we contextualize
> and explain the existences of
> others but cannot, on pain of
> infinite regress, be contextualized
> or explained ourselves?

Yet, while these seemingly profound figures nicely close down Wellman's hilarious look at the "State of the Onion," it is important to remember that in other cultures, such as in Japan, crows represent ominous forces of evil for the human species. One can only wonder, accordingly, whether the author is suggesting that in both Andy and Susannah we have lost, as a people, our only dreamers to realms that have no effect on our daily lives. Never mind, hints the witty writer, that these crows "look more like mynas or parrots than real crows: i.e., they're fake crows." In a world built of language anything is possible or nothing *is*.

Beware: the forces hovering over the second play of Wellman's quartet are Macaws.

LOS ANGELES, JANUARY 13, 2013
Reprinted from *US Theater, Opera, and Performance* (January 2013).

In 2017, after watching the Tony Awards, in which actor Reed Birney won a Tony for his performance in The Humans *on Broadway (a year after his equally acclaimed performance in the William Inge revival of* Picnic*), I wrote Mac a short and rather cryptic message:*

> *I turned on the TV last night and there was beautiful little Andy—all grown old. What a difference a few decades makes.*

When I didn't hear from him after a few days, I

wrote him again:

> *Since you didn't respond to my cryptic message of the other day about Reed Birney's winning a Tony, perhaps you may have forgotten that he was in your* Murder of Crows.
>
> *Also, I just saw David Lang's* Anatomy Theater. *How was he to work with? This new work is quite fascinating—although never saw your drama because Long Beach Opera couldn't get me a review ticket for a matinee. I just can't drive all the way down to Long Beach at night! And drive back yet, arriving after midnight.*
>
> *In any event...just curious how you are and what you're doing?*
>
> *Love,*
>
> *D*

I also reminded him that, at the time, he said that he wanted beautiful people in his productions, and Reed Birney, in his youthful days, was most certainly just such a person.

This time he did respond, explaining that my note was, in fact, too cryptic. Mac had also worked with the opera composer Lang on an opera, The Difficulty of Crossing a Field, *an opera performed for two years at the local Long Beach Opera, which I, as I explain above, had unfortunately missed.*

My life has always been lived according coincidence, and at the very moment I determined to add this note, in late afternoon, July 17th, Mac emailed me:

> *Douglas: And aside from all the Andies—how are you doing these days? Hope all is well! I'm taking it easy before I go to Italy for a week to teach in Umbria—ah yes! Love, Mac*

I took this as a sign, as always, that what I was writing about was connected with the world around me.

Music from Another World

MAC WELLMAN **THE HYACINTH MACAW** / PER-
FORMED ABOARD THE QUEEN MARY SHIP, LONG BEACH,
CALIFORNIA / THE PERFORMANCE I SAW WAS ON
MARCH 12, 2011

AS THE PUBLISHER of Mac Wellman's two-volume
set of plays *Crowtet*, and other Wellman fictions, plays,
and books of poetry, I have grown so used to the praise
that most often accompanies his performances and
publications that I was a bit shocked by the series of
quite negative reviews in the local press for the second
of the *Crowtet* plays, *The Hyacinth Macaw*, performed
recently by the California Repertory Company aboard
the Queen Mary ship in Long Beach.

I have always thought of *The Hyacinth Macaw*,
along with the first of the series, *A Murder of Crows*, as
one of Mac's best works, and I included that play in the
anthology we edited together, *From the Other Side of
the Century II: A New American Drama 1960-1995*. I

had seen *A Murder of Crows* at Primary Stages in New York City way back in 1992; the third play of the *Crowtet* quartet, *Second-Hand Smoke*, was performed as a reading by the Bottom's Dream group in Los Angeles in a series of readings over two years, which I co-sponsored. I also saw a reading of that play in New York. Bottom's Dream presented the premiere of the final *Crowtet* play, *The Lesser Magoo,* in 1997, a production which I attended. Accordingly, *The Hyacinth Macaw* was the only play of the series I had not seen, and I thought it a lovely idea to dine on the Queen Mary and stay overnight in the ship's hotel with my companion and friends Marty Nakell and Rebecca Goodman.

Like most of Wellman's work, *The Hyacinth Macaw* is filled with wonderfully irrational language along with what appear to be everyday aphorisms, parables, and commercial-like babble. The combination allows almost all of Wellman's works to straddle two fences: his characters and locale are often middle-class Midwesterners, behaving—or, at least, attempting to behave—like everyone else, while suddenly finding themselves in a tangled, bizarre series of metaphysical conundrums for which they have simply not been prepared.

In *The Hyacinth Macaw* the typical American family living in Gradual, Ohio (a town with "a gym, a school, a mall, all the normal things") comes face to face with Mister William Hard—representative clear-

ly of all the "hard" things they will have to face—who tells the daughter Susannah what she has always wanted to hear, that she's an orphan, a "useless yanked-up thing." Presenting a letter to Dora, Susannah's mother, he reveals, moreover, that the father, Ray, is a duplicate and is doomed to leave the family forever, which seems somewhat agreeable to both husband and wife. They are, after all, bored with the complacency of their lives, Ray revealing that years before, when he was "a kid," "I went crazy, and they hauled me off to a nut house." He tells of writing a perverted drama, "dwelling on the topic of lips and thighs." Over the years, although the urges have not abated, he has "trained" those urges with "patience, and little sweet gifts, cookies, chocolates and the like."

Dora reveals a longing to escape as well, and in the final act leaves her home with Mad Wu, who whisks her away to the nearby town of Moon Hat.

In the final scene Susannah and William Hard, her now surrogate father, bury the sick and dying moon, clearly suffering from the world's lack of romanticism.

In short, Wellman's play seems like Albee's *American Dream* blended up with large doses of soap opera events and coated with a thick compound of linguistic play and word wizardry which thoroughly amuses and confounds us. So  what's not to like? And why describe his play, as did the reviewer Joel Beers of the *OCWeekly*, as "an adolescent episode of theatrical dementia," or accuse it, as Greggory Moore of *Greater Long Beach*, of suffering from the "imitative fallacy," a work that in talking about boredom, imitates boredom?

The director, James Martin, has long worked with Wellman, producing one of the best productions, *Cellophane*, I have ever seen, and overseeing several others, including *The Lesser Magoo*. Yet here, I am afraid, he has lost some of Wellman's necessarily quick pacing, and by the last scenes the play begins to lag.

Certain scenes, such as the father's long and absurdly funny farewell, were played too much for laughs. In the script the father drinks only water, but in Martin's version, he increasingly imbibes wine, getting drunker and drunker in the process. The problem with such a literal reading as this is not only that it takes our attention away from the father's words, but seems to suggest his long-winded, somewhat meaningless chatter can be explained away: he's just drunk. In truth, Ray's speech is filled with a kind pathos that is crucial to our feelings for him:

> I see myself a feckless youth hardened by
> prolonged abstinence and chilblains, aghast,
> alone, in agony. I see myself, a young shoe-
> salesman on the windy plains of West Gradual,
> where the Bug River hyphenates the mighty Ohio
> with its moxie doodle, a cipher, a tragic hipster,
> a tramp. I encounter the notorious Mu Factor
> in the sad, shanty towns of Shenango and deem
> myself wise with the leer of unholy knowingness.

As in Allen Ginsberg's *Howl*, there is a sort of self-centered, self-loathing poetry in Ray's speech, a kind of poetic richness that transcends his ordinariness. Wellman's works are filled with these kind of poetic moments, when despite their drab lives, the characters speak out momentarily in a dream of wonderment.

Dora gets her turn in the next scene with her daughter:

> The time comes when you hear the music
> from another world. You know the
> music is from another world because
> it is so sad and strange you feel
> as if you awakened from a dream,

flung your fists out in a nightfever
and caught a living sparrow in your
hand. Only, the bird sings a piercing
wildnote threnody that drives you
unwilling straight to the center of
things.

Actress Lysa Fox in the production on the Queen
Mary played this scene nearly perfectly by performing it straight, as if she were saying the most ordinary
thing she might say day after day. Some of the others in
this production simply *acted* too much, which can kill
a Wellman play before it can puff up to its full poetic
confection. Or perhaps I should say, they tried *too hard*.
Like Mad Wu's song in the penultimate scene—

I sleep in the woods
    all day, all night;
If I don't finish this song
    There's no one around
To tell me I'm wrong;
    or, worse, that I'm right.

—there must always be a sort of casual insanity about
what is spoken in *The Hyacinth Macaw*. If the actors
take the lines too seriously, they destroy both the poetry and the fun.

I don't think that explains the hostility of the local critics, but it does account for their lack of comprehension. It's not that Wellman's plays are so difficult. They just have to be buoyantly performed in order to succeed—a hard thing to do in a country where acting is still somewhat attached to *method*. For there is no method to Wellman's sad and joyous madness.

LOS ANGELES, MARCH 18, 2011
Reprinted from *US Theater, Opera, and Performance* (March 2011).

You Can't Go Home Again

MAC WELLMAN **SECOND-HAND SMOKE** (PUBLISHED
IN *CROWTET 2*, LOS ANGELES: GREEN INTEGER, 2003)

IT MUST HAVE BEEN around 1996, the year in which
Mac Wellman's third work of his *Crowtet* quartet premiered at Fordham University, that I co-produced a
reading of the play with the theatre company Bottom's
Dream in Los Angeles. When I now look back on that
reading, I remember it fondly, as I did when I reread
the play before my Green Integer publication of the
work, along with *The Lesser Magoo,* in 2003. But reading it again, yesterday, I was struck by how little of this
rich text I had assimilated, the experience feeling as if it
were the first time I had encountered it.

I missed what was perhaps a wonderful production of it in New York in 1997 at Primary Stages, with
my friend, the legendary actor and playwright David
Greenspan, playing Mister Glitter, along with Vera
Farmiga as Linda, Johann P. Adler as Susannah, and

David Patrick Kelly as William Hard.

What really struck me this time about Wellman's whole *Crowtet* series is not only its nostalgic approach to an American landscape which the characters, young and old, can barely abide and which is not-so-slowly destroying them through its vast corporate greed and incompetence, but the radioactive quagmire into which it has been transformed. If the inhabitants of the dying community Gradual, Ohio are all rather strange, chalk it up to the effects of the toxic "smaze" which blankets the region, the gradual deaths imposed

upon its youths in the drudgery boredom of days working at Days Inn. Is it any wonder that the citizens of the region have all been transformed into mad bats, pesky rats, and roaming cats?

The local executive Mister Glitter begins the play buried in pseudo-scientific language which he clearly is unable to comprehend:

> Lever escapement. An escapement in which
> a pivoted lever, made to oscillate
> by the escape wheel, engages a balance

staff and causes it to oscillate.

A, impulse roller; B, notch; C, lever;
D, ruby pin.

So engaged in such seemingly meaningless instructions and equations $X = a \log (a + a^2 + y + a@\text{-}y)$ is Mister Glitter that he has no time and certainly no patience for traveling-salesman-like visitors such as Harry Custom, or even his own employee who is determined to introduce Glitter to the visitor, Mister Phelan.

Like most busy executives, Glitter is emphatically self-centered and determinedly rude, brushing off not only Custom, but the visiting Sylvia Palista, a representative of a federal agency of which even she cannot recall the name. If at first Glitter seems a bit more polite and inquisitive about the agency guest, it is only because she is an attractive woman who might bring back a negative report to her agency. But when he finally challenges her to produce some credentials, she is found not even to be listed in the agency book, and is even more rudely ousted than Custom, who has quietly remained at the center of power.

Suddenly, near the end of the day, all three men drop their pants, don "fustenellas and the tarboosh," close the drapes, and dance a "disturbing and gloomy rock song with the lyric":

Close the drapes
Aunt Wednesday
is changing.

If in the first play of the *Crowtet* Susannah and her crow-fixated father, Raymond, claimed that they had donned fezzes and outlandish costumes because they were gypsies in their early lives, the current denizens of Gradual and its nearby hamlets, according to William Hard in the third act of this play, "ape these things to appropriate what's foreign. Foreign-ness." Like small-town Shriners, the citizens of this festering "Land of Evening" simply make up the reasons for their strange behavior in their "Quasi-religious, quasi-mystical, quasi-scientific" Americaness, attempting to regain the "foreign and forbidden" that was once part of their immigrant pasts.

The more I see and read Wellman's theater, the more I realize that he has created a kind of grand world akin to Oz where everyone proclaims himself as a kind of wizard, growling out, as does Mister Phelan in the First Entr'acte, murky conjurations that keep the reality of their not-knowing at a distance.

In the terrifying second "rats" section of Wellman's touching inversion of Americana, two young girls challenge themselves to stay atop Mister Phelan's

 house as long as they possibly can, entertaining themselves and passing the time in absurdly childish and sometimes terrifyingly witty games that include every maxim, piece of jargon, advertising jingle, state slogan, cliché, and nonsensical patter that they have overheard from the surrounding adults. The be-fezzed Mister Phelan peeks through the blinds, conjuring up a magical weirdness that even these young girls, Linda and Susan, realize is utterly bizarre. But how else are they to entertain themselves in a world enveloped in such an "evil cloud." Their seemingly meaningless banter may sound, as the *Variety* reviewer Howard Waxman summarizes, like a dialogue that "melts into a jumble of syllables with mysteries we don't care to solve," but how better might they escape the shopping center realities of the world they inhabit? Indeed, I might suggest that the rhythmic chattering of these rats sometimes evolves into a kind a pure poetry that, as William Carlos Williams declared, represents the "pure products of America" gone crazy.

The play, in fact, ends in a kind of tragic dirge for howling "cats" as, from the opposite direction of the two young girls' binocularly-contained gaze, Susannah and William Hard of the previous two plays return to the place where their voyage has begun. Having failed in her attempt to find what Bishop Berkeley describes as "bedazzlement," to discover "a totally different place: where / angels sing, and the dialectical urge / may be laid to rest forever," the worn-out Susannah is ready to return to "The Junior college at Ping Pong, / ...to study typing, theater arts, and waste management," to work as all the others do, changing light bulbs at Days Inn.

Forced by her mentor, Mister William Hard, Susannah spends the last several stanzas of this sad soliloquy reciting the renunciations of her would-be teacher. Like the suddenly exposed Wizard of Oz, Susannah, in Hard's voice, surrenders her dreams, her magic, her perceived indifference to what she has attempted to leave behind:

I, MISTER WILLIAM HARD, Doctor of
    Divinity,
Gradualness and Equidistance, renounce
both river and craft. I surrender my
magical powers to Baron Samedi, Lord of
the Dead. I renounce both Bug River
and the needle of its dream. I renounce
slambang what is rigid and straight, and
what wiggles. And all the craft of Wicca,
whether of the Tribe of Gradual or the
Tale of the Bug.

I renounce all these because...my heart is broke.

What Susannah discovers, however, is what Judy Garland's Dorothy never quite came to realize: despite one's fervent desire, Wellman reiterates, you can never go home again, no matter how many times you tap the heels of your ruby-covered feet. For Susannah, "nothing happens." As the always on-the-prowl pedant Mister William Hard exclaims:

> This is what happens,
> Susannah, when
> the scene is too big for the frame;
> this is what happens when the frame
> can NEVER be filled.

No matter how much her heart is broken, no matter how few of her dreams have come to be realized, Susannah somewhat tragically discovers that her experience is now too large to allow her to slip back into the confines from which she has escaped.

LOS ANGELES, AUGUST 22, 2014
Reprinted from *American Theater, Opera, and Performance*
   (August 2014).

There are No Such Things as Crows

MAC WELLMAN **THE LESSER MAGOO** (PUBLISHED IN
CROWTET 2, LOS ANGELES: GREEN INTEGER, 2003)
MAC WELLMAN **THE LESSER MAGOO**, PERFORMED
BY BOTTOM'S DREAM THEATER AT THE IVY SUBSTA-
TION, CULVER CITY, CALIFORNIA, 1998

EVEN IF YOU cannot "go home again," Wellman suggests in the final installation of his astounding *Crowtet* series of plays, *The Lesser Magoo*, some few do slink
back into the fold, becoming re-assimilated into a
world even more brutal, perhaps, than the one they left.

The first scene of Wellman's play may read simply
as an intense interrogation of a man, Mr. Torque, who
cannot properly answer the questions because—just
like the audience—he does not entirely understand the
questions. However, I remember it (from the original
1998 production as performed by Bottom's Dream
in Culver City, California and directed by Katherine

Owens) as an intensely horrifying interchange between a would-be employee and his future bosses who can't wait to torture him. So absurd are the interchanges between Torque and Mr. Candle and his assistant Ms. Curran—to say nothing of the appearance of a former, now dead employee, Joegh Bullock—that we feel we have entered the territory of a spy story, where the hero (if Torque can ever be described as a "hero") must suffer a torturous interrogation to survive the insanity of the questioners and their assumptions. If in *Second-Hand Smoke* numerous characters, particularly those in high industrial positions, spoke in seemingly meaningless phrases, here they patter on as if they were speaking of some mythical world out of a fictional creation such as the *Harry Potter* tales:

> CURRAN: And, Mister Torque, do you know the
> precise location of the Bad Place?

That Torque has in fact gone to Princeton to obtain an education in these arcane facts turns the entire series of interchanges into a hilariously absurd situation, at which we can only nervously laugh, being totally un-educated in such a baffling illogic.

> TORQUE: The Bad Place lies deep within the Forest
> of Whim. In the deep, interior regions.

CURRAN: And?

TORQUE: And he holds sway there who stamps with a silver hoof.

If all their talk sounds a bit like a strange religion which employees are required not only to share but to reiterate as a creed of sorts, well...I am sure Wellman, given the concerns of many of his plays, would welcome the analogy. What began as a sort of collegial nonsense of shared social organizations akin to the Masons, the Odd-Fellows, or the Shriners has now become a required value system of dark magical beliefs unable to be questioned. The somewhat bizarre dances of foreign and forbidden phrases has hardened into required systems of fabrications which if questioned immediately define one as an "unusualist."

So terrifying are the beliefs uttered by Curran, her boss Candle, and even the interviewee that any theatergoer or reader of Wellman's four plays will cringe when we, soon after, come to discover that the mean-spirited Curran—whose questions Mr. Torque least understands—may be the lost dreamer Susannah of the plays previous.

If this first horrifying act is characterized by the author as a "bounce"—a bump or thump as a crate dragged down the steps (as defined in *Webster's New World Dictionary*)—the second longer act of this play is defined as being a series of "ricochets," as these monstrous beings and others—including Candle's wife Ruth, his daughter Tessara, an old speechless man, Mr. Foss, a mindless literary figure, Gabriel Pleasure, an ex-senator and country-cousin of Candle, Candle Prosper, and a strange woman from Central Asia, Aunt Sycorica—gather at Candle's country estate for an all-day dinner party. Like most such grand gatherings, no one says anything of value to anyone else; indeed hardly anyone can communicate for more than an instant. If Foss says nothing and the ghost of Joegh Bullock, despite his pleas, remains unseen and unheard, so too do all the attendees of the grand event organized by Mr. Shimmer (a relative perhaps of Mister Glitter in the last play?). Much like the two young girls, Susan and Linda of *Second-Hand Smoke*, who turn every sentence into a series of patter songs, Candle's guests grab every random phrase to bring it into meaninglessness through a musical concatenation, as did most early musical comedies which Wellman's play joyfully mocks:

> CURRAN: [*in response to a comment by Gabriel Pleasure*] How clever. First generation scarehead stuff. And I had you pegged as an unabhorrent. Albeit an unusual one.

> *Gives her a look, and*

then bursts into song:
GABRIEL PLEASURE: Scam. Scam. Scaly scam.
    Climb the side-pipes
        and back again.
    Oh, steady state. Steady state. Steady state,
    Steady state. Steady state. Steady state.
    My stick-dad named
    Pellagra.

This goes on for two more pages!

Among these *Midsummer Night's Dream*-like fools, only the innocent and young Tessara, the almost missing and always disappearing Foss, and the pleading ghost seemingly have anything to offer, and by Act III, they alone, followed by the all-too-knowing Curran, retreat into a glade deep within the interior of the forest, which may, in fact, be the location of the Bad Place.

It is only in Tessara's faltering perceptions and  self-evaluations and Curran's attraction to her that we finally realize that the formerly wild young Susannah knows that she has now completely lost her way, having turned into someone she used to so bitterly hate. And for the first time in the play, she admits, "I'm not so sure of a lot of things." Although that may be a good sign, it is also clear that she is now unredeemable, that she is now "odious and pathetic."

Only Tessara can see the dead, can hear the unwanted pleas of Joegh Bullock's ghost. And only Tessara is ready to admit that she doesn't know the language of those about her: "I don't even know what a Julia set is." The previously quiescent Foss speaks, declaring that Tessara, even if a little "piffle-headed," is too good "for this rat's-ass sewer of a Moonhat." Foss ends up even denying the route that Susannah had previously taken in her search for a way out: "There are no such thing as crows."

Just as Susannah had temporarily tried to escape the world in which she was entrapped, Tessara—like the small Roman tablet of wood or ivory that was used as a token—has a ticket to leave, to travel out of the ruined world inhabited and partially created by her father and mother.

A golden light surrounds her at the moment she transcends into the heavens, allowing, at least, Susannah's imagination to "carom," rebound into space, transfigured as another, before turning back into the whirling dance of death, like the *tarantella* she hints of in her last lines: "Taratantara. Taratantara. Taratantara."

LOS ANGELES, AUGUST 28, 2014
Reprinted from *US Theater, Opera, and Performance* (August 2014).

Two American Satires

Speaking in Tongues

FRAN ROSS **OREO** (NEW YORK: GREYFALCON
HOUSE, 1974); REPRINTED WITH A FOREWORD BY
HARRYETTE MULLEN (BOSTON: NORTHEASTERN UNI-
VERSITY PRESS, 2000)

I RECENTLY REREAD Fran Ross' wonderful satire,
Oreo, and enjoyed it even more than my original encounter. I first heard about this title at the Page Moth-
ers Conference at the University of California, San Diego, in March of 1999, organized by Fanny Howe and
Rae Armantrout. There Harryette Mullen spoke of the
book which she had accidently come upon, noting, as
she does in the Foreword to this new printing, that the
work failed to "find its audience,"

> possibly because in the process of commingling
> two ghettoized vernaculars, African American
> and Yiddish, the novel also draws on material

that both black and Jewish readers might find offensive, perplexing, or incomprehensible. Ross' double-edged satire includes a Jewish immigrant who retains a voodoo consultant Dr. Macumba; a reverse-discrimination tale of an all-black suburb where a local ordinance is selectively enforced to keep white people from moving into the neighborhood; a black radio producer's script of an advertisement for Passover TV dinners; ...and a fight in which Oreo beats a predatory pimp to a pulp while wearing only a pair of sandals, a brassiere, and a mezuzah.

Moreover, the stereotypes of racial jokes abound. "Dialects, bilingual and ethnic humor, inside jokes, neologisms, verbal quirks, and linguistic oddities" occur at regular intervals throughout the work. One might add that the heroine's brother sings his communications in a private language, while her mother transforms her difficulties into algebraic formulas. The book is not only filled with formulas, recipes, lists, questionnaires, and riddles, but it comically parallels the adventures of Theseus, his voyage to the underground, and his encounters with the Amazons, Phaedra, Hippolytus, Peretithous, Helen, and the Minotaur. Indeed Ross' work is not a novel, but a vast picaresque of the American landscape, with Athens transformed into New York.

It sounded like the perfect kind of book for Sun

 & Moon or Green Integer, and soon after, I found a copy of the original and devoured it; discovering the book's editor was listed in the New York telephone directory, I began the slower process of trying to obtain the rights; unknown to me, Harryette had already been in touch with Northeastern University Press, and before I was even able to make a formal offer, the book was published in their Library of Black Literature, an appropriate place.

I seems hard to believe, however, that *Oreo* has yet to find a wide readership, 10 years later. Ross' bawdy take on American life features a half-black, half-Jewish heroine who like a comic-book character successfully overcomes thousands of obstacles—lack of money, prejudice and hatred, sexism and abuse, and just plain ignorance—that face her upon her voyage to discover her identity. Oreo's greatest defense is what she calls WIT (the Way of the Interstitial Thrust), on the surface of the story a kind of mix of jiu-jitsu, karate, kung-fu, and numerous other movements; but in the work's poetic truth, WIT represents her ability to speak, parody, imitate, twist, mock, and translate almost any form of language she encounters. And it is this verbal wit that stands at the center of this book.

Indeed, Ross' jumps, splices, cuts, fissures, and all-out leaps of language might remind one of the slightly later experiments of "language" writing. Like that poetry, the reader has sometimes to make his or her own associations and choices of meaning in order to successfully maneuver Ross' pages. But the experience is always worth the trip:

Oreo on the subway

She was too preoccupied to observe noses, mouths, and shoes and award prizes. She did overhear someone say impatiently, "No, no, Mondrian's the lines, the boxes. Modigliani's the long necks."

And: "She a Jew's poker. Take care the sinny-goge fo' 'em on Sat'd'ys."

This gave her an idea whose ramifications she considered during the ride. Distractedly, she doodled on her clue list. Her basic doodles were silhouettes of men facing left and five-lobed leaves. Her subconscious view of her father as a mystery man? A pointless, quinquefoliolate gesture to the Star of David? No. Silhouettes and leaves were what she drew best. Next to her profiles and palmates, she made a line of scythelike question marks. Next to that, she sketched an aerial view of a cloverleaf highway, her gunmetal-gray divisions making a cloisonné of the ground. Then with offhand but decisive sweeps, she crossed "Kicks," "Pretzel," "Fitting," "Down by the river," and "Temple" off her list.

This event occurs after Oreo has described her hilarious life in Philadelphia for half the book and gone off to find her father, bedding down for the night in Central Park near a family of dog food-eating midgets, and battling it out with a pissed-off pimp and his long-hung monster sex fiend, Kirk.

The list she refers to above are some of the clues her father has given her to find him, and in her quirky searches, she somewhat reminds one of a Paul Auster-like detective, settling on chance. Ultimately she encounters him briefly just before his accidental death (an accident which she and a dog precipitate); in that short meeting, moreover, she discovers he has left something for her, the clue of which is hidden in one of her father's books.

Daring fate, Oreo sneaks back into his house, pretending to be a caretaker for his current wife's children. There she discovers the clue, unravels it, and collects her heritage: her father's sperm kept in a nearby clinic.

Sperm? This woman of wit has used her abilities to speak in tongues not only to overcome obstacles but, like some Amazon warrior, has been able to wrest reproduction from male dominance; by book's end, she is in control of the future, not only her own future but the possible future of others as she ponders whether to sell her inheritance to her bigoted Jewish grandfather or to destroy the stuff.

The chapter closes with her whispering to herself: *Nemo me impune lacessit* (No one attacks me with impunity). Like Theseus, Oreo has finally won her throne, becoming the King-Queen of her empire. Seldom have we witnessed such a powerful figure in American fiction, and none them has been as funny.

LOS ANGELES, FEBRUARY 12, 2010
Reprinted from *American Cultural Treasures* (February 2010).

Out of Step

DONALD OGDEN STEWART **AUNT POLLY'S STORY OF MANKIND** (NEW YORK: GEORGE H. DORAN, 1923)

AN EARLY FRIEND of F. Scott Fitzgerald's, Donald Ogden Stewart lived, for most of his life, in a charmed world. After graduating from Yale University, Stewart began writing satires in the manner of Ring Lardner, Dorothy Parker, and others, and, while writing for Broadway, become a member of the renowned Algonquin Round Table. After a stint in Paris, where he developed close friendships with Hemingway (he was the model for Bill Gorton in *The Sun Also Rises*), Dos Passos, Tristan Tzara, and numerous others, he returned to write screenplays for Hollywood, winning an Oscar for his adaptation of his friend Philip Barry's *The Philadelphia Story*. Previously he had also adapted Barry's *Holiday*, and written the screenplays for *That Uncertain Feeling* and *Life with Father*, among others. Djuna Barnes' interview with him in 1930 was brimming with sarcasm at his enormous successes. At interview's end Barnes finally comes full out with her disdain for him:

> We said: "Do you want to die?"
> "No," he answered lightly, "do you?"
> "We don't mind," we answered, stepping into the night.

One of Stewart's most noted satirical works, *Aunt Polly's Story of Mankind*, a seemingly gentle riff on WASP culture and values, sat for years in my library until I recently aired it out.

Aunt Polly, concerned about the education and behavior of her sister's three children, takes it upon herself over a period of a few weeks to share with them her version of the history of mankind, a delightfully Panglossian tale of the endless progress of man from caveman to the present day, culminating in the perfect family of herself, her husband Frederick, a banker, and her sweetly behaved son, David.

Sweeping them up into her limousine after school, Polly skims over various historical periods, "Egypt and Mesopotamia," "Greece," "Rome and the Christian Crusaders," and "European Monarchies and the American Revolution," portraying them each as a "step forward" to "The Glorious Present," a post-World War

I paradise of her family's wealth and privilege in a world where there will never again be war.

The perfect David is contrarily shown by the author to be an absolute monster who poisons his dog, begins fights from which he runs, and financially takes advantage of his classmates.

Meanwhile, his cousins Samuel and Samuel's two sisters, who have obviously grown up in a more liberal atmosphere, are naturally curious, and pepper Polly with numerous questions that she determines are certain signs of their impoliteness, discouraging, accordingly, any deeper entry into her bumbling recounting of the past.

> "Egyptians did build up a certain form of civilization although of course the wrong form and did not last."
>
> "How long did it last, Aunt Polly?" asked Samuel.
>
> "Why—I think about five or six thousand years," replied Polly.
>
> "That's longer than America, isn't it?" said

Mary.

"Why, yes, dear," replied Aunt Polly, 'but, children, you must remember that all that happened a long, long time ago when time didn't really matter so much.' ...An Egyptian didn't have anything to do all day compared to a person to-day. He had no magazines, no books, no shopping, no church work, no lectures, no social duties, so, don't you see, time didn't really matter."

Had Stewart kept his entire tale at this level, however, we might consider this a slightly humorous piece, without any serious satirical bite. But Polly's bland musings on "the best of all possible worlds" are constantly undercut by the series of good deeds she, the church, and the school inflict upon the children, with David as the centerpiece.

After the children are told about the Crusaders and visited soon after by a war veteran, her husband and her son cook up the idea of creating a crusader group of young boys, with David as their leader.

The boys proudly march for a while, but David's dog gets in the way, and the boys soon lose their patience with the child's pointless commands. A day later, the dog is found dead, and David insists it is the work of another school class. Now with an enemy on the horizon, most of the boys return to their marching. Frederick buys them uniforms, and, with his father's help, David purchases air-rifles at a discount, selling them back to the boys at the regular price. The crusader company is formed, and the other class develops its own competing group. When the church gets involved, they change their name to the Christian Scouts.

David's cousin, Samuel, however, refuses to join, and is labeled a "slacker" by David and the other boys, who refuse to speak to him. Joining up with the only black and Jewish boys in the school, Samuel begins a newspaper. Insisting that he intends to investigate the poisoned dog episode, David and others begin to fear what he might say, ultimately dressing, like Klu Klux Klan members, in white robes, beating up Samuel, destroying his printing press, and frightening his partners off.

The two competing Christian Scout troupes, meanwhile, plan to march in the Armistice Day Parade, to show themselves ready to fight. All the Allies are represented by flags the boys carry, but as they meet one another upon the stage, the two groups cannot resist an all-out battle; only David escapes unharmed. The book ends with him safely ensconced in his bed counting out the money he has earned from his rifle sales.

Stewart's parody, accordingly, has some tooth: not only does he comically predict World War II, but he unknowingly points to his own end. During the Mc-

Carthy era, Stewart was "named" as a Communist and was blacklisted in 1950. A year later he emigrated to England where he lived out his life. He died in 1980 at the age of 86.

LOS ANGELES, FEBRUARY 19, 2010
Reprinted from *American Cultural Treasures* (February 2010).

In a Tight Spot

JOEL COEN AND ETHAN COEN (WRITERS AND DIRECTORS) **O BROTHER, WHERE ART THOU?** / 2000

YOU CAN ALMOST hear the Coen boys giggling when they prefaced their comedic masterwork, *O Brother, Where Art Thou?*, with a translation of the opening line of Homer's *The Odyssey*, "O Muse! Sing in me, and through me tell the story...." The story they tell is not exactly Homer's, but it has enough clever parallels to please almost any classicist and pique the interest of almost any literate moviegoer.

The escape from the Parchman Farm by Ulysses Everett McGill (George Clooney)—chained, for life it seems, to the not so very bright Pete (John Turturro) and Delmar (Tim Blake Nelson)—begins with a hilarious attempt by the three to hitch a ride on a freight car. Ulysses (better known as Everett in the Coens' telling) makes it on, and finally Pete, as Delmar fails, pulling the other two back to earth with the recognition that, like the mythical man, the foolishness and mutiny of his crew will result in failure for the hero time and again. He is, after all,  the only one of the three with the ability for abstract thought.

Everett has told them he has buried $1½ million he has stolen from an armored car, a treasure that needs to be retrieved quickly before it is flooded over in the creation of a new hydroelectric project in Arkabulta Lake. Yet the three are apparently going nowhere—that is until they meet up with Tiresias, the blind prophet who predicts their future, while carrying them away on a slow-moving railroad hand car.

At Pete's cousin's house, they are freed from their chains, whereupon Everett carefully applies his Dapper Dan pomade (later the self-conscious lothario is seen wearing a hair-net), one of his ridiculous eccentricities that gets him into trouble throughout their voyage. And no sooner do they get a moment to rest in the cousin's barn than their Poseidon, the sheriff, rolls in, the cousin having turned them in for a monetary re-ward. If Ulysses was a hero, this modern-day version is a terrified fool, shouting over and over again, "We're in a tight spot!" Despite a fire, they escape.

They are now stuck in the middle of nowhere, sitting in a field as they ponder what each might do with their money. Everett will return to his family, he declares, while Pete is determined to become a maître d'; Delmar plans to buy a family farm.

Before long they are on the road again, this time to encounter the Lotus Eaters in a mass gathering of the religious congregation of seemingly hypnotized believers heading toward the river to have their sins washed away. The event is so mesmerizing that Delmar quickly joins in, joyful at having a chance for a new start.

Their accidental meeting with a young black man, Tommy Johnson (Chris Thomas King), who claims to have sold his soul to the Devil, leads the trio onward in the direction of a small radio station in the middle of nowhere, ending with their being paid to make a record, as the movie is transformed, in part, to a musical. Tommy, an excellent guitarist, joins the three, who now call themselves The Soggy Bottom Boys, in a rendition of "Man of Constant Sorrow." Unbeknownst to them, the song becomes one of the most popular pieces of music in the South. Indeed, the Coens' movie score, which includes dozens of bluegrass and country western classics, won a Grammy award for the Best Album of 2002, bringing platinum sales of 7,421,000 copies sold in the US by October 2007. Several of the film's real singers gathered for a concert tour, *Down from the*

 *Mountain*, which itself was filmed.

Other adventures follow. At one point a lone car arrives to save the day, but within, we soon discover, sits a young bank robber, Pretty Boy Floyd, as if the trio had suddenly entered another film like *Dillinger* or *The Grapes of Wrath*. Indeed they have, for the writers-directors have not only layered their comic froth with allusions to *The Odyssey* but riddled it through with a whole series of Hollywood films. The title itself is a reference to Preston Sturges' comic masterpiece, *Sullivan's Travels*, a movie whose scenes parallel those of the Coens' work throughout, particularly when they later sit in a theater where their former prisoner cronies are brought in for a moment of pleasure *en masse*.

Accordingly, it is not surprising that the three participate in Floyd's brazen bank robbery, following it up with another Odyssean encounter, this time with the Sirens. Upon waking in a daze, Everett and Delmar find Pete's clothes without him in them. When a small toad pops out of Pete's coat, Delmar is convinced that he has been transformed, as were some of Ulysses' men, into a beast—in this case into a frog.

The two soon meet up with a traveling bible salesman right of Flannery O'Connor, who promises to involve them in the business. But as soon as the two join up for a country picnic with the one-eyed salesman (the incomparable John Goodman), this Cyclops wallops them over their heads and steals their money.

A later hitch takes them back through the chain gang, where they discover Pete has again ended up, having divulged the secret of the treasure and their destination. By this time, however, the movie has grown so giddy (at least its creators have) that the hero admits it has all been a grand whopper; there is no treasure! He was arrested not for stealing but for passing himself off as a lawyer, and his goal all along has been to return to and reclaim his own Penelope, Penny (Holly Hunter), a woman who has told his children that he has been hit by a train and has taken up with Vernon T. Waldrip, an effete man who, we later discover, is involved with the Ku Klux Klan.

Another escape results in the three men's accidental confrontation with a grand Klan meeting, where they discover Tommy Johnson is about to be hung. This time, the reference is to another kind of musical, *The Wizard of Oz*, where, like the Scarecrow, Tin Man, and Lion observing the evil army of the Wicked Witch, they quickly change into the clothes of the enemy, grabbing Tommy and escaping once more.

Behind this new adventure lies a couple of battling governors right out of *Finian's Rainbow* (one of them

 the Grand Dragon of the Klan). The adventurers, transforming themselves once again into singing sensations, win the day for the good old boy incumbent, outing the would-be upstart. A full pardon is granted, but before the boys can let out even a Hallelujah, Everett's Penelope proclaims she will not take him back until he has retrieved her ring!

Strangely enough, accordingly, the Coens' shaggy-dog tale ends up in Wagner, as the three return to the very same cabin nearby where Everett once told them he had buried the treasure. The sheriff, having done digging up of his own, awaits their arrival, and this time it truly does look like they're in a tight spot from which they cannot possibly escape.

Remember that hydroelectric project? Well, today is that day! The water floods over the region, helping them to escape yet again, the ring safely in Everett's hot little hands, as our weary heroes return home.

But just as in *The Ring Cycle*, the whole thing has the potential to begin all over again, particularly when Penelope announces that he has returned with the wrong ring!

LOS ANGELES, FEBRUARY 21, 2001

Paranoia in the Library Stacks

DENNIS BARONE **TEMPLE OF THE RAT** (NEW YORK: LEFT HAND BOOKS, 2000)

OVER THE PAST SEVERAL YEARS Dennis Barone has proven himself one of the more interesting—and adventuresome—young American fiction writers. Particularly in his *The Returns*, published by my own Sun & Moon Press, and in *Echoes* (winner of the 1997 America Award for Fiction), Barone has charted out a quirky territory in fiction that is often a cross between a straight-faced and highly objectified realism and poetic fable.

In *Temple of the Rat* he attempts something similar. A young graduate student of history moves into an apartment only to be faced with a rat. A neighbor, Michael De Cordova, runs to his rescue, evicting the rat. The author immediately makes clear the fable-like structure he has in store as the narrator announces: "The little rat willingly suffered Michael's shoves because Michael De Cordova was the biggest rat around."

For the next several weeks, the narrator is forced to adjust to the ever-present existence of the De Cordovas: to the unannounced visits of Michael, who is both a brilliant cellist and a successful drug-dealer, and to the visages of Michael's younger and overweight brother, Clark, and mother, who spend most of their days on the stoop facing the narrator's window.

The narrator complains of their intrusiveness, of their constant observations of his comings and goings, but we soon recognize that Barone's history student is one of the most unreliable narrators—because he is so utterly self-deluded—that we have encountered in American literature for a long while. As he burrows into his escape from the world—work on his dissertation— the whole world seems to be peering in on him—even while he is also observing it, and in the process slowly being drawn into its arms. Having been insulated from most of life's experiences, he is shocked to discover that Clark, also a talented musician, has been beaten up at school and had his flute stolen. He is equally startled to hear of Michael's plans to escape to Bolivia, where he can play in the Bolivian National Symphony and simultaneously purchase large quantities of dope. He is scandalized by the fact that Michael has had sex with the previous tenant of his apartment—while forcing Clark to witness the event. Mrs. De Cordova's cryptic comments and her obvious preference for Clark over Michael further stir the narrator's indignation. In short, unable to face even the most banal of daily occurrences, the narrator nears the edge of a breakdown. Even the library becomes a terrifying place of possible destruction: while he puts his file cards in order, no writing takes place.

It is the return of Michael from Bolivia, drugs and bride in tow, and his ultimate rise in the real estate market, where he has invested most of his drug profits, that take the historian over the edge. As Michael invests heavily in his own, student-populated neighborhood, he becomes a brilliant slumlord; but when students rise up to protest, the world reels forward into utter absurdity, as the historian accidentally triggers events leading to the younger brother's death.

Barone has bet almost everything on the reader's perception of his narrator, but because he has so successfully grounded him in the realism of the situation—in the narrator's own context—it is often hard to know which world is more dangerous, that of the narrator or that of the De Cordovas. That tension is fine as long as it remains the impetus of events, but with the denouement, the tendons of the story snap, and with them the possibility of a coherent meaning, as the short novel flies off into the space of an almost cartoon-like fable. The reader has the strange sensation that he has been cheated, that this fiction has exploded before completing itself.

LOS ANGELES, SEPTEMBER 16, 2000

A Western Quartet

What the Night Does to a Man

BORDEN CHASE AND CHARLES SCHNEE (SCREEN-
PLAY, BASED ON A STORY BY BORDEN CHASE), HOWARD
HAWKS AND ARTHUR ROSSON (DIRECTORS) **RED RIVER**
/ 1948

HOWARD HAWKS' 1948 film, *Red River*, is certainly one
of the greatest of Hollywood westerns. If its plot and
even cinematography are a bit old-fashioned, the interrelationships between characters and the films presentation of a stampede, Indian attacks, and the plain dust
and dirt of a cattle drive are incomparable.

I've never truly been a John Wayne fan, although
I've enjoyed several of the movies in which he acted.
But here, as the autocratic rancher Thomas Dunson,
Wayne comes alive in the role, playing it at both ends,
from the hard-hearted, stubbornly overbearing settler
to the sometimes surprisingly tender and sympathetic

 man, worn out by the loss of his sweetheart to Indians and the years of hard work he has put into creating his ranch. As director John Ford is rumored to have said: "I didn't know the big son of a bitch could act."

Part of Wayne's power comes about because of those with whom he is cast. Walter Brennan, playing Wayne's right-hand man Nadine Groot, not only serves as chorus to Dunson's acts, but puts much of the serious goings-on into a humorous perspective. Without him, the entire film would be much darker, and clearly less enjoyable. Groot does his own serious mumbling—throughout the film Dunson demands he speak up and talk more clearly, but Groot has lost his teeth to Chief Yowiachie (Quo)—commenting on his employer's often brutal behavior. But his homespun observations pepper the action with a hardheaded wit, as when two strangers appear in the distance:

> Never liked seeing strangers. Maybe it's because no stranger ever good-newsed me.

At the other side of Dunson sits his adopted son,

Matt Garth (broodingly and beautifully played by Montgomery Clift). Although tough in his own way—after having seen the Indians destroy his family and,  later, having served in the Civil War—he is a far gentler and more reflective version of Dunson. Dunson has certainly plotted out his path in life, but Garth time and again describes himself as having "figured it out." Unlike Dunson, he has done serious thinking about the choices before him, and ultimately, despite his loyalty to Dunson and his love for him, it will be at the center of their parting ways.

Both writers and directors cleverly underline Garth's differences from Dunson by suggesting opposing sexualities. In fact, the film books report Wayne and Brennan did not at all get along with the homosexual Clift, keeping their distance throughout the shooting. Others involved in the film were worried that John Ireland (playing the cowboy Cherry Valance) and Clift might not get along because of their different and outspoken political views. But it is Valance and Garth, in this nearly all-male epic, who invoke any possibility of sexuality. From their very first meeting, the two obviously discover in each other a deep sensuality, which is played out in the nearly over-the-top exchange of guns and the shooting competition which follow, recently satirized in the Coen brothers' *True Grit*.

> CHERRY: That's a good-looking gun you were about to use back there. Can I see it? [*MATT turns, strokes his nose with his thumb and looks a bit amused, then hands his gun over. CHERRY takes the gun.*] And you'd like to see mine. [*CHERRY draws his own, and reciprocates by handing it to MATT. CHERRY examines MATT's gun.*] Nice! Awful nice! [*Looking somewhat sideways at MATT*] You know, there are only two things more beautiful than a good gun: a Swiss watch or a woman from anywhere. You ever had a good Swiss watch?
>
> MATT: [*pointing toward a tin can in the distance*] Go ahead! Try it! [*CHERRY fires a shot and knocks a can into the air. MATT also hits the can in the air with a shot of his own.*]
>
> CHERRY: Hey! That's very good! [*MATT shoots at another can, knocking it into the air. CHERRY hits it in the air with a shot of his own.*]
>
> MATT: Hey! Hey! That's good too! Go on! Keep it going!

It's clear that their shooting serves as a kind of orgasm

 that they hope will never end.

One can only presume, given nearly everyone's interpretation of this scene, that the people in the Hayes office were so literal-minded and stone deaf that they could not comprehend the loaded sexuality of the lines. In any event, from that first meeting on, despite Groot's prediction that the two will end up fighting, there is a deep relationship between them, including Matt's obvious jealousy when Cherry hooks up with a girl in a passing wagon train. Whether it's true or not, as the trivia people claim, that Ireland and Clift actually were having an affair during the shooting of this film (Ireland was married to Elaine Sheldon at the time), they hint at a simmering love on camera, or at least an almost uncontrollable fascination with one another.

This, in turn, further underscores the impending alienation between father and son. Dunson is a strong-headed conservative, determined to try no new routes to the Midwest, despite the near-starvation and exhaustion of his crew. Rules are rules and, as his cowboys sneak away, they are rounded up to be shot or even hung, after which Dunson, as he puts it, "reads over them," as if the burial service has redeemed his acts.

The more sensitive and thoughtful Matt, a soft-hearted soul, as both Dunson and Valance have described him, cannot tolerate the hanging of two defectors. Grabbing the reins of the cattle run and sending his own father off into the wilderness alone, Matt is determined to move in a new direction along the Chisholm Trail leading to Abilene where, it is rumored, a railroad now runs.

The question remains, of course, whether they'll get there before Dunson rounds up other men and returns to kill his "soft-hearted" son.

One of the most spectacular scenes of the film is the Texans' arrival in the city of Abilene, where they are heartily greeted as they drive thousands of long-horn cattle through the streets, accompanied, as always, by Dimitri Tiomkin's powerful score. The terms they're offered create a financial windfall for the cowboys. But vengeance, we know, is certain to rear its ugly head.

Dunson returns with new men intent upon accomplishing his blind, cold-hearted vision, despite the wise observations of Groot. Demanding that Matt draw, Dunson is ready for the showdown, which Matt refuses, throwing away his gun. Inevitability seems to have won the day, until Matt's new girl, Tess Millay (Joanne Dru), interrupts the fight by drawing a gun on both men, insisting that they face their love for one another.

It's an irony that strangely could never be played out in real life. It's also worth noting that Ireland divorced his first wife a year later, marrying Dru, as if she were a trophy won way from the Matt Garth character Clift portrays—a marriage which lasted until 1956, the year in which Clift's automobile accident basically destroyed his career, described as "the longest suicide in Hollywood history." Two years after his accident, Clift turned down the role in Hawks' *Rio Bravo*, a role reassigned to Dean Martin, a drunk with a clearly heterosexual history.

But let us forget all that: this film says everything that needs to be said.

LOS ANGELES, MARCH 4, 2011
Reprinted from *World Cinema Review* (March 2011).

Leaving Nothing to Chance

JULES FURTHMAN AND LEIGH BRACKETT (SCREEN-
PLAY), HOWARD HAWKS (DIRECTOR) **RIO BRAVO** / 1959

THE FIRST OF Howard Hawks' western trilogy, representing some of the last films he directed in his long
career, *Rio Bravo* is perhaps the best and most complex,
despite what at first appears to be a lightweight cast.
The idea of crooner Dean Martin, young singing-idol
Ricky Nelson, ingénue Angie Dickinson (playing the
role of a hardened gambling woman), and a slightly
overweight John Wayne teaming up to help save a small
border town from the clutches of the evil rancher Na-
than Burdette seems, on the surface, almost ludicrous;
and there were still titters in the audience at the Los
Angeles County Museum of Art's late Hawks' retrospective to justify those feelings. Nearly all film critics
agree, however, that *Rio Bravo* one of the better westerns in film history.

Hawks takes us through the few days between

the arrest of Burdette's brother, Joe, and the inevitable showdown, much in the way that Fred Zinneman did in the classic *High Noon*. But the differences between these two movies are crucial. While Gary Cooper, in his attempt to "save" an idealized and quite lovely small Western town from Ben Miller and his gang, is refused help from every citizen he asks to join him, Hawks, in response to *High Noon*, presents Wayne's Sheriff John T. Chance, supported at first only by his cackling old deputy Stumpy (hilariously played by Walter Brennan), as being ready to tackle the job almost by himself until he is joined by his alcoholic former sidekick, Dude (Dean Martin). The three of them spend much of the early part of the film prowling the streets of the gritty-looking, slightly seedy Rio Bravo, telling other folk to get out of the way.

If *High Noon's* Hadleyville is a spiffed-up village of wood-framed houses filled with proper middle-class citizens, Rio Bravo is as culturally-mixed as any border town probably was in its day: Carlos Robante and his wife Consuela run the local hotel in which the Sheriff sleeps, eats, and drinks; Burt, the local undertaker, is Chinese. Other than Chance, Dude, and Stumpy, it appears the only Caucasians in Rio Bravo come from the outside: Burdette's men, the cattlemen passing through, and the recently arrived card shark, Feathers (Dickinson). When cowboy leader Pat Wheeler is killed by Burdette's gang, one of his young assistants, Colorado Ryan (Nelson), casts his lot with the Sheriff, as he and Feathers save the Sheriff's life. In short, nearly everyone in this bustling little collection of low stucco buildings is willing to help, and even those who only watch the outcome help to save the Sheriff from being shot down on the street, since they might serve as witnesses.

Because the outcome of the final shootout, accordingly, is fairly apparent—justice will triumph—Hawks can spend most of his film revealing the interrelationships of these ragtag figures, demonstrating the power of friendship, loyalty, and love that connects them. And love in this drab outpost is not just reserved for the relationships between man and woman (Chance and Feathers, Carlos and Consuela), but—perhaps due in part to screenwriter Leigh Brackett's perspective as a woman—is equally expressed between the men, particularly through the complaining housewife-like role played by Stumpy (like many a Western husband the Sheriff has consigned his partner to the back room of their little "house" / jail cell, in this case armed with a rifle to protect it from all intruders), and in the admiration and love between Dude and Chance, the latter of whom has bought back his friend's gun and other belongings when, in his drunken nadir, Dude was forced to sell them. With the arrival of the young Colorado,

the prickly trio becomes a happier foursome, as Dude and Colorado break into song.

Music is quite essential in *Rio Bravo*; if the cowboy songs "My Rifle, My Pony, and Me" and "Get Along Home, Cindy" reveal the isolation and hidden desires of the singers, the enemy's repeated *degüello*, with its references to the battle of the Alamo, haunts these men barricaded in the jailhouse and torments them with their own failures. But their very fraternizing spirit ultimately strengthens them, cinematically revealed in the glass of whiskey Dude has just prepared to consume, successfully returned to its bottle without a spill. It is their love and friendship that save the day.

Only after normalcy has been restored to this village frontier does Feathers get her chance, in more ways than one. But it is she who does the proposing, leav-

ing nearly nothing to Chance, the man, but to bashfully accept their inevitable partnership.

The delight of *Rio Bravo* lies not in the characters' heroism, nor even in their dedication to justice, but in their own personal and often idiosyncratic connections with one another. Rio Bravo may be a rundown collection of desert dwellings, but I'd prefer it any day to the clean, white houses and churches of Hadleyville with its Sheriff's Quaker bride.

LOS ANGELES, MARCH 27, 2009

Geriatric Heroes

LEIGH BRACKETT (SCREENPLAY), BASED ON A
NOVEL BY HARRY BROWN, HOWARD HAWKS (DIRECTOR)
EL DORADO / 1966

SEVEN YEARS AFTER filming *Rio Bravo* Howard
Hawks produced the second film of his late Western
trilogy, *El Dorado*, a movie, as countless reviewers and
film historians have pointed out, extremely similar
to the previous one. Here too, a Sheriff (J. P. Harrah,
played by Robert Mitchum), in need of help to protect
his small community, gains the support of an older deputy (Bull Harris, humorously played by Arthur Hunnicutt), a former friend and top gunman (Cole Thornton, played by John Wayne), and a younger man who
becomes involved in the action almost by chance (Alan
Bourdillion Traherne, nicknamed Mississippi, played
by a youthful James Caan). The only superficial difference in the two films is that this time around the Sheriff
himself has become the alcoholic—also on account of

a "no-good" woman—allowing Thornton/Wayne to step in as a kind of symbolic Sheriff. Together this four-some, spurred on by the love of a local saloon opera-tor, Maudie (Charlene Holt), returns the town to order through a shootout between Bart Jason and his men, who are trying to take over the water rights of another local rancher-family, the MacDonalds.

The various vagaries of the plot, the fact that Thorn-ton refuses to sign on as Jason's gunman and accidently shoots one of the MacDonald boys, are of no great im-portance, for, once again, the theme here is friendship and the love and heroism it evokes. Indeed, as in the earlier film, the relationship between the men is em-bedded in a series of comical homoerotic metaphors. After an encounter with hired gunman Nelse McLeod and his gang, Thornton insists Mississippi wait with him while he warns McLeod and his men not to sign on with Jason. After insisting twice that the impatient young man wait with him in the bar, Mississippi blurts out, "Would you mind telling me why you have such a great passion for my company?"

Thornton has, in fact, saved his life; had Mississippi left the bar alone, others of McLeod's gang would have shot him down in the street. By saving his life, moreover, the two men are symbolically wed. Before long, Thornton, who has insisted upon going it alone, is joined in his journey back to El Dorado by the young man. As they head into town, Mississippi asks Thornton,

> Well, where are we headed?
> COLE: To see a girl.
> MISSISSIPPI: To see a "girl"?
> COLE: Yes, a girl! Don't you think I could know a
>   girl?

And when the two men are sworn in as deputies by Bull, the script even presents us with a metaphoric wedding ceremony:

> BULL HARRIS: Now, raise your right hand [*they do as they are told*]. I forgot the words, but you better say "I do!"

If in *Rio Bravo* the Sheriff and his gunman friend were getting on in years, in this movie Hawks practically turns them into geriatric figures. Thornton is shot early in the film by MacDonald's daughter, Joey, and suffers throughout much of the film from spasms, leaving his shooting hand temporarily paralyzed. Suffering from a home remedy for alcohol cooked up by the enterprising Mississippi, Harrah spends much of the later part of the film doubled over in pain, and, along with Thornton is shot in the leg. The final showdown is hilariously played out as both men hobble down the street on crutches, Mitchum's crutches sported sometimes on his left and at other times on his right; apparently Hawks shot whatever he felt looked best, and later was forced to add a line to the film noting the inconsistency, as if Harrah suffered not only from gun wounds but Alzheimer's disease.

The two Sheriffs may save the day, but by movie's end they are in sad shape. The next generation, represented by Mississippi and his potential relationship with the wildcat Western girl Joey, will clearly be different. While Bull and these men fight out of responsibility and honor, Mississippi, freshly in from the Delta, is fighting another kind of battle, a war of revenge. His best friend, a part-Cherokee river gambler, has been

killed, and over the years he has been seeking out and killing the murderers. This man of the new generation, moreover, does not even know how to use a gun; Mississippi prefers to kill his victims with a knife. Later, joining up with Thornton, Mississippi proves such a terrible shot that the older man buys him a double-barreled shotgun that splatters shots at everything in sight. Quoting Edgar Allan Poe's poem "Eldorado,"* Mississippi makes clear that his relationship to the West is a romantic one, that he sees Thornton as a kind of gallant knight who will soon ride through the Valley of the Shadow. Alan Bourdillion Traherne's refusal to give up his friend's river chapeau for a cowboy hat, makes it clear that, like the trumpet-toting Bull Harris—a remnant of the Calvary and Indian days of the early West—the values and heroism of Thornton and Harrah are almost a thing of the past.

———
*"Eldorado"

Gaily bedight,
A gallant knight,
In sunshine and in shadow,

Had journeyed long,
Singing a song,
In search of Eldorado.

But he grew old,
This knight so bold,
And o'er his heart a shadow,
Fell as he found,
No spot of ground,
That looked like Eldorado.

And, as his strength,
Failed him at length,
He met a pilgrim shadow;
"Shadow," said he,
"Where can it be,
This land of Eldorado?"

"Over the mountains
Of the moon,
Down the Valley of the Shadow,
Ride, boldly ride,"
The shade replied,
"If you seek for Eldorado!"

LOS ANGELES, APRIL 5, 2009

Irritable Comfort

LEIGH BRACKETT AND BURTON WOHL (SCREEN-
PLAY, BASED ON A STORY BY BURTON WOHL), HOWARD
HAWKS (DIRECTOR) **RIO LOBO** / 1970

AT TIMES IN director Howard Hawks' last film, *Rio Lobo*, it almost seems as if he is tempting the Hollywood idols. Except for the dozens of brilliantly comic one-liners of Brackett's script, the story is a shaggy dog tale without any "fur" to it. And it's hard to imagine a cast of less convincing actors than the Mexican heartthrob Jorge Rivero (who Wayne addresses as "Frenchy" throughout), Brazilian actress Jennifer O'Neill (*Rio Lobo* was clearly the best movie of her career), and future studio director Sherry Lansing. Publisher George Plimpton plays the 4th Gunman. Even Jack Elam (standing in for Walter Brennan and Arthur Hunnicutt) and John Wayne, here at his most laconic (in one of his first lines of the film Wayne reports to his soldier friend, "Ned, your neck's broken"), have seen better days. At one point, as the Rebels try to carry Wayne to his horse, they report what is obvious to all: "He's heavier than a baby whale!"

The film begins near the end of the Civil War as Col. Cord McNally (Wayne) and his Union soldiers attempt to transfer a large container of money from one town to another by train. The Rebels, headed by Capt. Pierre Cordona, whip up a plot to steal the money by greasing the tracks, rigging up trees with ropes, and tossing a hornet's nest into the armored car wherein the Union soldiers stand guard. The plot succeeds, and McNally, determined to seek out the Rebels, is captured and forced to lead them out of harm's way. But as he quietly leads them around a Union encampment, he shouts out for the troops, and the Rebels are foiled.

None of these series of high adventures, however, has any major significance for the rest of the film. The war is declared over the moment the Rebels are captured, and McNally treats his former enemies to a drink. Their actions, he reasons, were determined by war; the men he's after are the treasonous Union soldiers who clearly betrayed their own forces by leaking information to the other side. None of the Rebel soldiers knows the name of the two traitors. McNally charges Cordona and his friend, Tuscarora Phillips, to report to him through the sheriff of Blackthorne, Texas if they ever encounter these two men again.

In Blackthorne, McNally awaits the appearance of Cordona, while bedding down with a woman. Cordona has evidently encountered the men. Suddenly a gun-toting woman, Shasta Delaney (O'Neill), enters, demanding to see the sheriff: there has been a murder in Rio Lobo. Blackthorne sheriff Pat Cronin reports that it's out of his jurisdiction. Delaney reports, however, that the sheriff of Rio Lobo is corrupt and himself involved in the shooting. A posse from the nearby town arrives to take Shasta away. She shoots one of the men, Whitey, under the table, and McNally finishes off all but one of the rest; the final posse member is about to shoot McNally in the back when Cordona appears, pulling up his pants and shooting the other man dead. Whitey, Cordona reports, has been one of the traitors.

Shasta faints and Cordona insists that she should be taken to his room, as he dismisses the woman with whom he has just shared the bed. Shasta's awakening is one of the most humorous scenes in the film, and best conveys why *Rio Lobo* works despite its loony storyline and its unconvincing actors:

[*SHASTA wakes up in CORDONA's bed after fainting.*]
SHASTA: What am I doing here?
CORD MCNALLY: Well, you fainted after you shot
    Whitey, so we put you to bed.
SHASTA: Wait a minute! Where are my clothes?

Which one of you took my clothes?

CORDONA: I did.

SHASTA: Why?

CORDONA: Well, we flipped a coin and I won?

SHASTA: Where are your pants?

CORDONA: You're sleeping on them.

Brackett, in my estimation, should have won an award just for those lines!

Off go the unlikely trio, McNally, Cordona, and Shasta, to Rio Lobo, 70-80 miles away, to save the day and restore law and order. We know the formula: the three fall into a kind of erotic relationship that strengthens their determination to protect each other, drawing others to their side.

While, in the previous two films of Hawks' Western trilogy, Wayne was surrounded by weaker women and men, here McNally is himself a kind of agèd alcoholic, offering a round of drinks at every opportunity and demanding a swig of any liquor he can get. As the three spend the night in an old burial ground, McNally, sitting by himself in the cold, giggles in mysterious delight. Asked what he is so happy about, he answers: "I've had about the right number of drinks. And I'm warm, and I'm relaxed." Awakening the next morning to find Shasta by his side, McNally is startled. Shasta explains that she slept next to him because he was "com-

fortable." And it is clear that, if he is no longer a hero, he now represents a kind of irritable comfort, a safe place in a world of imminent dangers.

The rest of the story hardly matters. Of course they find graft and corruption facing them in Rio Lobo, as they are met with guns, imprisonment, and hate. A local bully, Ketcham, has installed his man, "Blue Tom" Henricks, as sheriff, and is trying to overtake the farms about. Tuscarora, Cordona's former Rebel partner, has been arrested on trumped-up charges. Visiting Ketcham's farm, the three overcome Ketcham, upon which Cordona reports that he is the second of the traitors. Forcing Ketcham to sign over the deeds of the stolen farms, McNally and his friends temporarily win the day. But, soon after, Cordona is taken by the bully's gang and an exchange, Ketcham for Cordona, is arranged. The local farmers join McNally and Delaney in the standoff, as Cordona dives to safety into a nearby river, and the evil gang is destroyed. Paralleling the plot of *El Dorado*, McNally, who has been shot in the leg, walks off using his rifle for a crutch, while Amelita (Lansing) runs forward to help him walk.

Few critics, with the exception of *The New York Times'* Roger Greenspun, appreciated the film. And Greenspun's faint praise, "The movie is close enough to greatness to be above everything else in the current season," evidently produced a flurry of angry letters. Despite Hawks' apparently lackadaisical attitude about his last film, the work is extremely amusing and was one of the biggest earning films of 1970.

LOS ANGELES, APRIL 18, 2009
All three essays reprinted from *Green Integer Blog* (April 2009).

What Isn't *to be Done?, or Take the Money and Run*

YUZ ALESHKOVSKY **KANGAROO**, TRANSLATED
FROM THE RUSSIAN BY TAMARA GLENNY (NEW YORK:
FARRAR, STRAUS AND GIROUX, 1986 / REPRINTED BY
NORMAL, ILLINOIS: DALKEY ARCHIVE PRESS, 1999)

WHEN YUZ ALESHKOVSKY'S *Kangaroo* was first published in English, a review in *The New York Times* described it as having "the stunning impact of a *Candide*,
a *Švejk*, a *1984*." Indeed the work may share many
qualities with these famous fictions, but *Kangaroo's*
hero, Fan Fanych ("alias Katzenelengogen, von Patoff,
Ekrantz, Petyanchikov, alias Etcetera!"), shares little of
the determined innocence and naïf belief of either Vol-
taire's Candide or Hašek's Švejk. From the 1949 com-
mencement of his story—which the narrator admits is
not really a beginning but a continuation of his ongoing
battle with Russian bureaucracy—to its Khrushchev-
era ending, Fan Fanych is portrayed as a man well aware

of the intricate insanities of a world to which he has resigned himself, perhaps, but which he is also able to magnificently manipulate. It is just this ability to twist an already twisted system to meet simultaneously his *and* its needs that animates the absurd humor of the book.

Having escaped a previous charge by the state, Aleshkovsky's "hero's" life has been put on hold, so to speak, by KGB officer Kidalla so that he may be charged later with a far more significant crime. Like Schweik, Fan Fanych is locked away in a kind of nuthouse—however, his KGB lockup is no dreary cell, but, as the collaborating prisoner has demanded, a comfortably decorated bedroom with numerous Soviet photographs of great heroes and significant events covering its walls (photographs which, within the paranoia of the situation, seem to be daily altered or switched). The narrator insists that he determine his own crime, choosing from the KGB files the most outrageous charge he can find, a "vicious rape and murder of an aged kangaroo in the Moscow zoo on a night between July 14, 1789 and January 9, 1905," in the hope, perhaps, that its very implausibility will save him from imprisonment or death. When he is told that the crime was created by computer, he and the reader recognize almost immediately that the authorities will now have to go out of their way to prove him guilty, if only to protect their commitment to the new—if slightly flawed—technology.

What follows is a long series of loony events, including an attempt by a scholar to indoctrinate him on the subject of marsupials—an elderly male virgin whom Fan Fanych introduces to the joys of the opposite sex; a foray into the psychological transformation of the prisoner from human being to kangaroo—which the "hero" undermines by acting out the expectations of the scientists; a presentation of a trial featuring a "documentary" film of the alleged criminal events—which the accused has scripted and in which he plays the role of the murderer; and an experiment in the effects of long-term space travel, where the subject is told that he is traveling to another planet in the period of a few days but actually travels over a period of weeks and months—a mystery our narrator uncovers when he finds that they have forgotten to cut one of his nails.

These events, if absurdly hilarious, do not permit us laughter, however, because of the rants and raves of the narrator which, in his philosophically inclined leaps of language, nearly take our breath away at the very moment of explosive relief.

You have no idea how cruel and dense a lot of people of good will can be, Kolya. They didn't waste a second worrying whether I was guilty or not. About ninety percent simply said my legs ought to be torn off my body. The remaining ten percent thought up original tortures, but only so I'd have to scream with pain for a good long time. Not one of them bright enough to suggest *eternal* pain and torture. I guess men always envy anyone any kind of eternal existence, even an agonizing one. The complex people—writers, artists, export managers, journalists, the rest of the dreck—every one of them proposed pouring vodka down me from morning till night without every letting me get over my hangover, until my heart just stopped. A horrible death, sure, but it needs complex people to think it up.

In the end, Fan Fanych outwits himself, as the Soviet authorities grant him his wish to be imprisoned with "notable" criminals, and he is locked away in a distantly located, dark hell-hole with former revolutionaries such as Chernyshevsky (author of the influential novel *What Is to Be Done?*), who in their continued support of the socialist cause, see even their own imprisonment as a betterment of Soviet ideals: "The sooner you get in, the sooner you get out!" The "hero" finds a way to better his life in prison by developing a "third eye," with which he more easily spots the rats that he and the other prisoners must destroy.

Unlike the more innocent and "feeble-minded" Candide and Schweik, moreover, Fanych, in part because of his crafty machinations, is quite an unappealing hero, particularly in his role as pickpocket (he pickpockets Hitler's wallet), determining, so the narrator reveals, Hitler's burning of the Reichstag, which leads to the Führer's Socialist party's rise to power. His vagrancy and self-protectiveness account also for his remaining mute about Stalin's secret plans at Yalta (and the increasing insanity brought on, in part, by the dictator's mortal combat with his right foot). Fanych, we recognize, is a survivor precisely because he is no innocent fool. The world into which he is finally released, accordingly, is radically different from the old only in the fact that it has wiped away all traces of a past that it is now free to repeat.

Indeed, Aleshkovsky's fiction ends with his embattled narrator even getting a reward for his participation in the government's labyrinthine evil plots; he is awarded £200,000 sterling for being "the first man of any nationality to rape and viciously murder a kangaroo" by an Australian millionaire suffering from kangaroophobia! Inevitably the government finds a way to strip him of most of the money. And just as inevitably, we discern that in Fanych's final toast to "Freedom" his tongue (be it Fanych's or Aleshkovsky's) is still planted firmly in cheek. In a country which, according to the narrator, has massacred 60 million men just to open up Beriozka stores, there is no garden left to cultivate. In such a morally bankrupt land, Fanych's choice obviously is the only one: take "the money and run."

Given the current situation in the new "freer" Russia—where the mafia and other men and women of greed siphon off much of the economy—Aleshkovsky's bitterly satiric tale might almost be seen, from hindsight, as a prophetic cry in the wilderness.

LOS ANGELES, JULY 6, 2006
Reprinted from *The Green Integer Review*, No. 4 (August-October 2006).

12 LAST DAYS OF THE SOVIET UNION

Day One: Gogol's Coat

AFTER MY FATHER's death in 2003, my mother gave me his dress coat, a long brown winter garment that I have only worn once—on a trip to New York in the middle of winter. It is quite out of character with my usual costume, considering my lack of fashionable dress, like something from another time and place.

A few years before, Howard had bought a blue-hooded cotton and nylon coat in Japan that I also sometimes use on my trips to Manhattan. Just as often, however, I travel with only a suit coat. I am known throughout New York as "the man without a coat"!

In 1989, however, I did not own anything but a spring jacket. And as I prepared for a trip to the Soviet Union with Lyn Hejinian, her husband, saxophonist Larry Ochs, and the ROVA Quartet, I bemoaned the fact that I didn't have one. "I suppose I shall have to go out and purchase an overcoat," I mentioned to Lyn in a telephone  conversation. "You most certainly will," she responded. "Leningrad is brutal in November! But my son has a coat. Why don't I bring you that?" "Wonderful," I responded. "That would solve the problem!"

Since I was in New York City just prior to the trip, I left with others joining us from that region on Finnair from Newark. On the same plane were poet Clark Coolidge and his wife, Susan, who in those days lived in upstate New York.

Unlike most American and other European airlines I'd been on, the many Finnish passengers, almost all tall, imposing men, walked up and down the aisles throughout the flight, using the back galley as a kind of bar. They drank all night. There was no possible way to sleep.

We were to meet the San Francisco contingent of our group—consisting of most of the 20 group travelers—in Helsinki. But we found no one to meet us at the airport, and soon thereafter, we discovered that the San Francisco plane had been delayed by an entire day or two! None of the few of us in Helsinki had ever been to the Soviet Union, and the tour guide, who might have led us through the difficulties of entering through Leningrad, was with the San Francisco contingent. We had no other choice but to proceed on our own.

Fortunately, poet and friend Arkadii Dragomoshchenko had been forewarned of our plight, and was at the Leningrad airport to meet us and help us through customs. He arranged for a bus to the hotel, where we were met also by ROVA photographer Peter Vilms, who was to be my roommate, and who had arrived earlier from Helsinki, traveling through his ancestral Estonia before arriving in Russia. The official Soviet tour guides were also there, and as soon as we had unpacked and showered, they took us out for a short tour. Suddenly, standing on a snowbank in the freezing winter, I remembered that I was without a coat; Lyn had what was to have been "my" coat with her!

The guides helped me to buy an Ushanka, the famed Russian hat, and one of them loaned me a scarf. I put on the heaviest sweater I had brought. But it was several degrees below zero Fahrenheit, and, despite my cheery bluff, I was absolutely freezing. Perhaps we were saved from more enforced tours that first afternoon simply because of the incessant chattering of my teeth. Besides, we needed the sleep.

I felt kinship with Gogol's poor character, Akakii Akakievich, a man whose coat has been stolen. But

then, I had never had one to begin with! I was even more of a fool than Akakii.

It took almost two days for the others to arrive, and the tour guides refused to let us remain inside. Yet I survived. Finally the coat, along with the rest of the group, appeared, and I was able to move through the city without fear of freezing. Indeed, somehow, I, who hate shopping and resist that activity at home, got the moniker there in Russia of "the shopper," since I visited dozens of out of the way Soviet shops.

What fascinated me about them was that in most of them there was simply nothing to buy, or they contained ridiculous items that had little at all to do with how they had advertised themselves. For example, what had been a jewelry store was suddenly filled with gym mats. The jewels, watches, and other things had never arrived or perhaps no longer existed, but the store had been shipped, perhaps by accident or by request, boxes and boxes of gym mats; and that, accordingly, was what they were now selling. How many customers they had for such a ridiculous object, priced out of range for most Russian citizens, I have no clue. But everyone from the neighborhood had seemingly come out to see them—as if perhaps the arrival of these bright green and blue mats was an indicator of better times to come; maybe the authorities might even ship them food! For weeks, so Arkadii told us, Leningrad had survived mostly on spaghetti.

So I walked and walked, one day even becoming lost, as I explain below in "Waiting for Tea." Now I was quite comfortable going about. Strangely, by the time our trip ended two weeks later, one by one everyone had come down with a cold—except me. I didn't even sniffle.

LOS ANGELES, JANUARY 7, 2010

Day Two: Waiting for Tea

OUR TOUR GROUP met together each day in the hotel dining room at a precisely appointed time for lunch and dinner. Food was not served outside of these set parameters, and if you were not punctual you simply missed out. Usually the meal consisted of some mix of salmon and herring along with a small serving of vodka, followed by a kind of meat patty and potatoes. Most of us chose to drink lukewarm Pepsi, since the bottled water was unbearably salty and the regular waters of Leningrad were so polluted that people not immune to them often developed stomach ailments including serious bacterial infections. We were warned never to drink water! The meal was followed always by ice cream.

After several days of being hurried from site to site by our Intourist guides, I decided to elude them one morning, setting out on a journey through Leningrad by myself. I brought along a piece of paper naming my hotel and bravely set forth, walking first toward the center of the city, following the famed Neva River, then turning and wandering down the vast Nevsky Prospekt. As the Russian author Andrei Biely described it:

> The Nevsky Prospect possesses an impressive quality: it consists of a vast expanse for the circulation of the public; numbered houses restrict it—this makes it easier to find any home we may want. The Nevsky Prospect, like any prospect, is a public prospect; that is, a prospect for the circulation of the public (not of air to be sure); the houses, which line it and shape its frontiers, are what give it substance—h'm...yes...for the public. In the evening the Nevsky Prospect is lighted by electricity. By day the Prospect needs no illumination.

Some of the grand buildings were still beautiful, but many had an almost fairy-tale like quality, the outsides appearing like stage-sets with nothing behind them. And indeed when I went into some of the grandest of these stores, there was nothing within. What had once been great groceries and clothing emporiums were now almost empty sets.

Still the Russians crowded through the doorways as if there might be possibly a new delivery of what they had lost. Throughout the city, double doors were being used to actually impede entry and exit. Wherever there were two doors, one was locked, so that people coming and people going were forced to wait for one

 another, as if the authorities were determined to hold those who were about to enter as long as possible from entering, while also stopping up the flow of those about to leave. At many doors, moreover, sat a man or woman on a stool as if they might check the passing crowd's papers. Yet they did nothing more than further block that furtive coming and going of the public mass.

At one point I stopped and ordered a small cup of something called "soku," a combination of crushed ice and fruit juice. I quickly drank it down, suddenly realizing I had just swallowed the polluted waters of the Neva. Would I survive?

A few yards further, I saw a long line snaking up to a little hut. The people in line, I soon realized, were waiting for tea. This impossibly long wait so intrigued me I decided I would join the line, just to experience the kinds of waits the Russians daily had to endure for anything they might seek. An hour later, I had a cup of tea in my hands, for which I was not even thirsty. I don't even like tea, but I drank it all up, embarrassed for having made everyone behind me wait. But through that event I realized how determined everyday moth-

ers and fathers, sons and daughters, had to be to survive. If you wanted to put food on the family table, the mother had to wait in line for hours; it you wanted to drink of cup of tea between work shifts, it was necessary to patiently endure the cold. It was easier not to survive than to continue the travesty of ordinary life. There was no ordinary life in Russia anymore.

Indeed, the whole city, despite its occasionally spectacular beauty, seemed destitute. And Moscow would later seem even more so. All those years, the United States' leaders' arguments for a verbal, financial, and militaristic war with this nation had been built, to my way of thinking, on a horrible lie. The Soviet Union appeared to me like a 19th-century country in a 20th-century cultural predicament. Yes, they had missiles, bombs of destruction, but what had it all been about? We had won the battle while losing our souls.

I walked on and on, visiting all sorts of stores, little shops, black-market kiosks (as warned, I bought nothing at these), tiny huts, even underground bathrooms, trying to find something that I might find familiar. Everything seemed foreign and cold. I realized that I could not survive in Leningrad—at least not in 1989—that, if I lived in this city, I couldn't be the man I was.

Soon I realized I had walked far from the center, and I no longer knew where I going. The light was beginning to fade, and I grew weary. How to return to the hotel? I tried to stop a person, showing her the name in Cyrillic on my piece of paper. But she could not or would not tell me anything. Hotels were off limits to the regular citizens, and perhaps they didn't even know what it was I was trying to ask? I became frightened. Would I be forced to spend the night on the freezing streets of Leningrad, without food and a place to sleep?

At a small kiosk, I pointed to a map, which I purchased, trying desperately to match the street sign beside me to a name on the map. Finally, I spotted a word that might be the same. I turned and walked in the direction of what appeared to be the Neva, after a long while reaching Nevsky Prospekt, feeling my way back to the hotel. I was hungry, but I had missed the appointed hour. Now I knew how it felt if one decided *not to wait*, not to suffer the daily indignities of the system. If I had had children, they would have gone hungry as well.

LOS ANGELES, JANUARY 11, 2010
Reprinted from *Green Integer Blog* (January 2010).

Day Three: Africa

ONE OF THE great treats of traveling with a jazz group was that every night I got to hear wonderful music. I never grew tired of the ROVA group, and I came to know some of their works quite well.

The first few days, moreover, during the Leningrad Jazz Festival, featured many of the top talents from around the world. The Festival was held on an island, which required one to cross a drawbridge, resulting, the first night, in my roommate being home long after midnight. A ship had become trapped under the bridge!

I attended the second day, truly enjoying the vast array of talent. One young Soviet saxophonist-violinist was particularly appealing, I recall, but now, some 21 years later, it is hard to remember any of the performances I witnessed. I believe I saw Viatcheslav Nazarov, the noted Russian jazz trombonist, as well as the Leningrad Dixieland Jazz Band. I vaguely remember that there was one group called Africa, which featured only white players, but seemed to have an appropriate

name nonetheless, celebrating the roots of jazz. Arkadii Dragomoshchenko later told me that there were a great many singers and groups in the Soviet Union who had taken on that moniker.

From time to time, I went to the nearby green room, which had a small café, and where figures from all the arts gathered to talk. Whenever my friend, Arkadii, decided to visit the café, he simply got up and walked across the stage instead of retreating through the back of the vast auditorium. It was his way of speaking out, I believe, against the authoritarian way of life in the Soviet Union, a kind a swagger, as if to say, "I'll go wherever I damn please." I always chose the long route.

At the café, Arkadii introduced me to several young

poets and two young curators, a husband and wife, who were planning a large international retrospective of contemporary artists. When I told them of my companion Howard's involvement with art, they immediately responded, "Oh yes, we know of him. We have his Robert Longo catalogue. Yes, we want definitely to include Robert Longo in our show." I grew interested, and we discussed several other artists they hoped to include. They often asked me what these people were like to work with. "That, I wouldn't know, except for hearsay. Robert, I believe, is usually a sweetheart."

After a while, I asked them what they were thinking of calling their show. Both quickly responded, "*AF-ri-ka*," emphasizing the first syllable.

"Africa?" I queried. "But you've named no African artists in your show, not even any blacks!"

"Oh, but you see, it is a world of pristine beauty. Of perfection. Of innocence. That's what we want."

"Oh dear," I pondered. "When I think of Africa, I think of all the destruction of land and cities caused by Western investments. I think of great poverty, of diminishing wilderness. Yes, I am sure there is much beauty in Africa, particularly in the protected parks and isolated sections, but so many scenes in photographs and films show ramshackle huts and tin-built canteens, crumbling cities. But then, I've never been there."

"Nor have we! But I am sure it is beautiful," insisted the male.

"It is as close to heaven as one can get," added his wife.

I smiled painfully. How do you argue against such a wonderful illusion? Given their own polluted rivers, rusting industrial complexes, they needed to believe that such beauty might exist somewhere, just as I had had to look elsewhere when faced with my childhood of suburban burger and pizza stands and chain shopping outlets.

LOS ANGELES, JANUARY 14, 2010

Day Four: Lives of the Artists

DESPITE THE APPARENT restriction of Soviet tourist hotels for Russian citizens, poet-friend Arkadii Dragomoshchenko joined us each day at dinner in the hotel dining room. His company was a joyful one, and he kept us abreast of Russian events and traditions. Clark Coolidge, Lyn, and I talked with Arkadii every day on various subjects. I particularly remember when the conversation turned to Women's Liberation, which was dismissed out of hand by both Arkadii and his wife, Zina. "We want to be pampered and not have to work," she declared.

Near the end of our stay, Arkadii invited us to a party at his son's art studio/apartment. The dilapidated space was like something out of the 1920s and 1930s collective housing, a place shared by four or five artists, each occupying a small corner. I recall a woman artist having only a small walking passage, a couple of artists sharing what might once have been a bedroom. Ostap shared the so-called "living-room." Several of his paint-

ings had been tacked to the walls.

Each of us, as expected, had purchased vodka and other foods (chips and candies) from the tourist shops, where, once again, Russian citizens were not permitted.

Zina had made a dish of chicken legs and wings soaked for days in a hot vinegar sauce, and served cold. The huge bowl of chicken, most of us realized, must have taken her several days, working with other women friends, to accumulate from the almost-always empty food stores. If it was not the best food I had ever consumed, it was, nonetheless, a veritable feast, given her few resources.

Ostap was a handsome young man, proud of his slightly abstracted figures on canvas. I was particularly taken by the brightly colored painting of two beefy wrestlers, and when I expressed my appreciation of the work, the artist immediately took it down from the wall, rolled it up, and handed it to me as a gift. I tried to pay for it, but he refused. Today, after these many years, it still hangs in my office, tacked to the walls as it originally was, in his studio.

The evening was absolutely splendid, but I could

not help but feel some sorrow for these young artists, who lived in frigid, walk-up lofts perhaps not so differently from young New York artists in the early 1950s. But each of

their spaces was so tiny it seemed that one might become claustrophobic if they all turned up on the same day to work. Perhaps they had planned it out that they would paint, draw, or sculpt at different times during the week. Yet they all seemed excited and proud to be able to show their art to a new audience whom we represented. Several works were purchased by members of our group. It was, in short, one of the most joyous evenings of our stay in Leningrad.

LOS ANGELES, MARCH 18, 2010
Reprinted from *Green Integer Blog* (March 2010).

Day Five: Hurry, Hurry!

ON OUR LAST day in Leningrad we were given a tour of the grand Hermitage Museum. I do not like tours, and this one had signified everything I hate about them.

We were first taken to see some of the classic paintings, particularly the Rembrandts. I was dazzled by his *The Sacrifice of Isaac*, but I believe we were all appalled by the realization that some of these paintings were shown in direct sunlight. I also recalled how only two or three years earlier, an insane attacker had thrown sulfuric acid upon the canvas of Rembrandt's *Danaë* at The Hermitage before cutting it twice through with a knife.

How long might these great works last in such a situation? we pondered. Was there anything that might be done? Certainly any comments we might make would be pointless, as our guide hurriedly rushed us in and out of rooms.

By the time we reached the modernist collections, mostly of great European art, we were literally being

 run from room to room, as if simply glimpsing paintings was the purpose of museum-going.

Clark Coolidge and I, fascinated by some of the art we had never before seen by Gauguin, Matisse, Kandinsky, Picasso, and French modernists, refused to budge upon the guide's call for us to "Hurry, Hurry," and the distressed woman returned again and again into the rooms where we straggled, growling at us to hurry along.

"We want to see the art," we insisted. Her sour look seemed to indicate that the art was not there for *us* to "see," whatever that might mean. We were meant, clearly, simply to witness the art, to observe the great troves of riches that the Soviet government had accumulated for the common man. It was as if the art were there simply as a kind of shrine, evidence of the Soviet's nationalization of the Impressionist, post-Impressionist, and modern art collections of figures such as Sergei Shchukin and Ivan Morozov.

The more our guide stamped her foot and insisted that we hurry, the more entrenched Clark and I became in our viewing, and I remember staring for long periods at works that I might never have noticed in my usual

run-throughs of galleries.

In that sense, what began as a kind of challenge to the busy guide, turned the visit into an intense viewing of art that revealed works, sometimes by rather minor French artists, in new contexts. Suddenly I could understand why, for example, Albert Marquet or Camille Pisarro were interesting artists.

"Hurry, hurry," she clapped her hands as if we were some misbehaving children. We clapped back and wandered slowly from room to room until she returned once more to scold us.

We left The Hermitage somewhat disappointed, but knowing we had learned, perhaps, more than she had intended us to.

Again, we realized why our Russian friends some-

times behaved in ways that at first seemed somewhat churlish with regard to personal movement. It was payback for the thousands of daily reminders that ingress and egress were always delimited and controlled.

LOS ANGELES, MAY DAY, 2010
Reprinted from *Green Integer Blog* (May 2010).

Day Six: The Train

FOR YEARS I believed that traveling by train, particularly long distances, was somehow romantic. Perhaps I had seen too many movies, or had been too strongly influenced by my favorite childhood book wherein a young boy takes a train ride with his mother to meet up with his father in a faraway state. Those trains, the trains of the 1950s Hitchcock films and within my little Golden Book, were glorious machines which combined dark green (one of my favorite colors) trimmed with oxblood accessories. Trains, particularly in which one had sleeping quarters, seemed like a little hotel on wheels, which thoroughly satisfied my peripatetic predilections.

So, when we were told that we would be traveling via overnight train from Leningrad to Vilnius, I was thrilled. Even after we waited in the cold night for hours until the train arrived, and had crawled up the stairs into what was clearly a derelict version of any train I might have conjured up, I still tingled with the

excitement of such a voyage. Each sleeping room contained four beds, and I, having spent much of my adolescence at the top level of a bunk bed, opted for the upper space.

On this train there was nowhere else to sit. The narrow halls contained only a couple of drop-down stools, upon which even the smallest child might feel ill-at-ease. Accordingly, we sat on our beds, chatting until we all were ready for sleep.

The gentle sway of the train soon lulled me into dreams. After a short while, however, I woke up with a headache, an array of uncomfortable odors in my nose. A couple of guys in our party had purchased a large bunch of garlic in Leningrad, and it hung from our ceiling. I love garlic, but this huge floral-like composition had clearly been soaked in some kind of herb or spice, and stank something awful. The next door bathroom—more an open privy than a toilet—added its own rankness.

I attempted to put the smells out of my mind, and let the rhythm of the rails lull me into sleep once again.

A few hours later, however, I awoke in a fit of coughing, my throat inflamed, my nose and eyes dripping. Was I getting a cold? It hardly mattered, for I felt as sick as if I had contracted some rare disease. I lay in the dark for a long while, but could no longer even doze, and, finally, I could no longer bear the prone position.

Slowly, as quietly as I could, I sat up, gathered my bag of books and papers, and jumped to floor, slipping out into the narrow hall, at the far end of which sat the carriage conductor. I tried as best I could to find some comfort on the tiny pull-down stool, but could hardly balance on the spot, let alone battle book and cough. I was miserable and wondered how I would withstand the rest of the tour. Had I been transformed into a vampire?

Seeing my discomfort, the conductor came forward, speaking Russian and waving his middle finger in a signal of "follow me." Given my "humpty-dumpty" position I had little choice, even though I was somewhat fearful of where I might be taken.

At the far end of the train car was a little door I had not previously noticed. He opened it, and I peeped in, discovering what was clearly his small office, consisting of a desk and a tiny bookcase shoved against walls covered over with magazine clippings and photographs. He signaled for me to sit, and I did, trying to convey my sincere appreciation for his kind act. I took out my notebook and began to write.

After a few minutes of observing my actions, he

imitated my insistent penmanship and shrugged his shoulders as if asking what it was I was writing. I pointed to him and smiled. "I'm writing of your act of kindness in my notes," I pointlessly reported.

But something friendly must have been conveyed, for he soon came forward, asking me a question in Russian. I shook my head, obviously not comprehending a word he had said. He came closer and for a single moment I wondered what was in store. He pointed to a small figure of Christ pasted to his wall, and to a reproduction of a painting of Mary.

"Christ," I responded, which brought a smile to his face, having interpreted my head-shaking as agreement.

"Christos," he proudly agreed.

"Yes, Christos. Da, Christos," I responded.

Suddenly he pointed to another figure a few feet away from the religious iconography, just as proud of displaying this clipping as he had been of his statements of faith.

I put on my glasses and carefully surveyed the figure: Einstein!

"Einstein?" I laughed.

"Da, Einstein," he laughed back.

Then he turned, almost as if embarrassed, and left me alone. I wrote a bit more in my journal, read some of my book, and waited for the morning to come and the others to wake.

Every once in a while the conductor returned as if to check on my well-being, which, in turn, somewhat troubled me. Was he trying to see if I had finally abandoned his comfy hole so that he might return? I certainly felt happy in this little spot, but I had no intention of putting him out of his little kingdom, and soon after I returned to the hall, standing near the window to look out at the vast white landscape lit up by the rising sun over what I presumed was Belarus.

Finally, the sun inched up a little higher in the sky, and my travel companions began, one by one, to emerge, congregating in the little wafer of space in which I stood.

"You're up early," the first to appear noted.

"Couldn't sleep," I grumbled.

"The smell is something terrible, isn't it?"

"Unbearable, in my case."

"Guess we shouldn't of bought that garlic, but my mother insisted I bring some back."

"I'm supposed to bring some Russian dolls for my grandmother! Haven't seen any yet."

When our tour guide appeared, she reported that she had just been told there was nothing to eat. "They forgot to load food on the train in Leningrad," she groaned.

I was nearly famished, and dreaded the hours we still had until we reached Vilnius.

Some time after, however, we were told to gather in the dining car. The cooks had discovered some beets, and, indeed, we witnessed a couple of bunches of beets laid out in the connecting links between cars.

We all eagerly crowded into the booths, where we were each served a bowl of borscht. At the bottom of each bowl sat a small piece of something that looked a little bit like meat. None of us dared say what we all feared. Yet that borscht was absolutely delicious, better that anything we had yet eaten in the Soviet Union. My cold melted away with each sip of the hot concoction, and by the time we reached Vilnius I felt much better.

As we left the train, I shook the hand of the obliging conductor, wishing him well. He once more beamed in quiet delight.

LOS ANGELES, MAY 19, 2010
Reprinted from *Green Integer Blog* (May 2010).

Day Seven: Too Many Churches

AFTER OUR STAY in the hotel in Leningrad, where even on the best of days, the elevators operated very slowly and the rooms were always overheated and dirty, and especially after our unpleasant train trip, we were all delighted by the towering, modern building where we were to spend some nights in Vilnius. I believe the hotel was what today is called the Radisson Bleu Hotel Lietuva, but I don't remember the name at the time of our stay. The first thing my roommate and I did was to take showers.

Upon inspection, soon after, the entire city of Vilnius seemed well-kept and spotless, a tourist's delight.

We were toured briefly through the Old Town, where the Jewish quarter was quickly pointed out to us. It seems hard to imagine so many important figures having lived in such a small area, but I'm sure it was a crowded few blocks even in the days that Vilna was described as the Jerusalem of Europe. Many of our

group wanted to see more, but we were hurried away, time and again, to inspect numerous churches and cathedrals. There are some 40 churches in Vilnius. (My essay on the Jewish poet Abraham Sutzkever and the Vilna community appears in *My Year 2010*.)

One evening three or four of us were invited into a Lithuanian home for dinner with an elderly couple. The couple with whom we were dining seemed quite literate, so I bravely asked whether there were any young innovative Lithuanian poets. Both husband and wife quickly answered, "Oh, no. Lithuania is a very traditional country."

Of course, this couple might have mentioned Tomas Venclova, although by that time he had already emigrated to the US; or they might have looked to the past for Oscar Milosz, Henrikas Radauskas, or the great Abraham Sutzkever, but it was obvious that they were uninterested in poetic adventurousness.

One day, however, we did catch a distinct sense of

change in the air. Our Lithuanian guide was explaining to us that, until very recently, Lithuanians had not been permitted to speak their own language, which, we had been proudly told by several Vilnius citizens, had its roots in Latin and even had connections to Sanskrit. The guide continued with a list of other restrictions put upon them by the Soviets, including the closing of several of their beloved religious sites.

Suddenly, one of two Russian guides stood up and went forward, speaking quite harshly, it was clear, to the Lithuanian speaker. It was apparent that the younger girl was being told not to continue criticizing the Soviets.

The Vilnius guide smiled and continued on with her catalogue of gripes. Clearly, she wasn't one little bit afraid of the ramifications. Perhaps that was the first time we all recognized that the Soviet Union would not last long, that its power in the Baltic States, at least, had already crumbled. We were all aware that only three months before, the Baltic countries had met to create the Assembly of the Baltic Independence Movements and created The Baltic Council, and this small

confrontation was one of its effects.

On another day, we were taken for a day trip to the nearby Trakai Island Castle, built in the 14th century. As we passed a woods just outside of Vilnius, many of our group asked whether or not it was the famous woods where a number of Jewish citizens had hidden and attempted to resist German occupation. Mightn't we be able to stop for a few moments by the side of the road? No answer.

Later that evening, when we were taken to yet another cathedral, several individuals in our party complained. "Not another church," a couple of them shouted. "Not another!" Some of their ancestors had lived in the Vilna Ghetto, and they were desperate for a different perspective.

Our feisty tour guides simply smiled.

Yet, despite the refusal of our guides to deal with the painful facts of the past, most of us did feel a sense of new possibility here in this lovely small city. Even the air seemed warmer than the cold stones of Leningrad.

LOS ANGELES, JULY 22, 2010
Reprinted from *Green Integer Blog* (July 2010).

Day Eight: Candies in the Snow

PERHAPS IN REACTION to some of our complaints, our bus trip to Riga, Latvia, was interrupted with a visit to the Nazi concentration camp in Salaspils. I imagine our American guide intervened in this case, insisting to the Intourist guides that this was a necessary change in the schedule.

The German Stalag-350-s began as a camp for

prisoners of war, and held approximately 43,000 Red Army soldiers and personnel. For that reason it was designated as an Arbeitserziehungslager camp, a work and education facility; which meant that instead of being administered by the Nazi SS (Schutzstaffel), it was subordinated to the HSSPF Ostland, the German police authority in the occupied Baltic countries. Himmler is said to have visited the camp often.

Sometime after its establishment, however, it began to be used for Baltic civilians, and by the end of the war it housed the largest population of Baltic citizens. All but 192 individuals were killed in this camp of 50,000 to 100,000 people. Early estimates of the population were continually upgraded as new information

was discovered, but the number is still the subject of much controversy. By the time of liberation, the camp had been burned to the ground by the Nazis and most of the records destroyed.

What has been revealed is that this camp was a particularly horrific place for children, of whom there may have been as many as 7,000. These were mostly the so-called "gang-children," young boys and girls without parents, housed in orphanages or working on farms. At one burial spot the corpses of 632 children, ages 5-9, were discovered. Eye-witness accounts report that numerous of the children were killed through medical experimentation, as many as 150 being killed every day. Others died of diseases and infection.

Most of us knew none of this when we arrived, and we were startled, I think, to find a camp whose only evidence of existence lay in the small memorials on the ground. Here also there is a terrifyingly beautiful tradition of which we had not known. In the field where the children's barracks had stood, visitors had strewn hundreds of pieces of candy, small wrapped packages that glistened in the snow. Others placed toys at one of the children's burial spots. This was the only moment during the exhausting trip that I broke down.

The camp also housed a rather informative exhibition in a small concrete hall that had been built near the entry, with the words "Behind this Gate the Earth Groans" attached. Dismaying to most of us, however, were the horribly kitsch sculptures built by the Russians, titled "The Mother," "The Humiliated," "The Unbroken," and "Solidarity," located near the center of what once had been dozens of barracks.

I believe we were all appreciative of this side trip into the painful past.

LOS ANGELES, JULY 24, 2010
Reprinted from *Green Integer Blog* (July 2010).

Day Nine: The Resort Hotel

AS I MENTIONED ABOVE, we took a bus from Vilnius to Riga, traveling along, at some points, the Black Sea in icy-cold weather. At one point we stopped by the sea just to watch the winter waves pounding the beach.

Arriving at one of the grandest and oldest hotels in the city, we were told only the jazz performers and their families could stay there. Although reservations had been made, there weren't enough empty rooms. What would the rest of us do?

We were shifted, via the bus, to what was described as a "resort hotel" in Jūrmala, a town between the Gulf of Riga and the Leilupe River about 20 minutes out of town. Certainly there were some grumbles about this new development, but we had, apparently, no choice.

The hotel was more like a college dorm, clearly built in the Soviet style. The bathrooms had only a drain instead of a contained shower stall, which troubled those of our group who had done little traveling previously. Perhaps the most disturbing aspect of this isolated

spot (although the on-line promotional sites describe it as the fifth largest Latvian city) was its darkness and desolation. A heavy snowfall had just descended upon the region, and, as several of us set out to explore the neighborhood, the entire area was so quiet and seemingly bleak that it felt somewhat foreboding, as if we had ended up in a town of the dead. Perhaps in the summer, it was beautiful and bustling, but its small dachas and wooden houses, lovely as they were, did not entice us. We couldn't know that this had been a particularly beloved spot for Communist Party officials such as Brezhnev and Khrushchev, and that over 400 wooden houses in the Art Nouveau style had been designated national treasures.

I recall seeing the so-called "House of the Benjamins," one of the favorites of the area, built in 1939, set darkly against the night.

When we returned to our concrete bunker of a hotel, however, we were not allowed to enter without our room keys and a passport. Like so many buildings in the Soviet Union, one door was closed, while in the other stood a guard. Access even to our beds was controlled.

When one of our group explained that his wife had the key, our friend was refused entry, despite our proclamations that he was "one of us."

"No. Nyet," repeated the guard.

I was angry. "He has to get in," I argued, "to dress

for the evening performance. Can't you comprehend that he is one of our party?"

"No," the guard insisted.

"We'd like to speak with your superior," another demanded.

"Nyet."

Finally our friend's wife arrived to save the day, and he, with some resentment, was allowed to pass.

The performance at a huge hall, the name of which I can't remember, was excellent that evening. And we were all fascinated by the formal stroll of the Latvian audience, arms around each other's waists as they slowly circled the halls. It was like something out of another era, like a formal dance.

But we were frustrated once again when, after the concert, we had no way to return to Jūrmala, since the bus had evidently abandoned us. Our Intourist male guide quickly flagged down several private cars, asking if, for a few American dollars, they would drive us to the resort. All but one agreed, and we finally reached our destination late that evening. Evidently, that mode of transportation was a fairly common one, for Leslie Scalapino reported to me that on a later trip to Latvia, during which she had also been forced to stay at Jūrmala, they too had had to flag down private cars. In 2008, bus service from the airport to the resort town was begun for the first time, and presumably, there is now bus service between Riga and Jūrmala.

By the next morning several inexperienced tourists among are group were boisterously angry, threatening to demand their money back and to cancel the rest of the trip. Those of us who had been in many countries, or were simply more able to deal with small inconveniencies, attempted to explain that a shower outside a stall was quite common in many parts of the world, that the guard's stubbornness was based on his attempt to protect us from black market dealers, and that the seemingly unusual method of conveyance was not a serious problem; after all we had been returned safely—and at only a cost of five dollars. One had to expect some difficulties when traveling throughout the Soviet Union. After a long conversation, they admitted that they had not been truly harmed.

The next leg of our trip was a fascinating journey to Estonia, of which I have already written in *My Year 2005*.

LOS ANGELES, SEPTEMBER 14, 2010
Reprinted from *Green Integer Blog* (September 2010).

Day Ten: Moscow Thanksgiving

AFTER A RELATIVELY pleasant time in the *moderne* world of Tallinn, it was quite a shock to return to the Soviet Union, where the 19th century seemed still to exist. The dust of the Moscow streets blurred our eyes, and the buildings, about which we had been forewarned, were notably Stalinist in appearance. Our hotel was the vast Rossiya Hotel, consisting of 3,200 rooms. Even the nearby Kremlin seemed lost in its hovering shadow. If one found one's way back to the room, it was comfortable enough, but almost unbearably overheated. In 2006 it was torn down to make way for a new, grander hostelry.

Although I continued the pointless activity of shopping in Moscow, it meant little. Hardly anything existed in the shops. Even in the famous GUM Department Store across from the Red Square there was not even a coat to be found. Numerous shops stood empty.

The trinkets left in the few open stores seemed value-less.

ROVA continued their concerts, thank heaven, which provided wonderful entertainment each evening, but in my daily walks I had grown tired of Moscow's ugly streets. I felt, after more than a week in this cold country, that we all wanted to go home.

One evening we were bused to a large theater on the edge of the city to hear Soviet poets read, our friend Ivan Zhdanov being one of the readers. But of course, the reading was in Russian, and most of us could not comprehend what was being said.

Lyn Hejinian met up with a young Russian writer there, whose name I cannot remember. He must have been still in his teens, a handsome and very gentle young man whom she invited for a walk the next day as well.

That day, November 23, 1989, was Thanksgiving back in the USA, and as a surprise our tour guide had ordered a special Thanksgiving dinner so that we might celebrate and be free, at least for one meal, of the standard Russian fare. After our walk, we encouraged our young poet friend to join us.

Russian citizens, despite Arkadii's rejection of the law, were not allowed in the international hotels; and the boy, accordingly, demurred. "Oh, I can't do that!" he insisted.

"Oh yes, you *have* to join us," Lyn insisted.

"Do come share dinner with us," I added.

"But I can't," he pleaded. "What if they find me out?"

"You're with us," Lyn added.

"But I don't speak English well enough."

"Yes, you do," I insisted. "Besides we'll do all the talking. Just pretend to listen."

And we quickly moved him through the lobby and into our dining room as we chattered away, placing him at the center of the long table the staff had arranged for us.

The dinner was edible, if I remember, although many complained loudly throughout. I believe chicken was served instead of turkey, stringy and without taste. But the potatoes were fine; even gravy. Did they add any of the other "trimmings"? I can't recall, but just having a change was good for the soul.

And despite regulations, black market dealers approached the tables with bottles of vodka and cans of caviar. I bought both, sharing the vodka.

Several of our group, however, grumpily continued in their commentary on the quality of the cuisine.

I turned to our young guest. "How did *you* like the food?"

He turned his fresh face in my direction, a smile creating a crater in its path. "It was the best meal I have ever had in my life."

He was serious! Tears welled up in my eyes.

LOS ANGELES, NOVEMBER 4, 2010
Reprinted from *Green Integer Blog* (November 2010).

Day Eleven: Breaking the Rules

FROM THE VERY beginning of our travels, we were told by our USA tour guide that there were two important rules when traveling in the Soviet Union.

One: We must never buy anything—as tempting as it might be—from the thriving Black Markets. "It is, first of all, against Soviet law, and, secondly, it is extraordinarily dangerous, given the individuals who sell the outlawed stuff.

Two: "Do not attempt to eat outside of the hotel restaurants. It's nearly impossible to get a reservation, and you never know what you might be fed or where it comes from."

Lyn Hejinian had added a third rule: "Don't ever get sick in the Soviet Union!"

The Russian tour guide suggested a fourth: "If you take a taxi, do not pay in American dollars." It was for that very reason that he had to hijack ordinary drivers to take us to our out-of-the-way resort spot in Latvia.

I am generally quite obedient, although I do have

a stubborn independent streak when it comes to being told *not* to do something while traveling, as I think I've revealed in these Russian memoirs so far. And these four rules all seemed to represent good advice. Why endanger yourself by buying off the street or in dark corners of a hotel? When I observed the seedy and surely sinister figures loitering in the dark stairwells of our Leningrad hotel, I had no desire to approach them, and I was more than a little bit frightened that they might try to approach me.

It was far easier to eat at the hotel dining rooms than to find an open or available restaurant, and after my "soku" incident, I had a great fear of unknown food stuffs.

It seemed ludicrous that taxi drivers waited to serve only "rich" Americans, leaving their compatriots to freeze on the streets.

And I had no intention of getting ill.

Yet, during our trip, I broke all but one of these sacred stipulations. It began in Latvia, when Susan Hopkins Coolidge, Clark Coolidge's wife, and I both speculated on the quality of Soviet restaurants. One of our group had gone to a restaurant before joining up with us, claiming it was an excellent experience. We were both curious and, more to the point, bored by our current repetitive fare. Consequently, we sought out a restaurant, and boldly entered. The place was utterly deserted, appearing as if it had never seen a customer. Approaching the man we thought to be the host, we were told we could not eat there.

Displaying my stubbornness, I asked, "Why not?"

"Because you do not have a reservation," snapped the host.

"How do we get a reservation?" Susan shyly asked.

"See the coat check," answered the uncooperative comrade.

We had experienced the coat check maneuver previously, when, at one hotel, we had found that we could get vodka at the coat check. At another inn, the coat check quietly arranged for cans of Beluga caviar to be sold at our table. Accordingly, we followed the host's instructions, and found a friendly face behind the empty coat racks.

"What time can we come for lunch?" we inquired.

He looked at his watch. "Two hours. You pay in advance."

"How much?"

He quoted a price in rubles that was something close to $10.00.

We readily paid, and returned precisely at the hour he'd suggested. We were quickly taken up to a pleasant table, but the room was still barren. Evidently, we were their only customers that day. But what a wonderful treat! The food was plentiful and excellent, exactly the

kind of break in diet we had been seeking. And it was, so it seems 22 years later, extraordinarily tasty. Our tip made everyone happy. I felt the experience was worth, this one time, breaking one of the rules.

By the time we reached Moscow, I had discerned that perhaps we had been somehow misinformed, that good things happened only when one *didn't* quite follow the rules. I had intended to bring back a Russian Babushka doll for my grandmother, a doll within which sits a series of nesting dolls. She had asked if I might get her one, but, clearly, none was to be found. As I have written elsewhere, most of the stores I visited were nearly empty, and when they contained products they were not what any tourist might desire. So one afternoon, meeting in the stairwell with two young Russian boys, I asked if they might be able to find the item for me. I was told to meet them in their room (Room 305) in about an hour.

Fearfully, I attended the appointment, knowing that anything might happen. I might be robbed, beaten, even killed. But no, there was the doll, and the transaction, for a few American dollars, went off without a hitch. My second such breaking of the rules was rewarded just as nicely as my first. Obviously, I might have purchased the dolls more easily in Los Angeles.

While I was in Moscow, I was determined to visit the major English-language bookstore, The House of Foreign Books. Yet, when I asked where it was located, I was told that it was quite a distance, and that I would be unable to walk. Taxis were just as hard to grab in Moscow as they had been in Riga. When I found a cabdriver willing to roll his windows down while remaining tentative about a stop, I quickly offered to pay in American dollars if he would wait for me, and, after I had visited the store, return me to where he had picked me up.

The cab door opened, and I was whisked away to Kuznetsky Most Ulitsa, where I spent more than an hour studying the shelves. Although I purchased only one book, I thoroughly enjoyed myself. And when I exited the place, there was the taxi, patiently waiting to carry me back!

I told no one about these transgressions, and Susan apparently did not mention our secret rendezvous except to her husband. As we gathered in the lobby to leave Moscow, however, the two young boys who had sold me the Russian dolls ran up to us, explaining to our US tour guide that I had forgotten my proof of purchase (obviously a fake document), necessary to take the dolls out of the country. The guide handed it over to me, tsking, "Douglas, shame on you, shame!" I bowed my head like the bad boy I was.

As I mention above, I obeyed only one of the rules. I had no intention of visiting a Soviet hospital.

LOS ANGELES, JANUARY 20, 2011
Reprinted from *Green Integer Blog* (January 2011).

Day Twelve: Trying to Leave

YESTERDAY'S BOMBING at Moscow's Domodedovo Airport could not help but remind me of our group's experiences at that same spot in 1989.

We gathered first in the large space where the bombing took place yesterday, checking our suitcases and other bags. Since I had brought a rather large sum of money which I had spent on trinkets, etc., a couple of the ROVA saxophonists asked if I might carry their cash. They had been paid in dollars, and could take out of the country only the amount with which they'd come in. I readily agreed, and we all moved forward to the large eating facility on the second floor. It was still early, and we thought we might get a bite to eat. It was just after noon, and our plane was not scheduled until 4:00.

Sitting at tables, however, produced no results. No waitress or waiter appeared. I finally stood and went over to a man who seemed to be dressed like a server. He joined me as we walked back to the group, telling our

 guide in Russian that he could not serve us without permission from the main office.

Where was the main office? I asked. He pointed, and a friend and I marched over to get the permission. There were two women behind the counter, but neither would come forward. As I had seen so many times in Russia, one of them turned away, hiding behind a small curtain, and the other just looked down as if we were invisible.

"Excuse me, I have a question," I pleaded.

I *was* invisible—and evidently mute.

"We can see you," said my friend, "even if you can't see us."

"We've been told we need to get permission here."

Neither of them moved.

"Permission to eat. We're hungry."

They had turned to stone.

My friend turned back to the group, while I went forward in the other direction just to explore. A few feet away, I found a small Japanese cafe, open, apparently, and serving. But, unlike the larger food court, wherein our group sat waiting, it was terribly expensive. Soups cost $20, some meals went for $50. I was hungry and sat down to eat a small bowl of noodles.

When I returned to the ROVA group, I told them about the Japanese spot, but none of them wanted to pay that much. Suddenly, as if a miracle had just occurred, the larger pavilion opened their windows and servers came out to take the group's orders.

While we waited, a message came over the loud-speakers—in English—that our plane was slightly delayed. Yet as soon as the food began to arrive, another message—this time in Russian only—reported that our plane would soon be ready to board.

Our guide, relaying this information to us, suggested we leave the food to face the interrogation of the passport inspectors.

Just as I have described in my 2006 volume about my visit to East Germany, the inspectors spent an inordinate amount of time stamping things and staring into our faces. The questions they posed were generally simple if somewhat inexplicable—"Why do you visit our country?" "Why are you leaving?" "What are you taking with you?" "What cities have you visited?" etc. The problem was that no matter *how* you answered, it appeared to be "incorrect." I felt as if they were attempting to keep me there until I confessed some criminal act or intention. It would have been comical except that it was so foreboding, and no smiles were encouraged.

Eventually, I was released along with Clark

Coolidge and several others. Yet we noticed one of our friends, my roommate Peter Vilms, was still being questioned, and Clark and I determined—unlike the others who had passed through the screening into another waiting room—to check on him. We stood aside for a long while, but he seemed to be making no progress, so I joined him at the window where he was held.

"They're evidently upset with me," he explained, "because I came into the Soviet Union on the ferry from Estonia." Peter, of Estonian ancestry, had arrived earlier than the rest of us so that he could visit relatives in his parents' home country.

Strangely, the inspector was speaking only in Russian, a language Peter could neither understand nor speak. The interrogation also included the requisite stares and stamping, but this was far more intimidating, and nothing Peter said seemed to help his situation. The man clearly was determined that something was "wrong" here, that Peter had obviously been "up to something," and there was apparently no way to change his mind.

For a few minutes, I tried to intervene, explaining he was with our group and visited Estonia only as a tourist. But that seemed to have an even more negative effect, so I ceased, and moved off to the sidelines where Clark and I continued our wait.

By now all the others had gone through screening

and were gathered on the other side of the glass wall for entry onto the plane. Peter was completely stalled, and there seemed no way to free him, until suddenly he was waved on. The moment the three of us began to go through screening, however, three soldiers blockaded the route, pulling down a small wooden bar.

"We have to join our party over there," we explained.

Their answer was "Nyet!"

We tried to get the attention of our friends, but everyone seemed oblivious.

Turning again to the guards, I tried to enter, but was barred yet again.

We had all had our breaking points during this Soviet trip, and Clark's came at that moment as he beat his head in frustration, again and again, against the glass. Finally someone from our group came up to the screening place.

"They won't let us in," Clark nearly shouted.

"It's okay," spoke the man. "The flight has evidently been cancelled."

A while later, we were encouraged to join the others, and we passed through without event.

Eventually, the plane was loaded. Evidently, there had been a threat of a strike in Finland, and the Russians were determined not to cross the strike line. We were just relieved that we had made it on board, and before long we were rumbling down the snow-covered runway to someplace else.

We had, however, missed our connecting flight from Finland to the US, and the Russians were forced to put us up for the night in a hotel, a very nice hotel indeed, the Helsinki InterContinental. Sitting down for dinner in the hotel's restaurant, we behaved like wide-eyed Russians visiting the West for the very first time. I think nearly all of us ordered up big steaks, with piles of potatoes and other sides. After dinner, we all took walks, amazed at the gleaming store-windows filled with stylish shoes, jewels, gowns, coats. Helsinki looked like a gem against the night sky. It was as if we had never seen such wealth. Indeed, in that year Helsinki was the most expensive city in Europe. In 2010, the most expensive European city was Moscow! In recent renovations, Domodedovo Airport has added 20 new restaurants and several jewelry boutiques.

LOS ANGELES, JANUARY 25, 2011
Reprinted from *Green Integer Blog* (January 2011).

FOUR FILMS BY ANDREI TARKOVSKY

The Star at the Bottom of the Well

VLADIMIR BOGOMOLOV, ANDREI KONCHALOVSKY, MIKHAIL PAPAVA, AND ANDREI TARKOVSKY (WRITERS, BASED ON A STORY BY VLADIMIR BOGOMOLOV), ANDREI TARKOVSKY (DIRECTOR) **IVANOVO DETSTVO (IVAN'S CHILDHOOD)** / 1962 / I SAW THIS MOVIE AT THE LOS ANGELES COUNTY MUSEUM OF ART ON JANUARY 23, 2010

IN ONE OF the most astounding film directorial debuts since Orson Welles' *Citizen Kane*, Andrei Tarkovsky startled the cinematic world with his first feature film, *Ivan's Childhood*, which won the 1962 Golden Lion in the Venice Film Festival.

As critics have pointed out, in this film we can already see many of the elements of Tarkovsky's later works: a detailed attention to nature, long focuses on isolate elements of a scene which generate a feeling of

abstraction, and scenarios suffused with visual images that generate emotional and psychological reactions, drawing the viewer into the frame or—as Bazin might argue—pushing the film from the screen into the real world.

From the very first frame of this film we already recognize its young hero as a ghost, a figure of another time, who has lost his way (along with his soul and sanity) in a cruel world from which he can no longer escape. Only in his fleeting dreams, or brief pauses to catch his breath in his run from German territory, does Ivan (soulfully played by Nikolai Burlyayev) get any respite from the realities of war and hate.

One of the earliest flashbacks (in a film that one might describe as one long flashback into a series of fragmented worlds) is a scene where Ivan and his mother stare down a well. The light emanating from the bottom, clearly the reflection of the sun, they concur, is a star at the bottom of the well. Despite the dark terror of the deep, for Ivan water represents a living force, almost his natural element, as we witness in the opening shot trekking through the swampy waters of the Dnepr.

At several points in his memories, Ivan is seen drinking from a bucket borne by his mother. Regularly the child calmly endures pouring rainfall. When he is finally  brought to Lt. Galtsev (Yevgeni Zharikov) by Russian soldiers, Ivan's face is almost a shrine to moisture, he himself having been transformed into something close to a star at the bottom of a well, a face shining through the water.

Galtsev is about to dismiss the urchin, but with a determined insolence, Ivan insists that he call Headquarters, Number 51, and report that he has arrived. The man at the other end of the line, Lt-Colonel Gryaznov (Nikolai Grinko), demands that Galtsev give the boy a pencil and paper so that he can make his report. Galtsev orders hot water, tells the boy to strip, and helps to bathe him. The child, refusing food, finishes his report, chews a few bits of bread, and falls asleep. Galtsev carefully tucks a cover around the child. Within just a few minutes he has clearly fallen in love with the waif.

Like Billy Budd, Ivan is outwardly a sign of beauty and innocence, naturally drawing people to him; within, however, and unlike Billy, he has become a machine

of hate.

We soon discover how this monster was created: his mother and sister have been killed by the Germans, and Ivan, joining the partisans, saw his new friends trapped and murdered. He has also seen, so he declares, the Maly Trostenets extermination camp.

In opposition to these realities, presented mostly in Ivan's dreams, are paradisical memories: a ride on the back of a truck filled with apples, which, falling to the beach, are joyfully gobbled up by horses. His sister and others innocently play hide-and-seek; Ivan thrillingly races across the beach.

Gryaznov and others try to convince Ivan to attend a military school away from the line of action, but he refuses, threatening to return to the partisans, and Galtsev and his soldiers are forced to take on the care and strategic use of the child.

Planning a surprise bombing of the German camp, Captain Kholin, Lt. Galtsev, and Ivan slowly retrace Ivan's former path of escape, the men at one point leaving Ivan to go forward on his own while they return, bringing with them two hanged bodies of their men.

Perhaps the worst thing about being at the front line are the intense silences. In the middle of the film, Kholin and the camp nurse, Masha, play out a game of sexual advancement and retreat within a frighteningly still beech woods, the very silence of that place hinting at the danger in their game. Now, the silence Kholin and Galtsev encounter as they quietly return to their bunkers represents the failure of Ivan's grenades which didn't explode. Despite their denials, they know, and we suspect, Ivan has been caught.

The last scene of Tarkovsky's painful love letter to a lost past takes place in Berlin at war's end. Together Galtsev and another of Ivan's former military friends peruse the scattered files of those caught and executed by the Germans. On the floor they miraculously discover Ivan's file, noting he has been hung. Like so many of Tarkovsky's heroes, Ivan is a victim of borders, being a child without a childhood, a man without manhood, an innocent filled with hate, a lovely being killed before he could come into full existence.

LOS ANGELES, FEBRUARY 2, 2010
Reprinted from *Green Integer Blog* (February 2010).

Creating the Impossible

ANDREI TARKOVSKY AND ANDREI MIKHALKOV-
KONCHALOVSKY (SCREENPLAY), ANDREI TARKOVSKY
(DIRECTOR) **ANDREI RUBLEV** / 1966 / I SAW THE FILM
AT THE LOS ANGELES COUNTY MUSEUM OF ART ON
JANUARY 30, 2010

LIKE THE ICONIC IMAGES of the artist upon which
this movie focuses, Tarkovsky's *Andrei Rublev* is less a
story or even a series of stories than it is a panorama
of stopped moments in time. Like the great films of
director Sergei Parajanov, *Shadows of Forgotten Ancestors* and two years earlier *Sayat Nova* of 1968, *Andrei
Rublev* is less a film about time than it is a series of emblematic images, scenes that in their slow resolution of
beauty and horror reveal a passionate and transforma-
tive experience that has little do with story or plot. And
in that sense, nearly all of Tarkovsky's works from this
film forward reveal themselves in formal cinematic patterns instead of narrative space.

Tarkovsky divides his film into nine parts: a Prologue, seven moments in time, followed by an Epilogue.

The Jester, Summer 1400
Theophanes the Greek, Summer-Winter-Spring-
    Summer 1405-1406
The Holiday, 1408
The Last Judgment, Summer 1408
The Raid, Autumn 1408
The Silence, Winter 1412
The Bell, Spring-Summer-Winter-Spring 1423-1424

Already in the Prologue Tarkovsky sets up a kind of abbreviated pattern for the rest of the film. Here Yefim, a creator on the run, is chased by a mob as he daringly jumps into his balloon, a hide-bound, medieval version of a hot air balloon. Amazingly, with Yefim hanging by the ropes, the balloon takes him up and away, revealing an entirely new perspective of the universe, as the frustrated mob below menacingly lift their fists into space. Yet, as in numerous occasions throughout this film, the miraculous creation is doomed from the start; Yefim and his balloon quickly come crashing to earth, sealing, it appears, his doom.

In "The Jester," Andrei (Anatoly Solonitsyn) and his fellow monks, Danil (Nikolai Grinko) and Kirill (Ivan Lapikov), leave their Andronikov Monastery

in search of work.
Forced by heavy rains
to seek shelter in a
barn, the three en-
counter a surly crowd
being rudely enter-
tained by a jester, who

mocks not only the approaching monks but all others
of social position and power, including the Boyars,
members of a social class similar to England's knights.
While Danil and Andrei watch the bawdy show, the
self-righteous Kirill, we later discover, secretly sneaks
away to report the Jester. Soon after, a group of soldiers
appears, beating the Jester and arresting him.

Here we see another kind of creator being pun-
ished for his art. Through this enactment, moreover,
we begin to perceive the harsh conditions of those who
must suffer at the hands of the powerful and rich. There
is clearly little room for even a joyous mockery of values
in this unjust society.

"Theophanes the Greek" explores the life of the
prominent master of icons. Visiting Theophanes, Kirill
is surprised to find the artist at a complete standstill,
all of his apprentices having abandoned him to watch
the public torture and execution of a criminal. To his
surprise and delight, Theophanes offers him a position
to become his assistant in the decoration of the Cathe-

dral of the Annunciation in Moscow. Kirill pretends to resist, but finally accepts the offer if Theophanes will come to the Andronikov Monastery and offer him the position in front of the other monks.

When the time comes, Theophanes instead sends a messenger, asking Andrei Rublev to be his assistant. Danil is angry and refuses to join his friend in the journey, but later relents and wishes Rublev well. Kirill, furious about the transition of events, not only hurls accusations at Andrei but verbally attacks all his fellow monks, leaving the monastery forever. Andrei has no choice but to take along a slightly oafish boy, Foma, as his assistant. Andrei realizes now that even joy can bring forth anger, jealousy, and loneliness, for it is clear from his conversation with Kirill that in the past the two have been deeply in love, with Andrei admitting that he has seen the world through Kirill's eyes.

"The Holiday" reveals another side of the highly Christian Russian world which Andrei inhabits. On a nighttime stroll Andrei encounters a community of pagan worshippers celebrating rituals of sensuality and lust. The celebrants run naked through the forest and fornicate openly on the beach.

As a voyeur to the festivities, Andrei is caught by a group of men, tied to a cross, and threatened with drowning. A young naked woman comes forward and frees him. As the sun rises a group of soldiers, clearly

Christian, begins to attack the pagans with the intent, apparently, of killing them. The young woman escapes by swimming the river where Andrei and his fellow men are gathered in a boat. They force the young Foma to look away as the naked pagans are rounded up.

Again a force of possible creation has been thwarted. Even a celebration of nature and the sexual body is dangerous in this highly divided and fragile world through which Andrei has silently passed.

Indeed what Andrei has witnessed in the various events of the film so far comes to influence his early statement of values in "The Last Judgment." Here Andrei and Danil have found an excellent job, the decoration of a church in Vladimir, but their work is not progressing, as Andrei, somewhat from doubt, but gradually out of principle, refuses to paint the topic he has been assigned. The horror of the subject appalls him, as he recognizes the theme as being another way that those in power terrify the common folk.

A young girl, a holy fool, enters the church, peeing at its entrance, desecrating the spot; yet her simple-mindedness and innocence allow Andrei to suggest the painting of a feast instead of a punishment. We never see him put a brush to paint, nor paint to wall, for it is not the act that matters but the significance of thought. Once again, creativity has been squelched by those in authority. But at least we now have a hero who may overcome the obstacles he might meet.

"The Raid," a series of absolutely horrifying images of rape, torture, and murder, seems almost to wipe out any possibility of creativity and hope. While the Grand Prince is away in Lithuania, his jealous brother (paralleling Kirill's jealousy of Andrei) has joined forces with the Tartars. Their invasion of Vladimir, replete with cows set afire, falling horses, and dozens of humans speared, knifed, and quartered simply for the sport of it, presents visually the world that Andrei had refused to paint. It is, in short, a hell on earth. As Durochka is taken away by a Russian to be raped, Andrei takes an ax to the perpetrator. In the end of this slaughter, only he and the now-mad girl have survived. Having been transformed from a spiritual being into a murderer, Andrei gives up any possibility of creation, abandoning both his art and his voice to the brutal world.

"The Silence" is just that, a long emptiness that has now settled over the Andronikov Monastery for four years and will continue to define Andrei's world for 12 more. It is a cold winter and the monks have little to eat. Old and physically destroyed, Kirill returns, ask-

ing to be taken in. He
is finally accepted,
but only if he will
copy the scriptures
15 times before his
death.

But even Andrei's silence cannot help. He has kept
Durochka with him. But when Tartars stop at the monastery for a water break, their leader carries her away
to be his eighth wife. The passive monks, including
Andrei, can do nothing to help, and the idiot child is
delighted by the act; now she shall eat, and live—if they
let her—an exciting life. For Andrei, however, it represents simply another failure; he cannot even protect the
innocent.

The final set of scenes is perhaps the most profound. Men are seeking a bellmaker for a new cathedral
being built by their prince; the boy they find at the noted bellcaster's hut tells them his father has died along
with the rest of his family. The only other bellmaker is
near death. They turn to go, afraid of the consequences
of having been unable to find a craftsman. The young
boy, Boriska, however, quickly tells them that he can
cast a bell, that his father has told him the secret upon
his deathbed.

The men are doubtful but have little choice, and
take him away with them. Now Boriska is caught up

 in something vast; he must find a location, the right clay to use, must dig a pit, put up molds, negotiate with the Prince and other wealthy figures for the correct mix of silver, melt the metals, and pour them into the molds. Nearly night and day, the young worker supervises and works without stop. Will the clay hold, will the bell, if it survives, actually ring or remain mute? Boriska knows that if he fails, it will surely mean his death. As he quietly observed the actions of the pagans, Andrei silently watches.

After months of this exhausting work, the furnaces are fueled and released into the mold. When it cools, the clay is chipped away. Now they must haul the bell, with an intricate series of ropes, across the stream and up into the half-constructed tower. Hundreds of men work against time, as the nobles gather to celebrate the bell's completion, many of them certain that such a clumsy child cannot possibly have accomplished the task. So frightened is Boriska that he can hardly participate, but he is ordered to come forward as everyone waits in anticipation.

The clapper is pulled, pulled in the other direction, returned, and pulled again. Finally, the bell rings out a somewhat deep, sonorous, clang. All are overjoyed.

The villagers applaud, the nobles smile and turn away to continue their celebrations in the castle.

Boriska is seen in this long-shot panorama walking alone into the distance. Suddenly he falls into a puddle of muddy water as Andrei passes. We observe the child weeping uncontrollably. Andrei goes to him, holding Boriska's head to his chest. The tears continue. "I lied," admits the child. His father told him nothing, left him in ignorance: "The skinflint," cries the young man. The bell has come into existence, clearly, only out of the boy's innate talent and faith. He has created the impossible.

Breaking his long silence, Andrei invites the boy to join him: "Come with me. You'll cast bells. I'll paint icons." Art may, after all, survive.

In a final epilogue, Tarkovsky transforms the screen into color, and gradually, in an almost abstract tracing of Rublev's images, shows us what resulted from that coupling, an incomparable visual splendor.

LOS ANGELES, FEBRUARY 9, 2010
Reprinted from *Green Integer Blog* (February 2010).

Hope

ARKADY STRUGATSKY, BORIS STRUGATSKY, AND
ANDREI TARKOVSKY (SCREENPLAY, BASED ON A NOVEL
BY THE STRUGATSKYS), ANDREI TARKOVSKY (DIREC-
TOR) **STALKER** / 1979 / THE SCREENING I SAW WAS AT
THE LOS ANGELES COUNTY MUSEUM OF ART ON JANU-
ARY 23, 2010

ANDREI TARKOVSKY's fifth film, *Stalker*, is, ostensibly,
a science fiction film, but viewers who seek out the *Ter-
minator* series and other action science fiction fantasies
need not bother. For this long, sometimes ponderous
work is a deep rumination, often using the genre of the
dialogue, to discuss weighty issues such as doubt and
faith, fulfillment and desire, art and science, and the individual and the collective. All of this is made palatable
and, indeed, becomes emotionally engaging through
the filmmaker's near-obsessive focus on images, the
screen often transforming into an almost abstract collage of the detritus of man-made machines, construc-
tions, and tools—used mostly for the rape of nature

and human destruction—set against the rejuvenating forces of the natural world.

In a small, crumbling village, just outside of the protected and prohibited "Zone," lives the Stalker (Aleksandr Kaidanovsky), his wife (Alisa Freindlich), and their mute and crippled daughter, nicknamed Monkey. The sepia color of the film gives the outpost (at least in the new print I saw at the Los Angeles County Museum of Art) a slightly sickly yellow tone. We know immediately that this town is deadly to its inhabitants. Three nuclear silos appear in the distance, the streets are littered with debris and filth, even the Stalker's house is perspiring with moisture. When the trains pass, the entire house rattles, moving a drinking-glass and other objects in its wake. This is a world on the verge of collapse.

Beyond it lies an even more "dead and deadly" region, the "Zone," site of a large meteorite or nuclear disaster, or....well, no one knows. The authorities know only that its inhabitants died, and when soldiers and others tried to enter, they never returned. Finally, it became apparent that the only way to keep people from doing harm to themselves was to fence it off, to prohibit entry. Policemen cruise the streets of the Stalker's small village, shooting anyone who may even appear to be trying to enter the "Zone."

In the Soviet period in which Tarkovsky made this film, the implications of the "Zone" were even broader. As Slavoj Žižek noted in *The Pervert's Guide to Cinema*:

> For a citizen of the defunct Soviet Union, the notion of a forbidden Zone gives rise to (at least) five associations: Zone is (1) Gulag, i.e. a separated prison territory; (2) a territory poisoned or otherwise rendered uninhabitable by some technological (biochemical, nuclear...) catastrophe, like Chernobyl; (3) the secluded domain in which the *nomenklatura* live; (4) foreign territory to which access is prohibited (like the enclosed West Berlin in the midst of the GDR); (5) a territory where a meteorite struck (like Tunguska in Siberia).

In short, Tarkovsky's "Zone" is any or all of these; it does not stand for one thing, and the essential fact is its prohibition, like so much else in Soviet life.

Following in the footsteps of a figure nicknamed Porcupine, the Stalker has learned some of the secrets of this forbidden place, and now, for a sum of money, he is willing to take people in and out of this prohibited space, facing possible death from the surrounding military (the Stalker has already spent long periods in jail) and, most of all, the shifting "death traps" of the "Zone" itself.

Yet some people are willing to take their chances; a writer and professor, each named after their profession, have heard that within the "Zone" lies a room which fulfills a person's innermost desires. Unlike the hopeless, hapless heap of rubble outside of the prohibited space, the "Zone," despite its treacherous potential, offers people the ineffable concept of hope.

In that sense, the "Zone" is the shadow of the "real" world which the Stalker, the Writer, and the Professor inhabit, a kind of dream landscape where, despite the evidence of disaster and the potential nightmares, imagination reigns, and human potential is a possibility. Yet, as the Stalker warns his partners in crime, not everyone will survive. Those who are the most wretched, who have the least ego and are most flexible, have the greatest chance of surviving, but even they are sometimes destroyed by the dangers that lie in wait. It is almost as if the "Zone" were itself a being, tricking those who dare to enter it into their own death.

After surviving the gunfire of the guards, the three escape via a railway handcar into a world that suddenly (as in *The Wizard of Oz*) shifts into color. Yet here no human beings exist, not even little ones. The plants have overrun the destroyed power lines and the tanks of the military, but their flowers have no scent. It is beautiful and, as the Stalker joyously proclaims, "absolutely silent," but it is a place without mankind, a world, in short, of death.

Almost immediately we realize that the two individuals whom the Stalker is guiding have little of what it takes to survive. The Writer is a worn-out genius, an alcoholic believing only in logic, and longing for the "magic" of the Middle Ages. His mantra is that everything is a triangle: A1=B1=C1. Despite the Stalker's stated restrictions, he brings with him a bottle of liquor and, as we later discover, a hand gun. The Professor is equally smug, insistently cynical of the human race and of any possible salvation promised by his own scientific kind.

Slowly they make their way toward the "room," seemingly just a few yards from where they stand; but both are frustrated with the Stalker's insistence that they cannot attempt a direct assault. Instead they must make their way around things in order to survive, turning this way and that, moving every few feet toward a cloth tied up with metal nuts, retrieving it, and throwing it out in another direction, before setting forth again.

Indeed the rules imposed upon this absurd journey often seem to be right out of Samuel Beckett's writings, and the two "tourists," arguing as they go, often appear to be playing out a variant version of *Waiting for Godot* or *Mercier and Camier*. So inconsistent seem the Stalker's rules that the Writer finally determines that he will disobey and move straight ahead; but when he attempts the maneuver, the house itself warns him to stay away, and he retreats, insisting that he was called back by his colleagues, they insisting that he spoke to himself in a transformed voice.

At one point, when the Professor disappears (against the rules, he has returned for his forgotten rucksack), the remaining two proceed through a rainy drainpipe, only to find him safely on the other side. It is as if space itself circles back. So exhausted are the three, they fall into a grumbling sleep, the two outsiders fighting like a long married couple until they collapse in a coma-like sleep, heaped each upon each, a stray dog hunkering down beside them.

Besides the simple beauty (and marked ugliness) of the landscape,* what helps the viewer to accept these somewhat academic dialogic encounters is the humor of it all, the Kafka-like ridiculousness of the men's positions, particularly given their improbable situation. What we gradually come to comprehend, moreover, is that despite their oppositional stances toward life, they

now have to obey the rules of a different world, and can make no progress without them.

Their final long voyage through a dark and filthy tunnel, although dramatically eerie, is less important. We know that despite their bluff, these "tourists" are both wretched men, unhappy even in their great successes. They will survive the trip, but will they survive the "gift" of the room, the realization of their "deepest, innermost" wishes?

As they reach the entry to the room, the Stalker once again explains what is about to happen before encouraging them to enter, reiterating that, having learned from the example of Porcupine (a stalker who entered in order save his brother, but instead became fabulously wealthy, and, soon after, committed suicide), stalkers are not permitted to set foot in this sacred space.

The Writer gets cold feet, realizing that the trap of the promised magic is that the innermost wish of any individual may not be what he consciously desires. It may be a destructive force, a petty wish that counteracts any human good within that being. No, he proclaims, he will not enter.

The Professor has already understood that such a force might be used by the truly evil men in society to take over governments, to kill thousands, etc., and he has brought a bomb with him to destroy the spot.

Terrified that this one last abode of "hope," the remaining "treasure" of Pandora's box, will be forever destroyed, the Stalker lunges for the bomb, but both the Writer and Professor fight him off. Again and again he tries desperately to save his world, but these are not men of belief, representing as they do the elite, the select yet totally disaffected Soviet upper class; whereas, in his blind faith, he is a muttering fool, a mere stalker, always on the search for something or someone.

Yet his fervor, his plea for the salvation of this sacred place, gradually wins them over. The Writer apologizes as the Professor disassembles the bomb, the camera focusing with intensity for several moments on the three men gathered at the future's gate, the floor of the room inexplicably flooding.

Returning home exhausted, the Stalker and his "passengers" gather once more at the local bar before his wife comes to fetch him. At home, he reports that he realizes he can never take another person into his beloved "Zone," that he must give up the one thing he was able to offer others because there is no longer anyone who believes strongly enough. When his wife proposes that he take *her* to the room so that she may achieve her secret desires, the Stalker admits he cannot dare that. Even he, it appears, does not have enough faith.

Has the "Zone" been his own fantasy, as the Writer and Professor have hinted, being the one thing in his string of life failures that he has been able to give, to create? We can never know.

His wife's monologue about both their sufferings and love which have allowed happiness and hope to co-exist, however, seems to point to their survival, perhaps even to their triumph over the difficulties they face. The rugged dreamer will ultimately accept the ordinariness of his life.

In the distance we hear the rumble of the train. Their deaf and crippled daughter sits alone at the table. First a glass, then a bottle, and finally a second glass slide across the table, the last falling to the floor. The train comes nearer, and with it, embedded deep within the rumble of the railway, a muted musical accompaniment from Beethoven's "Ode to Joy," which disappears as quickly as the engine passes. We now must ask ourselves, was it the train that moved the glass in the very first scene, and now these three objects, or was it an extraordinary telekinetic gift with which the child is possessed? There is no answer when it comes to such a question, only hope.

---

*Most of these scenes were filmed near Tallinn, Estonia, in an area around a small river with a half-functioning hydroelectric station. As sound-editor Victor Sharun has written:

> Up the river was a chemical plant and it poured out poisonous liquids downstream. There was even this shot in *Stalker*: snow falling in the summer and white foam floating down the river. In fact it was some horrible poison. Many women in our crew got allergic reactions on their faces. Tarkovsky died from cancer of the right bronchial tube. And Tolya Solonitsyn too. That it was all connected to the location shooting for *Stalker* became clear to me when Larisa Tarkovskaya died from the same illness in Paris.

LOS ANGELES, JANUARY 24, 2010
Reprinted from *Green Integer Blog* (January 2010).

Waiting for Something Else

ANDREI TARKOVSKY (SCREENPLAY AND DIRECTOR)
OFFRET (THE SACRIFICE) / 1986 / THE SCREENING I
SAW WAS AT THE LOS ANGELES COUNTY MUSEUM OF
ART ON FEBRUARY 5, 2010

COMPARED WITH the epic works such as *Andrei Rublev* and even *Stalker*, Tarkovsky's last film seems narratively simpler. His roving and constantly shifting images become, in the hands of cinematographer Sven Nykvist (also Ingmar Bergman's cinematographer), a series of longer and more focused scenes; in a film of 149 minutes there are, reportedly, only 115 shots.

Also because of its Bergmanian and, particularly, Chekovian influences, the narrative shifts from Tarkovsky's emblematic method of storytelling in his previous films to a more traditionally Western storyline—although Tarkovsky often purposely thwarts the more normative dramatic results.

Isolated on Bergman's island of Gotland, the fam-

 ily at the center of this film live, as does the family in Chekov's *The Seagull*, in what might be described as a summer house, but located by the sea instead of a lake.

Their home, a place that seemed to call out to both Alexander (played by Bergman actor Erland Josephson) and his wife Adelaide (Susan Fleetwood) upon their first encountering it, is something they both still love and yet it is a container for all their hurts and pains. Dressed almost as turn-of-the-century women right out of Chekov, both Alexander's wife and his daughter (Valérie Mairesse) quietly spar with each other. Indeed something seems to be sickening all the inhabitants of this house. The young son, nicknamed "Little Man," has just undergone some sort of throat operation, and is mute throughout most of the film. Alexander, a former actor, and now a successful aesthetician, journalist, and professor, is undergoing a kind of existential crisis, and is unable to find meaning or belief in his life. Alexander's behavior alternates between long philosophical monologues and self-consumed silence. As his friend Otto chides him, he is one of those desperately "waiting for something else" like a Beckett figure.

Otto, a part-time postman, collects strange incidents and falls into temporary faints. The Icelandic maid, Maria, to put it simply, is most strange. Yet, as their doctor friend and visitor, Victor, later reveals, it is Adelaide and her incessant attacks on her husband, and her outspoken dismissal of those around her that most make this house an unbearable place in which to exist. By film's end, Victor is determined to leave it (and, apparently, the daughter) for Australia.

The day on which the film begins is Alexander's 50th birthday, and all have gathered here to endure a celebratory dinner. At this point, however, Tarkovsky turns the tables, so to speak. What has been a Chekov-like family comedy-drama is suddenly transformed into an international event as the radio and television, in blips of static, report that the world is in the throes of another great war, with the certainty of a nuclear holocaust.

Adelaide lapses into a fit of terror, screaming out for the men "to do something," as Alexander retreats to his room upstairs, pondering the unbearable wait of the next few hours. This, he is suddenly certain, was what he was waiting for, a call to action. Although he has previously described himself as a nonbeliever, he now intensely prays to God, insisting that he will give up everything he loves, his son, his house, his life, if only the holocaust can be averted.

While we hear the roars of jet planes flying overhead, the family, some now sedated by Victor, quietly wait out what is suddenly a *real* trag-edy, reiterating their personal pains and failures. Otto, who has previously left, climbs secretly through a second-story window to ludicrously reveal to Alexander that he must go to the house of the Icelandic maid—who is a witch, but of the right kind—and lie with her through the night in order to save the world.

Suddenly we begin to suspect that Tarkovsky is pulling out the rug from his story once more. Just as we might have imagined that the original tragicomedy has reverted into an allegory of horror, by now combining pagan acts with Christian prayers, we begin to see another kind of comic potential in this work.

In his essay "Zarathustra's Gift in Tarkovsky's *Sacrifice*," Gino Moliterno convincingly argues that Tarkovsky is reiterating in his film Nietzsche's Zoroastrian notion of the Eternal Return that Tarkovsky intimates at the beginning of the movie with a reference to Zarathustra's dwarf. Alexander, he argues, who has come to the crossroads of his life (like Tarkovsky, who himself was dying of cancer at the time of the filming), is by

film's end willing to say, "Is that life? Well then, once again!"

I argue that Tarkovsky purposely combines both the pagan and the Christian worlds, symbolized by the gentle drama of the turn-of-the-century combined with images of the horrors of 20th century wars. What some critics have complained is a murky mix of paganism and Christianity or a narrative incongruity is, in fact, a kind of delicious *pot au feu* in which Tarkovsky's character pluckily mixes religions of the present and the past, represented by various dramatic genres, in order to transform the present into another kind of reality, pointing up both the past and the potential for a different future. The witchcraft of Maria weaves its spell, just as the Christian moral choices of abstinence motivate Alexander's acts.

Waking the next morning, the electricity has returned, and all seems like it was earlier the day before. The other figures quietly share a breakfast table, seeming to have forgotten what they have undergone during the night. Was it all just a dream, a horrible nightmare spawned by Alexander's troubled mind? The house is still sick, the patients still in need of a cure, even if the world at large has been salvaged.

Tricking them to take a morning walk, Alexander dances and trots around the house, almost comically snacking on tabletop leftovers as he prepares a fire which, once he has set, quickly creates an inferno.

As family and friends come running back to the burning pyre, an ambulance miraculously arrives to cart off Alexander, a man apparently gone mad. Such a truth-teller must be put away immediately. Whether or not he has redeemed their lives, has managed to resurrect the lives of his family and friends, he has redeemed his own life; for once he has acted instead of passively waiting for the end.

Tarkovsky's brilliant film closes with a scene in which "Little Man," a future Alexander, lies under a tree which the two of them have planted in the very first scene. The child, in his first and only lines of the film, speaks: "In the beginning was the word...why is that, papa?" If Alexander is determined to spend the rest of his life in silence, to give up all that life has meant, the boy will continue to speak in a dialogue *with* and for him in the next generation with its new possibilities. The magic, Christian or pagan, has been accomplished.

LOS ANGELES, APRIL 15, 2010
Reprinted from *Green Integer Blog* (March 2010).

When I first saw The Sacrifice *years earlier, I was immensely moved by it, and had the feeling when I fell asleep that night that I dreamt the movie all over again, as if it had somehow rewound itself in my head. I did not know at that time that Tarkovsky had had a somewhat similar experience occur during the work's filming. When his crew first attempted to film the burning house, the camera jammed, and they lost the crucial shot. At great expense and time that Tarkovsky, ill during the shooting, did not have, they rebuilt the house and filmed the scene again with two cameras.*

Moliterno points out that this ironic situation might have reiterated one of Tarkovsky's themes: "Is that life? Well then, once again!"

LOS ANGELES, APRIL 16, 2010

Index

Green Integer
On   Net

"*Go In*" and visit our new on-line book publishing venture on our website (www.greeninteger.com). Green Integer is publishing several new, older, and out-of-stock Sun & Moon, Green Integer, and other archived titles online.

Ordering through PayPal, customers will be provided with a PDF link within 24 hours of payment so that they can either read the books on the computer or download them to print to other media.

We believe that this service will help make titles available for general readers, classroom students, and scholars.

SELECTED "ON NET" TITLES

David Antin *Definitions* [na] $5.00
Charles Bernstein *Dark City* [978-1-557131-62-1] FREE
Paul Celan *Lightduress* [1-931243-75-1] $8.00
Clark Coolidge *Solution Passage* [0-940650-55-X] $5.00
Arkadii Dragomoschenko *Xenia* [1-55713-107-4] $5.00
Alfredo Giuliani (ed.) *I Novissimi: Poetry for the Sixties* [978-1-55713-137-9] $10.00
Peter Glassgold *Hwæt!* [978-1-933382-41-8] $5.00
Lyn Hejinian *My Life* [1-931243-33-6] $5.00
Ko Un *Songs for Tomorrow: A Collection of Poems* 1960-2002 [978-1-933382-70-8] $5.00
Lucebert *The Collected Poems: Volume 1* [978-1-55713-407-3] $10.00
F. T. Marinetti *The Untameables* [978-1-933382-23-4] $5.00
Douglas Messerli *Dark* [978-1-933382-14-2] $5.00
Amelia Rosselli *War Variations* [1-931243-55-7] $5.00
Gertrude Stein *Tender Buttons* [1-931243-42-5] $5.00
Stanzas in Mediation [978-1-55713-169-0] $5.00
Guiseppe Steiner *Drawn States of Mind* [978-1-557131-71-3] FREE
Susana Thénon *distancias / distances* [1-55713-153-8] $5.00
John Wieners *707 Scott Street* [978-1-557132-52-9] FREE

GREEN INTEGER
SELECTED NEW TITLES

2011

±**Julien Gracq** *The Peninsula* [978-1-933382-39-5] $12.95
Richard Kalich *Penthouse F* [978-1-55713-413-4] $15.95
Joe Ross *wordlick* [978-1-55713-415-8] $11.95
†**Nelly Sachs** *Collected Poems 1944-1949* [978-1-933382-57-9] $13.95
Ko Un *Himalaya Poems* [978-1-55713-412-7] $13.95

2012

Blaise Cendrars *Films without Images* [978-1-933392-55-5] $14.95
Jean Frémon *The Botanical Garden* [978-1-55713-411-0] $13.95
Peter Glassgold *Hwæt!* [978-1-933382-41-8] $12.95
Douglas Messerli *Dark* [978-1-933382-14-2] $12.95
    Reading Films: My International Cinema [978-1-55713-427-1] $29.95
Jules Michelet *The Sea* [1-933382-11-2] $15.95
±**Ivo Michiels** *Book Alpha and Orchis Militaris* [978-1-933382-15-9]
    $12.95
Yuri Olyesha *Envy* [978-1-931243-12-4] $13.95

2013

Eleanor Antin *Conversations with Stalin* [978-1-55713-420-2] $14.50
Ascher/Straus *Hank Forest's Party* [978-193338-247-0] $12.95
±**Reiner Kunze** *Rich Catch in the Empty Creel* [978-1-933382-24-1]
    $15.95
Lucebert *The Collected Poems: Volume 1* [978-1-55713-407-3] $15.95
Douglas Messerli *My Year 2003: Voice Without a Voice* [978-1-
    933382-35-X] $15.95
Xue Di *Across Borders* [978-1-55713-423-3] $12.95

2014

Lee Si-young *Patterns* [978-1-55713-422-6] $11.95
Robert Musil *Three Women* [978-1-55713-419-6] $12.95

<u>2015</u>

Ece Ayhan *A Blind Cat Black* and *Orthodoxies* [978-1-933382-36-4]
   $11.95
Kim Soo-Bok *Beating on Iron* [978-1-55713-430-1] $12.95
Sigmund Freud / Wilhelm Jensen *Gradiva* and *Delusion and Dream
   in Wilhelm Jensen's Gradiva* [1-892295-89-X] $13.95 [REPRINT]
Douglas Messerli *My Year 2002: Love, Death, and Transfiguration*
   [978-1-55713-425-7] $15.95
   My Year 2007: To the Dogs [978-1-55713-424-0] $15.95
   My Year 2008: In the Gap [978-1-55713-462-4] $15.95
Paul van Ostaijen *The First Book of Schmoll* [978-1933382-21-0]
   $12.95

<u>2016</u>

Jim Gauer *Novel Explosives* [978-1-55713-433-2] $15.95
Douglas Messerli *My Year 2009: Facing the Heat* [978-1-55713-429-5]
   $15.95
F. T. Marinetti *The Untameables* [978-1-933382-23-4] $12.95

<u>2017</u>

Régis Bonvicino *Beyond the Wall: New Selected Poems* [978-1-55713-
   431-8] $12.95
Lee Seong-Bok *Ah—Mouthless Things* [978-1-55713-440-0] $12.95
Lucebert *The Collected Poems: Volume 2* [978-1-55713-434-9] $17.95
Ern Malley *The Darkening Ecliptic* [978-1-55713-439-4] $12.95
Douglas Messerli *My Year 2010: Shadows* [978-1-55713-432-5] $15.95
Steven Moore *My Back Pages* [978-1-55713-437-0] $30.00

† Author winner of the Nobel Prize for Literature
± Author winner of the America Award for Literature